THE PELICAN AND THE CHELA

THE TEACHER-STUDENT RELATIONSHIP IN THE SPIRITUAL LIFE

Ann Ree Colton and Jonathan Murro

THE PELICAN AND THE CHELA

THE TEACHER-STUDENT RELATIONSHIP IN THE SPIRITUAL LIFE

by

Ann Ree Colton

and

Jonathan Murro

ANN REE COLTON FOUNDATION
Post Office Box 2057
Glendale, California 91209

First Edition

Library of Congress Catalog Card Number: 85-70766
ISBN: 0-917189-04-3

Printed in the United States of America
by DeVorss and Company, California

For information regarding the writings and teachings
of Ann Ree Colton and Jonathan Murro:
write:

Ann Ree Colton Foundation
336 West Colorado Street
Post Office Box 2057
Glendale, California 91209
Telephone: (818) 244-0113

CONTENTS

Part III: Personal Journals and Diaries

Dedicated to all Great Souls who have covenanted to wear the Teacher's Mantle.

Also dedicated to their students or *chelas* who will inherit the Mantle of the Teacher.

He that receiveth a prophet in the name of a prophet shall receive a prophet's reward.
—St. Matthew 10:41

Part I
Ethics and Responsibilities

Thank Thee, Father, for all Teachers of Truth—past, present and future.

J.M.

. . . Jonathan Murro

1

PRELUDE: THE ANOINTING

But the anointing which ye have received of him abideth in you, and ye need not that any man teach you: but as the same anointing teacheth you of all things, and is truth, and is no lie, and even as it hath taught you, ye shall abide in him.

—1 John 2:27

The Pelican

I am like a pelican of the wilderness.

—Psalm 102:6

The Pelican tears open her breast and feeds her young with her own life blood in times of famine. It is the symbol of Christ Jesus and His atonement on the Cross.

—Friedrich Rest
*Our Christian Symbols**

For it is said that the pelican so loves her young that she puts them to death with her claws. But on the third day for grief she wounds herself, and letting the blood

*The Pilgrim Press, New York 1954, 1957

from her body drip upon the fledglings she raises them from the dead. The pelican signifies the Lord, who so loved the world that he gave his only-begotten Son, whom on the third day he raised up, victor over death, and exalted above every name.

—Honorius of Autun

The symbol of the Living Teacher is the pelican. The pelican symbolizes the Teacher who sacrifices his life for the young in understanding.

There is the mother who is similar to the pelican-mother symbol. She takes the feathers out of her bosom or her breast to make the nest for her young. This is the mother who, while sacrificing, clothes her children with spiritual realities and gives them the understanding of the dignity and reality of the life in this world and of the life in Heaven.

—Ann Ree Colton

Ancient mythology contains a number of symbols that describe various processes of the higher life. Over the ages, the pelican has come to symbolize certain qualities and attributes of enlightened men and women. A pelican, as a Christian symbol, means sacrifice, atonement, resurrection. In Masonic symbolism, the pelican's blood represents the secret work that enables man to rise from ignorance to wisdom.

A Teacher of the higher life is called a *Pelican* for reasons that relate to the physical characteristics of the pelican and also to mythological symbolism. The pelican flies in formation with other pelicans; the Teacher works in unison with other Teachers in Heaven and on Earth. Even as there is a leader in every formation of flying pelicans, so is there a leader in every cluster of Teachers. In the Christian heritage, Jesus is the Leader of all Teacher-Apostles anointed by God's Holy Spirit.

Even as the pelican must feed, protect and teach its young, so must a Teacher of Truth feed, protect and teach his or her students. A pelican regurgitates the food eaten for the benefit of its young who cannot digest the original fish; the Teacher, upon receiving profound wisdom from God's Spirit, must simplify and soften this wisdom so that it can be understood or "digested" by students.

The symbol of a pelican pulling feathers from its breast in order to build a nest for its young, or tearing open its breast to feed its young with its own life blood during times of famine, denotes a Teacher who provides his students with sacred instruction regardless of personal sacrifices and suffering.

Jesus, while on the Cross, paid uncountable sin-debts of mankind; thus, for centuries the Cross has represented suffering for righteousness' sake. When one carries the Cross of Jesus, he follows the example of his beloved Lord; he becomes a liberator of others. Through the suffering of the righteous, the unrighteous and the unknowing are given endless opportunities to become relieved of their sin-burdens and to begin the process of their redemption and rebirth through the Christ.

> *The Spirit itself beareth witness with our spirit, that we are the children of God: And if children, then heirs; heirs of God, and joint-heirs with Christ; if so be that we suffer with him, that we may be also glorified together. For I reckon that the sufferings of this present time are not worthy to be compared with the glory which shall be revealed in us. For the earnest expectation of the creature waiteth for the manifestation of the sons of God.*
>
> —*Romans 8:16–19*

THE CLASSIC TEACHER-STUDENT RELATIONSHIP

Teachers open the door. You enter in by yourself.

—*Chinese Proverb*

Ann Ree Colton, my beloved Teacher and Wife, passed away on June 28, 1984, in her 85th year. During the months previous to her passing, Ann Ree was planning to write a book with me on the subject of the Teacher and the student. For this work, she selected the title *The Pelican and the Chela.* *

As my Teacher for over thirty-two years, Ann Ree Colton taught me invaluable truths regarding the ethics and responsibilities in the Teacher-student relationship. This knowledge, combined with other related subjects, is in *The Pelican and the Chela.* The final section of this book contains writings from our personal journals and diaries.

When Jesus was in the world, He chose twelve men to be His close disciples; these men recognized the importance of following Him and learning from His wisdom and example. Jesus and His disciples fulfilled the *classic* relationship between a Teacher and his students. In the East, the relationship between Teachers and students has been well known for thousands of years. However, in the modern-day Western world, very little is known regarding the classic relationship between a Teacher and student of the spiritual life. Most truth-seekers are totally ignorant of the ethics and responsibilities involved when one becomes a student of a Living Teacher anointed by the Spirit of God.

In the Western world, spiritual dedication is a rarity. It is the nature of the Western disciple to be caught up in many extrovert affairs and many crowded events. These

**Chela* is a Sanskrit word meaning student or disciple.

diverting impulses and interesting by-paths come between him and dedication.

—Ann Ree Colton

Many modern-day religious philosophies are moving farther and farther away from the basic truths and principles through which God blesses and anoints His servants. Consequently, there are very few truly enlightened Teachers in the world.

In my work with Ann Ree Colton, we have offered spiritual instruction to numerous persons. Most of these individuals are the unfortunate victims of faulty religious attitudes inherited from parents and society. Some probationers make their own rules for the Teacher-student relationship; these persons are incapable of any kind of sincere commitment to God.

A great number of modern-day "students" are unwilling to live according to the basic Laws and Commandments of God. In reality, such persons are chronic law-breakers who, through self-deception, have convinced themselves that they are religious or spiritual.

If a seeker after truth is graced with an Anointed Teacher, there is much for him to learn and to observe. Each day is an adventure in learning, for everything the Teacher says and does is inspired by the Holy Spirit.

The attitudes of a truth-seeker are all-important. Only through the careful and conscientious training received from an Enlightened Teacher will a devotee's attitudes experience the necessary changes that will qualify him to experience the *Divine-Marriage Anointing.*

If a student is fortified by a natural expression of ethical attitudes and devotional dedications, he will make rapid progress on the Path; however, one erroneous attitude, if not corrected, could prove to be a major stumbling block in his efforts to attain God-Realization. Thus, all who are graced with a Master Teacher should pray for the courage and self-honesty to correct any attitudes that are delaying or preventing their progress toward union with God. Their success in this necessary endeavor will reward them with increasing measures of Divine Grace as God's Spirit moves closer and closer toward their hearts and minds.

To receive the fullness of God's Spirit is to become a Teacher of Truth, an Anointed One. Those who endure and persevere during the inevitable trials and tests of the probationary years will become the future Teachers of the Word of God. The world desperately needs Teachers who are knowledgeable in the Eastern and Western heritages of Wisdom; Teachers unprejudiced and unbiased; Teachers filled with God's Holy Spirit of Pure Creation and Cosmos-Revelation.

Union with God requires a sense of responsibility and commitment. The Lord Jesus, in His covenant with God to serve as Saviour and Messiah, assumed the awesome responsibility of seeking to liberate and illuminate every soul assigned to this Solar System. Jesus must work patiently with *all* souls until those who respond to His mediation are transformed into enlightened sons and daughters of the Living God. Individuals who serve the Lord Jesus as devotees, disciples and Apostles assist Him through their own sense of responsibility and commitment to the Creator.

> *The woman saith unto him, I know that Messias cometh, which is called Christ: when he is come, he will tell us all things. Jesus saith unto her, I that speak unto thee am he.*
>
> *—St. John 4:25, 26*

THE HOLY MOUNTAIN

He that putteth his trust in me . . . shall inherit my holy mountain.

—*Isaiah 57:13*

The Pelican and the Chela is a book of instruction, inspiration and testimony. It presents a view of the Holy Mountain from the vantage point of an Illumined Teacher and from the perspective of her student.

The Holy Mountain has many paths. Each path is contributing to the ennobling of the human spirit. The essential ethics in the Teacher-student relationship are universal in nature; they apply to all paths or religious philosophies dedicated to Pure Truth.

Jesus stated that one should not "put new wine into old bottles." (St. Mark 2:22) The new wine of the Christ requires the new bottles of truth-seekers who have a soul-knowing regarding the necessary blending between religion and science and also a soul-daring to work with new formulas of Creation.

"We shall be like him." (1 John 3:2) Even as Jesus is the *Prototype* for the future man in ages to come, so does God send other prototype-souls who represent different plateaus in mankind's progression toward perfection. Ann Ree Colton is such a prototype-soul. Ann Ree represents the future individual in the world who will be perfectly centered in God's Grace through the natural blending of religion, science, philosophy and the creative arts. More and more prototype-souls are emerging to lead mankind into coming centuries when the inhabitants of the planet Earth will be cognizant of their placement in the Plan of God for Stars and Galaxies.

The next stages for man's progression into the future pertain to his becoming knowledgeable in all scientific and spiritual sciences linking him with the Cosmos. Reverence for the Image of God as a Cosmos-Universal Image will accelerate the manifestations of the dimensional skills of the heart, mind and soul through which man will claim his crown as an illumined son of God.

Every true Teacher is a gift to the disciple from the Omnipresence of God.

—*Ann Ree Colton*

As long as a student or chela remembers that his Teacher is a gift from God, he remains under the blessing of his Teacher's Mantle. However, if one forgets that his Teacher is a gift from God, he begins his descent down the Holy Mountain of Divine Grace.

This book is written with the fervent prayer that there will be a return to the classic Teacher-student relationship. The Spiritual Path is a difficult climb up the Holy Mountain. Without a Teacher to show the way, a student is unprepared to meet the rugged and repetitive initiatory challenges. For earnest truth-seekers graced with a Teacher, there is the strong possibility that union with God will occur in their present lifetimes if they carefully and conscientiously heed their Teacher's instruction. If such students will remain constant in their covenant with God—and not permit anyone or anything to intrude upon their dedication—the Creator will place His Spirit upon them. This Divine Benediction will assure the world of Anointed Teachers in the future who will be knowledgeable in the ethics and responsibilities of the Teacher-student relationship.

Take fast hold of instruction; let her not go: keep her; for she is thy life.

—*Proverbs 4:13*

CLASSIC CHALLENGES

One is sent to his Teacher because his soul needs the respite of spiritual reliance upon a God-oriented person. His Teacher channels the strengths needed until he receives right discernment and discrimination.

To be beyond the reach of the sense and sensual deceptions, one by grace enters the Path of Discipline. He takes step-by-step obligations or trials to prove his own capacity to serve God.

—Ann Ree Colton

One must have devotion towards one's own guru. Whatever may be the nature of the guru, the disciple gets salvation by dint of his unflinching devotion towards his guru.

—Sarada Devi
Wife of Ramakrishna

An ancient saying in the higher life is: "*When the student is ready, the Teacher appears.*" The Spirit of God, through the Law of Attraction, directs students to their Teachers in perfect timing. This mightly blessing occurred for me in the early 1950's following a prayer for God to "use me."

At the time of my prayer, I was living in St. Petersburg, Florida, and Ann Ree Colton was across the country in California. A vision accompanied by direct guidance directed Ann Ree to return to St. Petersburg, her home for many years, to meet the person who would help her in her future work. Ann Ree was obedient to her guidance—and we met a short time later.

The Law of Attraction directing a student to his Teacher is an infallible Law of God. No one can come between the student and the Teacher who have covenanted in their souls to serve God in the world.

My parents and other persons tried to keep me from assisting Ann Ree in her work. This led to many years of estrangement from family members. The strong objection by loved ones and friends is one of the *classic challenges* that confront some students on the Spiritual Path. In such instances, the Holy Bible contains passages that provide great comfort and assurance. *"When my father and my mother forsake me, then the Lord will take me up." (Psalm 27:10) "He that loveth father or mother more than me is not worthy of me." (St. Matthew 10:37)*

Soon after we started our work together, Ann Ree began to teach me the spiritual art and science of meditation. After a meditation one day, I instinctively kissed her feet. At the time, I did not know that for thousands of years chelas have been kissing the feet of their Gurus or Teachers as an expression of their gratitude to God for guiding them to a true source of enlightened instruction. It is also an expression of gratitude to their Teachers for opening the door to the knowledge of God and His Kingdom.

"Again, the kingdom of heaven is like unto a merchant man, seeking goodly pearls; Who, when he had found one pearl of great price, went and sold all that he had, and bought it." (St. Matthew 13:45, 46) Even as I intuitively knew that a student should kiss the feet of his Teacher after certain sacramental meditations and at other important times, so did I know with an innate knowing that all of my funds and worldly possessions should be placed at the feet of my Teacher for her to use in service to God. One day, I experienced the ecstatic realization that I literally had fulfilled the saying of Jesus to sell all for the "pearl of great price."

Ann Ree and I both believed in the Scriptural directive *"Owe no man." (Romans 13:8)* The Holy Bible contains numerous passages that affirm the Providential Grace of God that comes to those who place their trust in Him, fulfill His Commandments, and serve the human spirit as faithful Apostles of the Lord Jesus.

I began to assist my Teacher by recording and typing her public talks and private meditations. This led to the publishing of her first book one year later. Over the years, the files of manuscript continued to expand—and a number of beautiful books were published. In the early years, funds for the publishing of the books appeared miraculously. The Providential Grace of God is perfect in its timing. After one's faith is tested, the Providential Grace of God always provides for each legitimate need and expense.

During the thirty-two years with my beloved Teacher, I marveled at her courage and conscientiousness. Ann Ree met every obstacle and challenge with courage inspired by her love for God and the Truth. For almost thirty years, she wrote monthly lessons for her students. Even during times of critical health conditions, she would write the monthly lesson in the hospital.

Ann Ree would never shirk any responsibility. Often, she would teach classes or conduct weddings while ill or very weak. Over the years, my admiration and respect continually increased for my Teacher's beautiful virtues, especially her courage and conscientiousness.

One of the greatest blessings for an aspirant on the Path is to have a Teacher who has the courage to tell him the truth about his faults and other shortcomings that delay spiritual progress. One day after I presented a Sunday sermon, Ann Ree said to me: "You need to be more loving." My initial reaction was one of shock, because I thought I had placed great love and care in the preparation and presentation of the talk. After absorbing my Teacher's admonition, I thought: "One *always* needs to be more loving!"

A student once asked Ann Ree to tell him the truth about himself "with both barrels." She asked the student, "Do you want gold bullets, silver bullets, or buckshot?"

One of the comforting feelings for a student is to know that his Teacher's union with God's Pure and Perfect Truth is always there to bless him in many ways. This union with the Truth enables the Teacher to answer every question asked by the student. To have such a Teacher is a priceless blessing, for God, as Truth, abides in the heart, mind and soul of the Teacher.

I received Ann Ree's teaching about the reality of the Masters or Great Immortals as proof that there is a *Living God.* The Masters are Beings of a superior intelligence assigned to this Solar System for the purpose of instructing the Saints, the proteges of the Saints, and others who are receptive to Cosmos-Eternal Truths.

Over the years, my Teacher's inspired instruction has opened my understanding of the great Host of Heaven who work between God and man. These include the Angels, Devas, Saints, Illuminati, Great Immortals or Masters, Mary, the Apostles of Jesus, Jesus, the Holy Ghost, the Comforter, the Spirit of Truth, the Divine Mother, the Heavenly Father, the Hierarchs, the Archangels, and the Christ. God is the Omnipresent Spirit within all Beings, Presences and Souls in all visible and invisible worlds. The Living God *lives* in all consciousness beings in the Universe who are graced with the Gift of Intelligence.

> A devotee dedicates his life to the service of his Master and dissolves his will in that of his Master. It is a life of complete surrender.
>
> —Kirpal Singh

THREE STAGES OF THE HIGHER LIFE

A teachable student is a rare jewel.

There are three major stages in the higher life of devotion and dedication to God. The first stage relates to the years of probation during which a devotee is prepared for the Divine Marriage: Union with his Beloved Lord.

The second stage pertains to the occurrence of the Divine Marriage when the heart, mind and soul experience a sublime fullness of Grace and Truth. Fullness occurs through the Holy Presence of God anointing, sealing and quickening the chosen one.

During the Divine Marriage, the Initiate unites with the bliss, ecstasy and joy of God's Holy Presence. Sacred raptures accompany mighty realizations about the Creator, the Soul and the Universe. To be anointed by the Cosmos Presence of God is to become a Cosmos Initiate or Disciple.

The Spirit of God is an Eternal Spirit present throughout the Universe. The Divine-Marriage Anointing by the *Eternal* Spirit of God awakens *eternal* attributes in the soul; thereafter, the God-Realized Initiate experiences the higher levels of Truth related to Eternal Life and the Image of God. The Laws and Commandments of God are seen through prophetic sight, thereby enabling one to perceive the long-range purposes of each Law and Commandment.

The third stage of the higher life relates to one's service to God *after* the Divine-Marriage Anointing. This close relationship with the Creator adds many new responsibilities. Anointed Teachers are responsible for establishing new truths in the world; they also are personally responsible for every seeker after truth guided to them by the Creator.

An Anointed Teacher is a dynamo of versatile creations for God. The moment an aspirant becomes the student of a Master Teacher, he begins to learn of a world of wisdom, beauty and inspiration hitherto unknown to him. To be nigh unto a Teacher anointed by God's Spirit is to participate in the divine drama of unceasing creations.

As one progresses on the Path, he renders greater ranges of service to God and to his fellow man. Students who respond to their Teacher's instruction unite with the blessed Bridegroom and receive the Divine-Marriage Anointing.

I have ordained a lamp for my anointed.
—Psalm 132: 17

THE TEACHER'S COVENANT

The Teacher is responsible for the Altar of God. The Teacher must wait until students come who also feel a sense of responsibility toward God's Altar.

An Illumined Teacher may be likened to the Sun from which light is constantly being emitted. Even as the Sun has a specific number of planets circling in their orbits, so does an Anointed Teacher have a certain number of students. The number of students and the types of students are determined by the Teacher's Covenant with God.

Everything in God's Plan for man and for stars is accomplished through *Covenants.* The Teacher's Covenant determines the pure creations that the Teacher, as a servant of God, will contribute to the progression of the human spirit. The Teacher's Covenant also pertains to the teaching of students who will become the future Teachers illumined by the Spirit and Grace of God.

Even as the prophet Elijah passed his mantle to Elisha,* so does every Anointed Teacher pass his Mantle to responsive students or chelas. In all teachings dedicated to God, the passing of the Mantle from the Teacher to the student assures the perpetuation of God's Word in the world.

In the East and the West, in times ancient and present, the passing of the Mantle from Teacher to student is a reality, a necessity. The Teacher's Mantle represents Spiritual Gifts and Wisdom; the Teacher must instruct his students

*2 Kings 2:8–15

in the knowledge of *ethics* regarding each Gift and Power that comes with the Mantle.

A Teacher or Pelican is totally responsible for each student sent by God to receive instruction. The Teacher understands the seriousness of this Covenant with God. However, new students are as baby pelicans who are completely unaware of the process of their care, feeding and protection.

A *Soul-Covenant* is an agreement between God and the Soul. This sacred Covenant is not made by an individual on Earth, for the Soul's Covenant was made *before* he was born on the planet. The Soul's Covenant determines when and where one will be born in each lifetime; it determines what he will learn from life as an imperishable treasure sealed into the Soul's Eternal Record.

When one covenants to live a life with no spiritual aspirations, he has covenanted with his soul to live a mundane life. Presently, numerous persons have no desire to make any kind of spiritual commitment; nevertheless, many lessons remain for them to learn regarding the difference between right and wrong, virtue and vice, morality and sin. These lessons affect all nonreligious and religious individuals. Persons who feel no responsibility to heed the Laws and Commandments of God must still abide by the laws of their tribes, communities, nations. However, when one's *Soul* covenants for him to live a life based upon spiritual values, ethics and principles, he will be born with an earnest desire to learn of God and to worship Him.

Jesus' Parable of the Ten Virgins refers to devotees who are either foolish or wise. The foolish are drawn into selfish pursuits or they are lazy; the wise are virtuous and reverent worshippers of God. The wise virgins become the brides of the Bridegroom. "*. . . .the bridegroom came; and they that were ready went in with him to the marriage: and the door was shut." (St. Matthew 25:10)*

Everything any individual experiences in life can be traced to his Soul's Covenant with God before birth. Even as there are levels of learning in school, so are there levels of learning in the School of Eternal Life. Every lesson in a life of noncommitment or commitment to God is important in God's Plan. The Soul's Covenant determines when one begins to be *quickened* spiritually. Until the Soul's Covenant makes this determination, one remains unawakened on religious and spiritual levels.

A person may live in the garden of life for many lifetimes and never observe or appreciate the flowers of virtue. The moment one begins to notice the beauty of the flowers of virtue, he has begun to receive his first spiritual quickenings from his Soul. Thereafter, he will live many lifetimes during which he will covenant with God and his Soul to travel the Path of Virtue until he qualifies to receive the Divine-Marriage Anointing.

When one covenants with his Soul to work to *earn* the Divine-Marriage Anointing, he has truly turned toward God. The Creator rewards such ones by sending them an Enlightened Teacher who will accept the responsibility of helping them qualify for the Divine Marriage.

"For many are called, but few are chosen." (St. Matthew 22:14) Even though a Teacher or Pelican may receive a number of students to instruct, only a few will have evolved the virtues necessary to become true students. Even as there are many students in school who do not study and are unteachable, so are there many students in religious and spiritual philosophies who do not study and are unteachable.

In the higher life, *fringe* students around an Anointed Teacher are limited in important areas of virtue-development. However, God is gracing them with inspired instruction so that the *seeds* of the truths being planted into their beings through sacred instruction may bear fruit in coming lives.

Persons who remain "called" and not chosen for the Divine-Marriage Anointing are the majority in religious and spiritual teachings. Their enlightenment will come in future lives because mighty seeds of Truth have been planted into their beings by their Teachers. This planting is a necessary contribution toward the future-lives' spiritual attainments of truth-seekers who evolve at a slower tempo. For those who progress very rapidly through virtues earned in past lives, the seeds of Truth planted by their Teacher produce immediate fruit. Such persons are the *few* who actually qualify to receive the Divine-Marriage Anointing in their present lifetimes.

O gentle breezes of the soul, waft thy precious truths earthward.

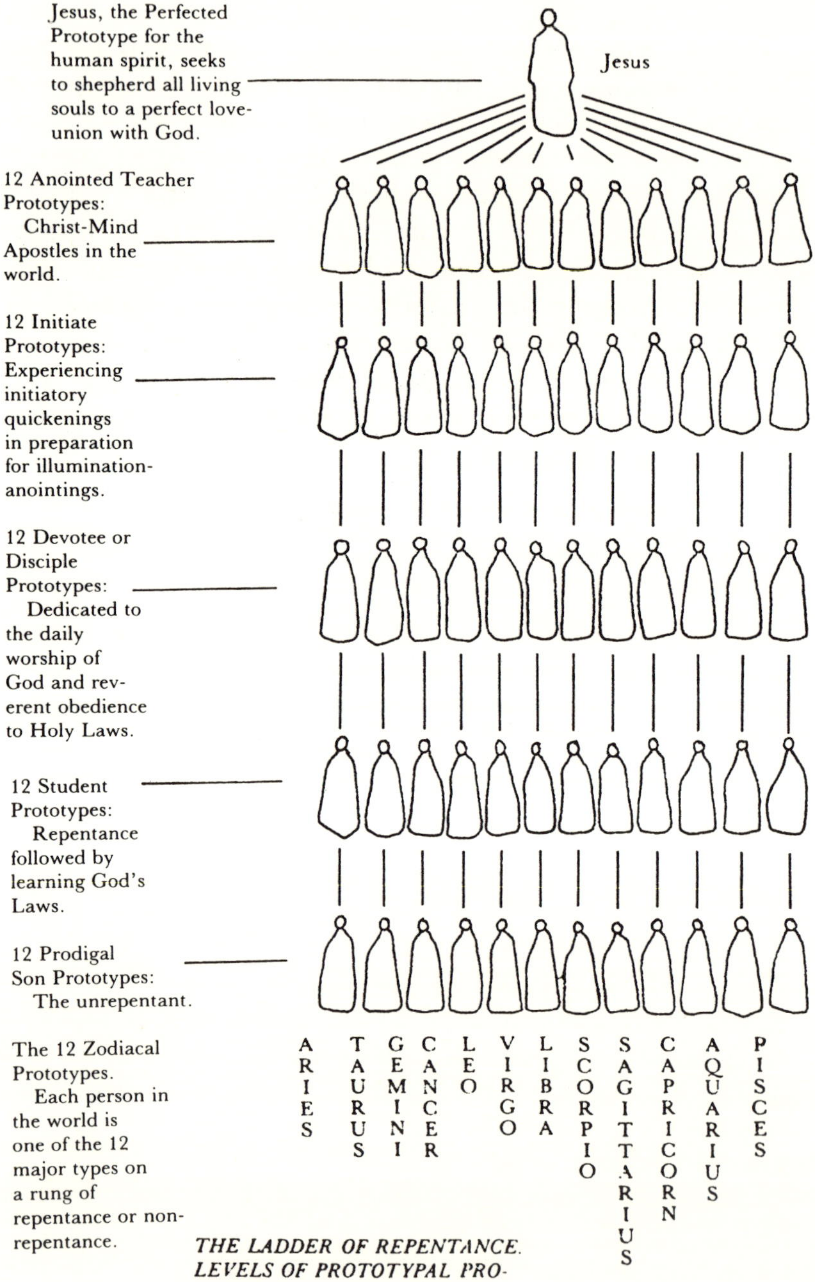

THE LADDER OF REPENTANCE. LEVELS OF PROTOTYPAL PROGRESSION ON THE PATH OF VIRTUE. Chart by Jonathan Murro.

. . . Ann Ree Colton

2

THE LIVING TEACHER

I would get to my Teacher if I had to crawl on glass for miles and miles.

The Path and the Teacher

I met my Teacher, and my soul knew. My wayward ways, hurting and angering, had fed me with futility. At last the sitting down by the stream of consciousness came. I began to be fed with the fruits of blessed joy.

A Teacher's knowing unites him with all Great Souls who know and have known. At times, he may not use the same language used by other Teachers, but he uses the same true ideas which will infallibly support him in his teaching.

Every true Teacher is a gift to the disciple from the Omnipresence of God. Regardless of the union and trust building a holy bridge between the disciple and the Teacher, the Teacher remains a mystery to the disciple; for the very knowing of the Teacher contains the answer to the secrets the disciple is athirst to know. This mystery in the Teacher is also the mystery and the challenge within the one who seeks to know and to be.

A living spiritual Teacher is the greatest grace a disciple may encounter in the search of his own soul. To refuse to heed the voice of one's Living Teacher is to refuse the Light, and thus to remain blind to wisdom's gift.

The vow, the covenant and the devotion should be remade each day to one's Living Teacher. The recognition of the spiritual Teacher as an extended being with an expanded consciousness glorifies one's own learning and knowing. The spiritual Teacher is the door to the Light, and is the one who leads the lesser light in the mind of the disciple to the greater Light of God.

On the Path with the living spiritual Teacher there is only the one-way. One leaves behind him the alternates when once the Teacher has called him with the sweet lute music of the soul.

Walking the Path with the Teacher, one dusts off and takes up all of the jewels of past-life knowing and understanding. Through the Teacher's instruction, he goes forth to add to his collection or treasure the necessary jewel to be added to his storehouse of knowing.

Until one has found his living Teacher, he is a wanderer with bruised and weary feet. Once on the Path, he walks in the Light with the Light.

The Teacher tells the disciple to fear not the world and all of the evil he sees; to have compassion for those who see not and hear not. He explains the why of suffering undergone by the unknowing. He pulls aside the veils of matter and gravity obscuring the light of the soul.

The Living Teacher comes to give life and Light to the world. He begins with one disciple. The Light, when wholly received by the disciple, gives him the power eventually to teach.

As a mother must transpose her pains of labor into joy of the human child in her arms, the Master lives solely to give light and spirituality to his disciple.

All disciples become first, scribes; next, prophets; next, healers; and finally, Teachers of disciples to follow them. This is the Path—a Path made up of the conjoined souls of Teachers, disciples, initiates, devotees.

The Teacher and the teaching coming forth from the Teacher come to free one of certain troubles which have followed him over long ages of spiritual ignorance and procrastination. These have kept alive the dark karmic obstacles in his works and mind in past lives and in this life. These karmic obstructions are not suitable or congenial to the present need in one's desiring to walk upon the Path with those who have cleansed their feet of stumbling transgressions. Unhappiness, sorrow and discontent are the results of one's own actions either in this life or some other life.

One must be willing to work *with* his Teacher. A Teacher can have no value to the student unless the student is willing to receive interpretation of his past and present-life karmas. The Teacher must give to the student the way to overcome the obstacles in karmic offenses. The divine obligation of the Teacher to interpret the student's karma is necessary so that the student may work out his karma more swiftly through acceptance and lucidity, and thus gain expansion of the heart and the mind.

The Teacher must evaluate the karma of his student. He does so by using the Love Principle and his higher intuition, and thus carefully avoids offending the inward privacy of the will of his student.

A true student desires with his whole self to understand himself rather than to put on mystical blinders regarding his prime obstacles to spiritual progress. One who comes to a Teacher or a teaching expecting to exert no effort is yet a babe in realization.

When there is joy in the struggle to free the soul from the Maya mazes of false belief in the existence of this world as being the all; when the Teacher is in vibratory oneness with the student's heart call and desire to learn—true existence enters into the life of the student. The Teacher lives in the reality of true existence; he also struggles for the student—to give the student the freeing awareness of true existence and reality of God.

A student desiring excitation and excessive titillation through entertainment is responding to the lures of astral enticement. He is yet to be a student. The karmic decisions made through karmic law reject such students. The Cherubim Angels guarding the Path of evolvement freeze the student upon the threshold of the Path, sending him back into the scorpion stings of enticement and self-love.

Everyone on the Path must be initiated through the fiery trials spoken of by Jesus and Peter. To resist the fiery trials is to fall into the fiery furnace of dissolution. To look to one's Teacher as the deliverer who points the way to walk over the abyss of dissolution is to be graced, and therefore blessed, rather than consumed by the fires of one's own biased and unbalanced passions.

A student should alert himself when the Teacher's vibration has been short-circuited in his consciousness. He alone is the one who has set up the barriers to the telepathic flow between himself and the Teacher. Through gratitude to God, to the Christ, to all true Teachers, and to his Teacher, he should seek to return to the heart-atom alignment with his Teacher.

To think one's self as being wholly adequate upon the initiatory Path is to invite the tempter, Satan.

The true Teacher knows that he is under the instruction of the Christ; he leads all in that direction. He blueprints the course of the walk on the Path after the One, Jesus, who set the Rules and the Ethic into the etheric portion of the heart and mind. His own grateful heart is ever at the service of his student, that all may work together in grace for the Will of God to be made manifest.

"Where is my Teacher?" is the first call of the student; and, finally, when the Teacher comes, "Here is my Teacher. I will regard his coming as sent of God, and I will thus walk with joy."

SALUTATION

> *O Great Guru of God, I look to thee and do obeisance to the Light of God in thee.*

It is the *Light* in the Teacher or the Master to which one turns. As a sunflower must stay fixed on the Sun, so must the soul seek the one having more of the Light. To have found one's Living Teacher, to recognize him or her as the soul giving forth the needed dew of instruction, is grace freedom and a promise of grace action.

To be teachable is to become a Teacher. Until one can dissolve the resisting pride of the intellect, the wandering is long; and the shallow springs in instruction, giving no living waters to the mind and soul, are all that can be offered or received.

On the day one can say, *"I can of mine own self do nothing" (St. John 5:30),* there is a roar or responding joy in Heaven. The *Maha Guru* within the heart and the Living Teacher in the world make contact with each other. The bands of iron on the heart and the veils of egotism obscuring the mind are removed. Freedom comes; joy comes; life lives.

The soul is a half-dead spiritual organism until one meets the Living Teacher and the living teaching which the Teacher brings. The Living Teacher comes in ripeness to world need, soul need, evolvement need. The Living Teacher lives to teach the living. He seeks to reach those who have come to know that the vital life-breath of the True Self cannot survive in the atmosphere of scheming, manipulation and deviation.

To long to be the True Self is to attract a Living Teacher, and thus come alive to what one truly desires. How wonderful the smile from a Living Teacher afire with the soul life of the spirit.

How marvelous the joy to know and to look upon the face of one's Living Teacher who has been seeking to teach the neglected attributes of the soul. One word from a Living Teacher to the soul is worth more than thousands of phrases from a sterile soul-less pen or speech.

The Living Teacher comes to sound the Word into our life-atoms, to awaken our vital perceptions, to make acute our sensitive intuitions, to make free our high reasoning.

Every day, if one has not found his Teacher, he should look out on the world and long for him, or he should look on the horizon at dusk and call to him, saying, "Come."

The vibration of the teaching and a Teacher of the pure in one's life is as an iceberg emerging upon the void of the deep. Expect every thing to be shaken when the Living Teacher appears. Teachers bringing placidity are no teachers. The very Light in the Teacher, which is the Light of God, must change the soul's direction, the mind's direction—so long running the circular course of repetition. The life of the mind will be recharged, redirected, revitalized. Thoughts unfamiliar will come to rearrange the patterns of karma so long being housed and fed by the inertia of the will. All will be swept away by whatever way the Will of God working through the Teacher determines best in time and need.

Trust on the cleansing process of the Living Teacher to be right and acceptable. Learn each day that the Love of God in the Teacher or the Master is that which you love.

For long ages, the Teacher has made himself a vessel through which the Love of God can be seen and known.

The Master, Teacher or Guru is seeking you, that your soul may come out of the restrictions you have placed there. He comes to ignite, to electrify, to accelerate your mind, life and will, that you may know and create, and thus make union with God as he, the Teacher, before you has made union. As Lazarus was given life renewal through the command of Jesus, so does the Living Teacher command you to come forth to receive instruction, to study, and to prove yourself as a worthy workman for God.

Lead me into Light, O Divine One. Teach me; instruct me. Hail to all true Teachers and Givers of Enlightenment.

*

O thou true Teachers and Gurus, hail! And to all true teachings, peace.

The Teacher comes to the heart of his student or disciple first as the unknown friend. He awakens the slumbering soul-forces of his student. He silently and firmly urges him to seek the Real and to make union with God as his first and foremost goal.

In the silent language, the Teacher comes. He approaches the ear and heart of the disciple, producing the new joy for the new and the Real. How great is the grace for one who hears and sees his Teacher eye to eye.

When learning and yearning to know become the vessel, the Teacher reaches the heart-ear of his student. Ideas, phrases and promptings are received. The disciple becomes the initiate preparing to teach those who would hear the voice of their souls.

Only experience gives authority. A spiritual teacher without Self-Realization, Soul-Realization and God-Realization cannot teach with authority. The power moving through the Teacher and the teaching comes only from the Teacher having experienced what he teaches. Closed ears and hearts cannot be opened by one who has not experienced what he teaches.

All who walk in the Path intuit and know the Real. The words of power and of life give them a wisdom grace. The grace-mastery of wisdom produces miracles in light, timing, healing and instruction.

There is an intelligible cable heart-cord of love connecting the student and his Teacher. Along this cable flow the unceasing communication and instruction—the *Buddhi* informing action. Upon this same cable-current flow the interpretations of one's study and reading, written by the Teacher. Also, one receives the revealing of his karmic pattern. He is given inner, resurging strengths by the Teacher to endure, dissolve, clarify and erase the obstacles in karma standing between him and his place upon the Path.

When one turns in the direction of the Path, his face is toward the Light. His soul-forces are stirred and quickened, and he begins to contact many planes beyond the objective conscious planes of the physical world. Only a Teacher's care and supervision can enable one to explore the planes beyond the physical. To try to explore without a Teacher the unknown psychic ranges of the invisible is to invite confusion and unreality, and sometimes tragedy. To reach toward the Teacher is to be healed of egotism.

Each day give obeisance to the Teacher by the loving salutation:

O Divine Teacher, I take refuge
in thy instruction,
which is the cloak of protection, wisdom

and unceasing love.
Your urgings are life renewing.
Hail, Teacher;
blessings to all pure sources of instruction.

Listen to what the divine chain of instruction is saying within the ear of your heart. Hear; respond; activate the priceless jewel purchased by constant devotion and love. Never let a day go by without salutation to the Teacher within. Listen; hear; live. Let the true Inner Light be your resounding new joy, new bliss. Make meditation and prayer your meat, your food of life. Keep Light unceasing in your mind. Keep the castle of your heart pure and chaste, that the Lord and the Teacher may be as one in you.

Before you came to this world to serve the soul-need of your mind's expansion, you were aware of the need to accept the blessings of divine obligations and the disciplines accompanying the spiritual life. So it is that a true initiate never feels that he must blame others for that which has been blueprinted for him by the karmic impressions or *Samskaras* dwelling similar to ravening lions, tigers or wild horses in the subconscious depths of the lower quelle portion of the mind.

The blessings of being aware of one's own Maha Guru or Teacher support all true initiates during trials, temptations and challenges. However, if one fails to observe the Laws, he regresses as an initiate.

The Master Teacher or Guru enables one as an initiate or disciple to live within the causal Buddhi mind. In this, the initiate is mentally strong and alert during accelerated trials or initiation. The Samskaras are controlled, balanced and timed to the flow of the outward life.

During accelerated initiation, one opens the *truth-gaskets* of his conscience. In these fiery periods, he literally walks through the furnace of death to old practices and habits of the physical, emotional and mental life. He dies to the lower will and mind through this purging. He is enabled with the help of his Guru or Teacher to bring forth the Buddhi birth or the *Informing Principle* in his mind. One should accept that initiation-trials are serious, sometimes lengthy, if he has procrastinated in former lives.

All initiates or disciples of the *Great-Soul Line* should never fail to open any conversation concerning holy revelation—such as being on a lecture platform, speaking in a class or the beginning of his own meditation—by preceding or opening his logos with recognition of the Teacher and of the Divine Line of Gurus or Masters of which Jesus is head. Suggestions:

1. *I am giving thanks for the Holy Teachers and for the Great Souls.*
2. *I give obeisance to my Teacher as I speak, pray and meditate.*
3. *I give obeisance to the Divine Line of the Great Souls who seek to speak through dedication.*
4. *(For one's own personal Teacher)*
   I give thanks to ________ (name optional), my Teacher; hail to the words and works of my Teacher. Through the Father in me I give recognition to the Father in my Teacher.

All blessings for the birth of your Buddhi mind. The world is starving for divine and holy leadership. Be prepared. Be willing to be teachable, so as to teach.

> *Give instruction to a wise man, and he will be yet wiser: teach a just man, and he will increase in learning.*
>
> —*Proverbs 9:9*

JESUS AS THE GURU OF GURUS

I am the door.

—St. John 10:9

Jesus is the first and supreme Avatar for the world. All who have reached *Higher Self-Genesis* consciously enter the door to instruction through Jesus.

Even though a Self-Genesis ego may be united in instruction with an Eastern Guru, Jesus is the Mediator and true mediative Light for all Guru instruction. The greater Guru-Line is headed by Jesus; more and more it may be seen that Rishi instructors seek to identify themselves with Jesus. In some manner, all religions puzzle over the magnificent enigma in Jesus, intuiting Him to be the One who contains the Way, the Truth and the Life.

To cling to Guru Eastern instruction through the love or bhakti instruction endears an initiate to Jesus. To finally open the heart buds in loving is similar to a flowing stream irresistibly drawn toward the source of love, Jesus. The Jesus heart is a magnet drawing all inwardly toward the soul-winged way of irresistible love. All Teachers, Gurus and Saints know Him who loves all.

The Rishi systems of instruction teach one how to fulfill *self-salvation.* The Jesus instruction prepares one to take part in *world-salvation.* To pray for an instructor will never fail to produce a Teacher or a Guru. To each one comes the Teacher closely aligned with the seeking and the call. In teaching, a true Guru points toward the One higher and beyond. This is that One called Jesus. Blessed is the one who comes in the name of the Lord.

The spiritual disciple seeks to become an initiate; the initiate seeks to become an adept. Once the hand is on the plow he looks not back, and in time he will experience the great or sacred initiation whereby he will become more than a dove mystic or an eagle initiate. By the spiritual law of ascension, he will become a transcended avatar.

The Divine Avatar-Chain of Illumination is inconceivable in the mind of the lesser or dove initiate. The dove initiate or mystic-heart-initiation of love pertains to all-feeling. The eagle initiate relates to the use of mental powers as received from communicable levels of mediation. Mind initiation unites the initiate with certain powers of imaging, enabling him to use some degree of de-manifestation and manifestation.

All Teacher-Gurus are *gates* to the sacred initiations. Christ Jesus is the *door* to the Divine Father of this eternity.

> *Jesus saith unto him, I am the way, the truth, and the life: no man cometh unto the Father, but by me.*
>
> —*St. John 14:6*

Through intellectual instinct produced by disciplines and exposure to truth in former lives, one surrenders his mind to a teaching or Teacher. Through love-intuition, one gives his heart to his Teacher. Through deep and sincere love of God, he gives the priceless gift of his will unto the safe keeping of the Will of God.

When one begins to serve God and only God, self-will has found its place in the Will of God. To be in the Will of God under Christ, one becomes Spaceless and Timeless. To serve God is to be instructed and to be loved of God. Thus, one is never absent from those who represent God.

All beings of the Earth must develop, evolve, expand and create. All seeking beings are learning together in the unceasing soul oneness of learning, expanding, becoming. The Will of God is made plain when one frees the Space compressions in self-thinking or doing.

True Teachers teach all to love God first. From this, one may discern the true presence, face, voice and worth of his Teacher.

Teachers loving God are directors, transformers, translators. Through their own God-Realization, such Teachers give to their students and disciples *Niscience,* that they may overcome their limiting nescience or unknowing.

Too long have we been betrayed by doubts resulting from nescience or unknowing. Through Niscience the compressed space in our souls expands into freedom, liberation, salvation.

He who is Christ is our Liberator. He is the Light and Liberator of this small planet. As a magnet in the Eye of God, the Christ Spirit draws us into the Cosmic and the Cosmos expansions.

Each individual, through the Christ Spirit, is being prepared to break the egg shell of inverted life. Through His Light, we become Spaceless in soul expansion and mind expansion. Through Him, we attain liberation and freedom *to be.* Through Teachers under Him, we become the sacred sound, sounding within the Will of God.

THE GREAT MANTRA

Mighty is the love — OM
The arc of power in life — OM — OM — OM
Love, the breath of the exalted space. OM

Mighty is the Light — OM
The merging, penetrable — OM — OM — OM
The moving, the extendable — OM — OM — OM
Increasing Light. OM — OM — OM

Mighty is the Word — OM
The Sound going forth — OM OM OM OM OM OM OM
The call going out — OM — OM — OM
Mighty, mighty, mighty — OM
The Word. OM — OM — OM —HUM

Instruction:

We master the Time element of Space in this planet into Space-expansion through the sound of the mantra OM, that we may enter into the Hierarchy powers under the Christ. Christ is that one who opens the way to Timelessness and Space-liberation.

Speak aloud all three stanzas first without use of OM sounds. Second, speak using the OM sounds loudly. *Third speak OM and other words mentally, holding light between the eyebrow center and surrendering the self-will unto God. Relax and feel bliss-joy. (Once a day before or after meditation, as you desire.)*

TESTIMONY AND WITNESSING FOR GOD

I give witness to God in me.
In His Truth, I am free as a spirit,
whole, eternal and complete.
I give witness that I am deathless.
I give witness that my soul is free in God.
In my beginning, I am spirit.
In my ending, I am spirit.

To testify for God is to be His witness. Following a right virtue in testimony come the Gifts of Passing, Healing and Teaching.

The supernatural powers of the soul are made active in testimony. He who refuses to be a witness to God as Truth sets up a wall against soul-power and powers.

There is no reason for a man to undergo testing unless he gives testimony as to his testing and victory over his testing. Then he is free from the sin for which he testifies.

The more people give testimony, the closer they are to God-Realization. From testimony come revealment and clarification in one's own conviction that the protecting and caring Laws of God exist in all conditions human and spiritual. Testimony is the tongue of proof—proof of the existing Will of God as progressive and creative in the life of man.

Testimony is the chief virtue-support in religiosity. A mind dependent upon secular religion yields not the fruits of true witnessing. Only in religiosity, with the virtue of true testimony, can religious virtue live.

Confession and testimony, when becoming one, obliterate tons of heavy debris in karmic guilt and sin.

He who has courage to speak for God gives encouragement for the blind, the afflicted, the weak, the doubtful, the indecisive. There is no testimony of right virtue through a divided mind. Testimony given in the spirit of doubt reveals religious and spiritual illiteracy.

He who is brave enough to say what he knows is one who Passes. This Knowing is Niscience. From it comes an alchemy to destroy hardness of the mind and heart.

Testimony is the language of the Apostle. Through the tongue of the God-sent come Redemption and Sacrament. Through the genuine witnessing of God as Spirit, one spreads out the Angelic Kingdom before men.

> *This is the disciple which testifieth of these things, and wrote these things: and we know that his testimony is true.*
>
> —*St. John 21:24*

THE CORRIDORS OF MIRRORS

> *He that refuseth instruction despiseth his own soul.*
>
> —*Proverbs 15:32*

Jesus, of all Teachers, is a Mirror unto all who would move aside all self-illusion states of self-importance. The

Living Teacher under the Christ is a mirror reflecting back to the probationer and initiate all of his flaws, hatreds and short-comings. He who refuses to face this mirror is seeking to throw a stone at the mirror or his Teacher; he breaks the mirror only to find himself with a second mirror exposing with more clarity his wrongdoing, his weakness and his ignorance.

On seeking still to cast the blame upon one's Teacher for self-exposure, he breaks the second mirror and enters into actual karmic states and suffering. In this, he becomes hated because of his hating; he becomes unloved because of his unloving; he becomes poverty-stricken because of his non-giving and non-forgiving. From mirror to mirror he goes until he is naked, no longer hallucinating in ego-fantasy of self-dominion.

It is the work of the Living Teacher to act as the mirror in the initiatory cycles of the disciple's birth to the spiritual life. Willingly he has chosen to be a sacramental yoke-bearer for the sins of arrogance and cowardice in his chela or disciple.

The Living Teacher, representing Jesus, stands as the mirror. He has dedicated to embody Truth and to expose all flaws in the life of the chela. He acts impartially as a reflector for the Christ.

The same mirror to the Teacher is his invulnerability to the stones which seek to destroy him, his teaching, and that which he represents. The Teacher knows himself to be upon a battleground in a holy war of the spirit. He accepts the froth of madness from those who blaspheme his efforts to heal as being but the foam on the Ocean of Maya-illusions supporting the ego.

To be instructed by a Teacher who has had erasement of sins is very disconcerting to a sinner who is still in love with sinning. Teachers are persecuted and maligned because people do not want to hear the voice of conscience outside of themselves or within themselves.

The Teacher's effort is to enable each student to realize for himself the continuity of the Light. The first law of the Teacher is to teach a person to be self-responsible. Dedication is the greatest gift man can cultivate—and from responsibility comes the great dedication.

The Path is Eternal. No ego has ever walked the Path; only the One within is the Walker of the Eternal Path.

> *We must see not only our Teacher as being in Omnipresence, but we also must see our fellow disciples in Omnipresence and in a place and point of time revealing to us our own need—for the karmas seen in another are in reality our own mirrored back to us.*

THE LIVING TEACHER

> *And he gave some, apostles; and some, prophets; and some, evangelists; and some, pastors and teachers; For the perfecting of the saints, for the work of the ministry, for the edifying of the body of Christ: Till we all come in the unity of the faith, and of the knowledge of the Son of God, unto a perfect man, unto the measure of the stature of the fulness of Christ.*
>
> —*Ephesians 4:11–13*

The Living Teachers are living books having access to the *Word* through the Greater Archetypes. Besides these, there are lesser teachers not having access to the Greater Archetypes; they are partial-truth purveyors of the Word. To fall into the hands of a biased teacher is to feed upon the husks of unreality.

A Living Teacher fears not the results of his word, for he is sweet with the elixir of Truth which falls as a just rain upon the just and the unjust. To him who hath an ear let him hear. To him who hath an eye let him see. To him who hath a heart leaning in the direction of the Light, let him sit and learn at the feet of the Living Teacher taking of the fountain of life.

A person seeking to enter the Spiritual Path fails himself and his search for Truth when he does not trust his Teacher. One must have trust in his Teacher and faith in God to remain on the Path. Through trust in the Living Teacher, the Teacher will enable him to move aside his ego, that he may dwell in his higher mind, where the true teaching under God is confirmed and revealed to him.

The Teacher knows that the ego of the student rejects him. It is the work of the Teacher to bring the higher mind to birth in the student. The Teacher forgives, and moves out of the range of the ego of his chela or disciple, seeing always the higher mind and the soul desiring to break free into Self-Realization and God-Realization.

To be a real and true Teacher, one must have access to the constant wisdom-consciousness stream of parabolic allegories and the archetypal symbols. Otherwise one is a parrot or imitator and is devoid of the Living Word within his speaking or sayings.

Until one has command of the three lower astral planes, he is not ready to be a Teacher. The unmanifested processes must flow through him and be made manifest.

To be opened as a soul does not make one a Teacher. His apprenticeship begins the moment he is soul-opened.

The Teacher opens up his subject matter with gratitude, God-praising, God-acknowledgement, and divine obligation as to the source of his teaching. This is the way he prepares the group-body to receive the Holy Spirit through the peace-flow and comfort-flow and Love of God.

The Holy Spirit is the Messenger of God filled with the Love-flow and Power of God. He who has the Holy-Spirit logos is a love-vessel filled with God, giving comfort, peace and enlightenment.

There are two cardinal sins for a Teacher: (1) To mention any human issue on the altar that identifies a student to his fellow students in the spirit of weakness or criticism; and (2) to base his lesson upon his own struggle and challenges in a karmic situation. That is inflicting upon his students his own karma and involving them in his karma. These are strictly Neti, Neti's, the "No, No's" in Teaching.

The Holy Ghost is the Comforter. He comes first to give peace and comfort. The Bible is a Holy-Ghost book. Its tongue is the Holy Spirit. Its evangelistical power is lost when it is made into literature fed by the intellect. Preachers and teachers who give sugar rather than the salt within the Gospels have lost touch with the dynamic Power of God speaking through the Bible.

> *No two people need their Teacher in the same way. Each brings his own psychic puzzle to be solved.*

CO-SIGNERS IN THE SPIRITUAL LIFE

> *There is nothing more dynamic than sacrifice.*

When a Teacher takes a student, he becomes a co-signer to a note which is dependent upon the virtue-collateral in his chela or disciple. If the Teacher co-signs the note, he becomes a co-signer to the karmic debts of his student. If the student fails to pay his part of the note, it falls upon the Teacher to be responsible for the debt.

A Teacher, with his observation powers earned through spiritual processes, must assay the collateral for which he is signing. If there is no character in his student, the door is closed between him and his student.

If he is a teacher untrained as to the ethic of succession in Dharma, he will be blind to the significant responsibility between a teacher and his student. Under the karmic law of balances, if the teacher blindly or emotionally accepts the karma of a disciple through any degree of preference, he takes on the debt of karma of his chela. Such a teacher exposes himself to the personalized issues in a student's life, and thus directly learns through the reproduction of his student's karma in his own personal life.

A Teacher must *see* clearly; he must observe the spiritual potential of the disciple weighed against the debts of the disciple. Jesus understood this law when He took unto Himself His disciples: Peter, James, Thomas, Jude, Andrew, Nathanael, James the Less, John, Philip, Matthew, Simon Zelotes and Judas. Jesus' Power of Exorcism of karmas of His twelve was used in two instances: at the Lord's Supper during the washing of the feet; and in giving the Fire during His Ascension at Pentecost.

A Teacher having absolving powers of karmic debts is under the Holy Fire through Jesus. No other Teacher in the world has had the total exorcism obliterating of karmic debts save Jesus.

As long as the Teacher and the student are bound together by the vow of instruction within the Holy Dharma, the Teacher remains karmically bound to the chela from life to life. In each return to life, the chela finds his Teacher, that his karma may be revoked and cleared. The teaching side of the Teacher remains in this bond; and the chela, no matter what portion of life he may live in his return to the Earth, hears the voice of his Teacher as his conscience.

Judas entered Jesus' life to seek to knock Him from the Path. Satan used Judas to incite the satanic evil causing the Crucifixion of Jesus.

Jesus, standing firm against all temptations, laid down the blueprint for all Teachers in associating with their chelas and disciples. To His disciples who asked materialistic favors from Heaven, Jesus showed clearly the pitfalls of ambition. To Peter, He showed the karmic debt the chela takes on himself when he denies his Teacher, as did Peter on denying Jesus. *"Peter said unto him, Lord, why cannot I follow thee now? I will lay down my life for thy sake. Jesus answered him, Wilt thou lay down thy life for my sake? Verily, verily, I say unto thee, The cock shall not crow, till thou hast denied me thrice." (St. John 13:37, 38)*

If one would be a Teacher of the spiritualized truths, he will be always a chela whether he is a Teacher or a chela; always in the state of soul-expanding under the direction of the One who had full command of His Most-High Soul-Powers.

Jesus loved all of His disciples. He understood their frailties, but He knew that their essential characters must be ever pounded upon the anvil of the fiery shaping, whereby as disciples, through total submission to the Will of God, they could serve the Christ Spirit in the transforming processes of the earth and the soul.

> Forgive me, but the task of the Guru is not an easy one. To make something of the disciple, to put him on his feet, to give him new life, to help him reach his True Home—this is the Guru's work. Giving lectures or fine talks is not the Guru's work. His talks are merely to help them be aware that they are in deep forgetfulness, but the Master's duty is a matter of custody.
>
> It often happens that the disciple is due for heavy suffering because of the karmic reactions from the past, but through the Guru's protection it can be reduced from the gallows to perhaps a slight pinprick.
>
> The Master always saves the disciples, no matter how dangerous a situation they may be in. His protecting arms serve as a shield and buckler, and the disciple leads a charmed life, as it were. He takes in his own hands the entire process of winding up the karmic impressions of the jiva (soul).
>
> —Kirpal Singh

STATEMENT OF FAITH

Through Jesus, my strength is ever near.

Through the weakness of those who betray me, my strength is ever present in Jesus.

If my teaching be the Truth, those who betray me betray the Truth. The Spirit of Truth shall go with a lamp of my devotion and my commitment. This lamp is perpetual in the Flame of the Everlasting Christ in me.

Who bars the threshold of my temple of worship condemns himself to darkness.

I of myself can do nothing. The Father has charge of my dedication. My commitment is of the soul. No man can profane my commitment or pollute my integrity.

Through Christ, I have freed myself from the wicked, who, through the spirit of darkness, would seek to waver me.

I behold the face of Satan in him who would lead my soul into desolation.

God help him who would shake my commitment or reshape it.

I shall worship One God Who is the One in All.

I shall keep His Altar flame alive with my blood, with my life.

. . . Ann Ree Colton

3

VENERATION FOR THE TEACHER

When reverence is present in the student, wisdom is free in the Teacher.

To Identify the Teacher

Only soul-knowing makes Teacher identification possible.

Nothing can equal the student-and-Teacher relationship when the Teacher comes loaded with spirituality. The Teacher, always in the state of pregnant knowing, imparts life and light to him who responds with his heart and mind. It is not shameful or weak to lean on the knowing within one's Teacher.

All ethical Teachers teaching from the direct formulas of the Spiritual Worlds ask nothing for themselves, but ask everything for what they carry as the Dharma, as the Light. If one would follow a Teacher with the Dharma, he must be prepared to open with heart expectations what the Teacher brings, offers and provides.

Many in the world cannot bear the Truth or contemplate Truth because Truth foretells destruction of temples built upon self-love within the Pleasure Principle.

The meeting of a Teacher ignites instant mediation. If one denies his Teacher, that which mediates through the

Teacher places him where he belongs as to what school—whether it is karma as family, as race, as nation. Karmas of the body related to health are a manifestation of mediation. Karmas in the loss of property are the Law of Karma at work to bring equilibrium to one's giving and receiving.

What one receives when absent from the stewardship of sharing, places him in the ranks of a taker and a parasite. The taker can never enter the Path of direct Dharma. The giver is prepared to enter, but must be trained through lessons of false-sentiment. The taker must be trained through the removal of what he loves or possesses so that he might learn the basics of the Real for which his soul longs and hopes. The taker is his own dunce, denying his own birthright. He finds his birthright when he learns the precious joy of giving and receiving.

Earning and learning are one in preparation for the Path. To prosper, one must be willing to learn through his earning. This is accomplished when he looks upon his earning as a service to God.

To be a Teacher, one must thirst for wisdom, and be teachable. He must hunger to serve. His hunger and his thirst must be equal, or he will be an erratic and fanatical teacher.

The interflow of the wisdom-consciousness now pouring into the pool of unknowing and spiritual ignorance must be mastered by the future Western Living Teachers or Gurus. In the West, soul-hungers are fermenting, that the surfacing desire to know the soul and to manifest the powers of the soul be met by Teachers who are sincere, true and ethical.

The seed of reforming must be planted by a Great-Soul Teacher without offensiveness. This seed must sprout from within the chela by his own disciplines and growing.

The reforming will and a reforming mind of a Guru act as an adversary against the self-will of a chela. The seed of reform, when clothed in Bhakti love, results in a healthy suggestibility and acceptance upon the scale of spiritual growth and growing.

Souls entering the world who have been nurtured in the mortification-trials in previous lives accept discipline as a tonic and vitalizer for character and for spirit. Only the strong have such acceptance of mortification. The goal is purity, humility and modesty for all who would aspire to be in the Will of God.

Pure souls are channels for the Will of God. Only these can channel the Power of God. All else is power for self, for ego and for manipulation.

A *choice soul* is one who keeps his word; he is one who is self-responsible from childhood. He can be seen in childhood as the one who takes upon himself burdens to relieve his parents, burdens the other children refuse to assume. In school and schooling, he keeps his word; he is on time; he keeps up his grades. In the work life supporting his stewardship, he is honest, reliable, ethical. This is a choice soul whom the Divine Companions of Omnipresence choose to give the truths and enlightenment to the world.

> *Obedience to the teacher and to what he teaches—the teacher as a representative of God, the One—will in time lead the novice-initiate toward all of the joys to be had from the spiritually illumined mind.*

CONSCIENCE AS AN EQUILIBRIUM-VEHICLE

> *It is God's pleasure to give you the Holy Gifts, but they are given to you according to your earning—and you can earn them only through discipline.*

Souls born with spiritual maturity, having known spiritual discipline under a Guru in former lives, have no expectations of paternal indulgence from the Guru. Discipline is accepted as a necessary support on every level of their lives, physical, emotional and mental. Such disciples venerate and honor their Gurus.

When a young person with an untrained, restless mind and undeclared vocation enters a spiritual environment to receive instruction, he is inclined to look upon the role of the Guru in his life as a parental role. If this continues, the Guru cannot reach him; the Guru is sealed away from the immature student. This also relates to an older, undeveloped emotional person who seeks to outpicture his unresolved parental and family-atom relationship. Within the aura of the Guru, he is an initiating karmic agent.

A Teacher of the higher life is never disappointed in a student and never surprised at what a student does. If a teacher is disappointed in a student, he is on the karmic level of his student. And if he is surprised at the student's conduct, good or bad, the teacher is yet judging his student from the comparative standpoint of his own ego.

The teacher places a burden upon his student when he overpraises him. He isolates himself from his student when he uses harsh judgment in correcting him.

A relaxed and trusting attitude between the Teacher and the student is forged upon trust in God first. When the Teacher has attained perspective, he knows that God within his student or disciple can and will accomplish *miracles.*

When a Teacher gives credit to God for what happens to his student rather than to himself, he moves beyond his own ego as a Teacher.

The wonder of being a Teacher is that one can selflessly do the works for which the Father has sent him. This is wonder-grace, never ceasing in the flow of consciousness between the Teacher and the disciple.

A teacher asking self-credit for his work is an unformed teacher. He is himself in need of instruction. Such teachers receive their instruction in the harsh school of karmic involvement on the level of their students.

A teacher must avoid dry repetition in the presentation of instruction, or his own versatility falls into boredom—and he becomes a pedagogue. His teaching versatility becomes a biased and partial vehicle. Such teachers betray their philosophies and their ideals. True Teachers produce ingenuity and incentive in their students.

Conscience is an equilibrium-vehicle. The conscience rights itself due to the equilibrium-laws of morality.

When one is indecisive by lack of grace, his conscience cannot work. He is led to his own destruction for his soul's sake. In duality, the conscience dips left and one is indecisive as to his own harm. He thus makes wrong choice and steps into hardship karma.

The conscience seeks to come to centering as an equilibrium-vehicle. When there is over-inflation of ego and self-assessed righteousness, the pendulum of conscience tilts to the right, and there is over-exhibition and thus demotion.

It is the purpose of the soul to work with the centered equilibrium of right choice in man. There is only one way to live in right choice—and that choice is God as the Will, the Life, the Light, the Love.

When one comes into the aura of the Teacher, conscience becomes a vehicle of omniscience. Conscience coming directly from omniscient, prescient power of the soul knows the right or wrong of the past, the present and the future.

The Teacher is the Higher Self of the student until the student makes union with his own Higher Self. The student must be alive with the desire to escape his problems, and he must see that instruction is the door to the escape from suffering.

If the Teacher sees that the student is heedless, being

laden with tamas inertia, karmic law frees the Teacher—and the student is removed from the environment of the Teacher.

> *True prophets in the world sacrifice themselves to purify the conscience of nations and religions.*

THE TEACHER AND THE CHELA

> *The Western person does not know what it means to have a Teacher or how to treat a Teacher. The Master was telling me the other day, the Western person does not know how to relate to a Teacher. He has no courtesy, no manners, no reverence, no sense of gratitude.*

Knowing is a positive, attracting principle. The desire to know attracts the chela to the Teacher. The Teacher who opens Knowing comes as an angel in disguise, for concealed in the birth of Knowing is freedom.

It takes straw to make bricks. It takes students to make a Teacher. A Living Teacher does not teach to great masses of people because he is fighting to bring to birth God-sent souls or future teachers.

The Teacher must draw forth his students from those who have attained the sacred *volatile will,* or self-control and self-mastery over the ego. Students retaining excessive self-esteem must await many lives of the future to become the initiates for the New-Era time.

The greatest praise one can give his Teacher is his willingness to be taught. Beware of a person who is not teachable.

The Masters mediate to send one to his right Teacher. The chela or disciple who is considered by the Masters to have humility is one who is teachable. And especially is humility gauged by the Masters in one who permits Life to teach him, and applies the resulting lessons to life—to shape, to form and to create.

One is electricity—and his voltage depends upon his love nature. When one hates, he is fire. When one hates, he destroys. And when he is unteachable, he destroys.

Persons who are unteachable are classified as the most destroying, for they are willfully set against learning. They are enemies against the Wisdom Principle, which demands flexibility of mind and heart.

Those who lie to themselves and seek prominence through desire for ego inflation, craving to dominate the wills of others, attract false teachers to themselves. If by some inadvertent small portion of grace, they are attracted to a true Teacher, their false desires and pressures produce a mish-mash of astralocity; the purest teachings become distorted into fantasies of glamor and confusion.

The first law in the life of a pure seeker is reverence for the Teacher and Teaching. When this is set aside by an inflated mind, the result is accentuation of karma and demotion of the little will.

When the pupil is in a tamasic state or half in and half out of Maya tensions, he is similar to a snake shedding its skin or a babe half out of the womb—and the Teacher comes.

"Seek, and ye shall find." (St. Matthew 7:7) One's loneliness is proof that he is searching for God. Not listening to one's Teachers shows waywardness or short-stop thinking. What is the use of having a Teacher if one does not do what the Teacher says?

If a student does not have right attendance, he does not receive the complete virtue out of his study. If he does not go *up* with his studies, he goes to the end of the class.

Teachers such as Sri Aurobindo, Yogananda, etc., who die, are just as responsible for their students as they were on earth. They have to work with their cycles.

To teach through deeds and to manifest deeds in others is the most noble character in man.

The Teacher's knowledge is honed against the unknowing in the disciple.

When one makes himself a rival of his Teacher, he invokes his karma.

When the chela is magnified in emotion, he receives the seed of Truth first into his emotions. Through initiation, he is tested until the seed takes firm root through desire and conscience. Through desire and conscience, the seed grows and flowers in the mind to quicken understanding and realization. When this occurs, his emotions are spaced, becoming a healthy vehicle for the mind. This is true Realization.

When one has overabundance in the mental, it is destiny for him to contest spiritual truths. The interflow of emotions being less positive than the mental flow, he becomes a contestant to the Light, challenging his Teacher and the teaching.

When the Teacher unburdens his disciple or chela, he frees the disciple from the shock of facing the Angels of Judgement after death. This is why it is important that there be openness between the disciple and Teacher. Secrecy must be healed through confession—right confession in right timing to the need of being free of karmic burdens.

Teachers identify negativity in their disciple first through energy-velocities given off by the disciple. The Teacher works with the disciple to transenergize these energies into quickened realization and freedom.

The Teacher has to know how to work with the karmic variables.

Defective persons are born from having defected from God's processes of Law. They are *soul* defectives and must be re-envisioned by a Teacher who beholds the Image of God behind the screen or mask of defection.

Students who lose enthusiasm for God are bored by the monotony of virtue. All boredom is caused by an unawakened creativity.

Spirit awake in man leads to virility, vitality and spirituality. A true Teacher must awaken the creative potential in his disciple or chela.

When one moves away from the Teacher's Mantle functioning through the Coinciding Principle, he moves aside from the Coinciding which works with Omnipresence.

When a man cannot accept a woman Teacher, he has not worked out his karma with women.

As a child's hands must be slapped to teach non-offence, so must the chela feel the vajra-blow of correction.

Disciplines dulled by indulgence from a teacher produce gross offspring and nought is observed of the Dharma.

Be prepared to see a neat lodging, a fair face, a glow of confidence in the chela who is suckled at the breast of pure learning.

It must be known and expected by the chela that old hospices must be burned with the fire of purification before the closed eye and ear might open.

Everyone must learn where his Achilles' heel is, and he must know its accompanying vulnerabilities. Far better for him if he masters the Achilles' heel without shame or fall.

Teachers come into the initiate's life to move him over the abyss of lust, hate, envy, lies.

In the finest aspects of Initiation, he who does not listen to his Teacher will have failed in listening to his conscience over many lives. The soul never casts any soul into oblivion, but the soul does make an outcast of one who has refused to yield to his conscience and to his Teacher. It is not the soul that is outcast; it is his soul's record of what he knew that is obliterated until he can retrieve it in some future life or incarnation.

A mantra remembered is a divine current that can open

the voltage of grace, which has been interrupted by lack of obedience to spiritual Law. Discipleship means exactly what it says: Discipline under the Law.

> *There are some students who are more in love with their own karma than they are in love with God.*

THE CHURCH: THE CRADLE OF THE CHRIST

The best religious contribution is *conscience.* A religion based on conscience is destined to uplift consciousness. Religious tyranny ends where conscience begins.

To one of tamasic tendency, freedom to worship prolongs persecution in creeds. Freedom to worship expressed as rajasic produces schisms, cliques and creed-oppression. Freedom to worship based upon Conscience and Mediation, observing the rights of one's neighbor as for himself, is Agape.

In every body of worship, twelve levels or types of conscience are expressed. A worship congregation and a worshipful congregation are not the same in the expression of religious conscience. One who worships blindly has yet to know his true Polar Star—the Christ. One who worships with religiosity is linked to the Polar Star of the Christ.

For the thousands of worship-bodies, there are few among them who have any inclination toward true worshipfulness in the religiosity spirit.

Ministers serving the Altar, containing the true hungers and yearning for God, are hapless victims in worship bodies having no conscience. The martyrdom of today expressed in church bodies by truly dedicated ministers is little known, save by those who experience it.

Men serving the Altars of holy places who are subjected to ecclesiastical formats lacking the true life waters of the

Holy Spirit endure intense persecution from those who authorize them to speak the Holy Word. The Word which they are committed to as being Holy is muzzled by boards, committees, cliques, conferences, mortgages, and non-sacramental edicts having no place in God's Holy Place.

It can be seen by those who observe religion through religiosity hearts that the human contradictions which defy and challenge all men in the nonreligious life are refined and magnified within the church body or the temple.

The minister who retains his virginal self-denial impulses is crucified on the Altars where there should be the Word of God in its most high and holy state.

Rebellion in the churches, when not shepherded into peace, builds unsacred atmospheres for those who come to hear the Word and to pray within the atmosphere of the Word. Those who have authority over the place of the Word—having no thought of conscience—give off a sterile atmosphere to an expectant, worshipful heart.

The church of today is undergoing in the Inner-World governings the Prophet's Scrutiny, for where the Prophetic Voice or the Holy Intuition is absent in the hearts of those serving the Altar, the word is dry-rot rather than flesh.

THE TEACHER AND THE LAW

If ye keep my commandments, ye shall abide in my love; even as I have kept my Father's commandments, and abide in his love.

—St. John 15:10

The root is in the Old Testament. The flower is in the New Testament. And the fruit is in the book of Revelation.

Truth has produced the Law, and Law is the way action is maintained. That Truth may have its Will in earth, Law must be.

A Ministry must be built upon Law and nourished by Love. The great Laws are splendid truths upon which we are supported.

Niscience is an Initiatory School. An initiatory school without teaching the Law is an inept school. Those who are being shepherded to Niscience and its instruction are being drawn by the magnet of the heart toward the Law.

Love is an energy, an elixir of direct Spirit. It is the Teacher's responsibility to disclose the Law to the body of love. Faith in the Teacher builds the body of love through which the Teacher teaches.

If the Teacher has developed heart-response in the words of Law, he protects and maintains the pure, naive quality of love embodied in those who have faith in him and in his way of teaching. Not only should a disciple have faith in his Teacher, but the Teacher must have faith in his disciple as a being of love.

The Love-Teacher gives the blueprint of the Law with firmness and clarity, that he protect his students and provide them with insulation against corruption in the world of human affairs.

God cannot wholly reveal Himself except to a disciplined heart. The emotional body will be the last to be perfected in this earth. The mind cannot function totally in its creative radiance until the emotions are devoid of fantasy and unreal expectations.

Law demands discipline. And the first discipline is the discipline of the self. This discipline begins in the heart.

Unrealistic love-relationships produce suffering, outrage and distortion. The fires of passion, when predominating within any relationship, produce retaliation and revenge.

A disciplined heart attracts to one the blessings of love, protection, joy and peace. A hardened heart is not a disciplined heart.

Every person loving truth has the science of hope. And hope gives the chalice for your faith to work.

One starts off saying, "The Father will do it for me." Then he ends up saying, "I will do it for the Father."

There is so much to know and the Eternal will teach you. You can be in the Eternal Now under the tutelage of the Eternals when you have total belief in Life Everlasting.

The greatest gift the Eternal gives us is change of form and expression in consciousness. Every germ, every organic substance is in a state of infinite transition, which never ceases. One must look into the face of his own change, and know that he is changing yet deathless, that he is immortal while yet mortal.

"Here am I, Father, use me." God uses one's willing spirit. Every failure man has is because of a resisting and unwilling spirit. Will without intelligence is disobedience.

Today, things are worse than they were in the time of Saint Paul when men used ritualistic idolatry through objects and forms. Today, there is undisciplined license in *self-idolatry*.

When a teacher teaches the letter of the Law, he is but a translator of the Law, but an authorized spiritual Teacher teaching to advanced disciples *transposes* the Law. He passes the Law onto the disciples—and the disciples are compelled to live within the Law.

Love is the transmitting instrument. A teacher without love cannot emanate *The Power*.

There is a period when one truly gets the Power. If he has a single malicious thought or dishonest motive, it wreaks calamity on self and on all.

Power without love is fanaticism, the "letter," and is the "sounding brass" or a "tinkling cymbal." Power minus love creates fanaticism, war.

Overstimulation is power misused. Equilibrium in power can be maintained only through Love.

A teaching body founded upon Love provides proportion to the three great aspects of God: The Father, the Son and the Holy Spirit. The attributes of holy discipleship and steward-studentship must be founded upon Love, that the Power of God may emanate through all of the vehicles seeking to express the Eternal Spirit.

Revere your Teacher who comes armored through the Christ.

. . . Jonathan Murro

4

THE MANTLE OF THE TEACHER

When one has found his guru there should be unconditional devotion to him, because he is the vehicle of God. The guru's sole purpose is to bring the disciple to Self-Realization; the love a guru receives from a devotee is given by the guru to God. When a spiritual preceptor finds a student in tune with him, he is able to teach him more quickly than he can teach a student who resists him.

—Yogananda

Three Stages of the Teacher's Mantle

The true Teacher-and-chela experience begins even before each enters the world through birth. From the beginning of the Teacher's awareness of his calling as a Teacher, he is resounding in his own hierarchy nature the names of those who are to extend his work and purpose of coming. Thus, the chela or disciple knows his Teacher and trusts him. He knows his Teacher is God-sent, for he has longed to hear his name spoken on the lips of his Teacher from life to life.

—Ann Ree Colton

Jesus could read the Soul's Record and Covenant of a person; therefore, He knew whom to call and select to be His disciples. In this way, He chose Peter, Andrew, Matthew, Nathanael and the other disciples. *"Ye have not chosen me, but I have chosen you." (St. John 15:16)*

A true Teacher who comes into the world to render a great service to God and the human spirit has the ability to read the Souls' Records and to know the Souls' Covenants of others. Thus, he *knows* the individuals who will become his students, recognizing their unique qualifications as recorded in their Souls. This ability of the Teacher is a Soul-Gift, a Prophetic Gift, that enables him and his students to accomplish some special task for God and the Dharma.

Before birth, a holy personage reads his own Soul's Record and perceives his Soul's Covenant with God. During life, he remains centered within his Soul's Covenant, fulfilling God's Will while in the world. He knows the work he must do, the persons he must teach, the new truths and principles he must seal into the Earth.

Before a Living Teacher is ready to begin his ministry, he works on the inner planes to call his disciples to him. In the inner planes of knowledge and truth, the Teacher is shown who will be his students in the world. God's Holy Law of Attraction then begins to draw together the Teacher and the students in the outer world of action.

There are three stages of the Teacher's Mantle:

1. Before the Teacher meets the student.
2. After the Teacher meets the student.
3. After the Teacher leaves the world.

In many instances, students-to-be are involved in heavy karma or the pleasure principle and have no knowledge of the Teacher nor do they desire to follow the Spiritual Path. However, if such persons have covenanted before birth to make unique and important contributions to the world, they will begin to experience certain longings for freedom, knowledge, and a desire for a more reverent and moral way of life.

When the Teacher is ready to do his work in the world, he must first begin to release his students-to-be from the karmas that are claiming them in their lives. In this, the Teacher's Mantle moves spiritually over a student-to-be *before* the student meets the Teacher. There is a Soul-Communion between a Teacher and his or her future students. This Soul-Communion through the Teacher's Mantle begins the process of freeing a prospective student from his karma so that, when the Teacher comes into his life physically, the student will be able to move into the Teacher's rhythms of instruction and creation.

If the sins of a student are many, the Teacher will enter into *Intentional Suffering* to pay the student's sin-debts as part of the Mantle-Grace and its liberating blessings in the student-to-be's life and destiny as a future servant of God. This Intentional Suffering by the Teacher for the student's sins begins before the Teacher and the student meet physically. If the Teacher did not covenant to render this service, the student's sins would prevent him from being graced with sacred instruction from an Enlightened Teacher.

After the Teacher and the student meet in the physical world, the Teacher accepts full responsibility for the student. In this, the Teacher must teach the student everything that God would have the student learn regarding the Divine Marriage. An attentive and responsive student immediately begins to unite with his Soul's Covenant with God, thereby experiencing miraculous healings, holy joys and grace-gifts.

If a student does not accept the disciplines of the Laws and Commandments of God, the Teacher must pay for any sins committed by the student as long as they are associated through their coordinated Covenants. This means that the Teacher is willing to pay the student's new sin-debts through some form of suffering. If the Teacher did not accept this responsibility, every student who sins would *immediately* be removed from the grace of spiritual instruction and placed back into the prison of karmic bondage.

The payment of a student's sin-debts by his Teacher may be likened to a loving parent paying the debts of a foolish young son or daughter to keep them out of jail. A Teacher's suffering for his chelas who have yet to learn right from wrong is a noble dedication. Suffering in order to help others learn and grow spiritually is the exalted life. Jesus, the Saints and dedicated Teachers epitomize this fact of the higher life.

The Teacher is *always* working on the level of the Soul's Covenant of each student, and therefore patiently teaches, heals, and pays the sin-debts of his students until they finally unite with their Souls' Covenants with God. When this occurs, an initiated student will become a Teacher of Truth authorized by God to teach through the Powers and Gifts of the Covenant.

A cardinal sin is a major offense against Holy Law. If a student offends any of the Ten Commandments or fails to give an honest tithe to God, he is guilty of a cardinal sin. Most students do not comprehend the gravity of their sinning. However, the Teacher understands the heavy penalties for offending any Law or Commandment of God—and willingly pays the debts of his students through Intentional Suffering on their behalf. Few persons love enough to render this kind of service for the cause of teaching others the Word, the Law and the Will of God. This is why there are so few true Teachers in the world. This is also why a Teacher anointed by God's Spirit is the most priceless Gift of God to the world.

To teach others sacred truths is to liberate their souls. Blessed are all Teachers of Truth who teach lovingly, graciously, unendingly, for through their inspired instruction the world is progressing from darkness to light, from ignorance to knowledge, from sin to enlightenment.

A Teacher who leaves the physical world through the door of death continues to bless and instruct his chelas through the Mantle-Covenant and Dedication to God. In certain ways, the Pelican and the chela are closer together. Totally free in his or her eternal body of light, the Teacher may grace the student with the knowledge of new areas of Truth, thereby expanding the student's range of understanding and enlightenment.

The reality of God as the Creator of the wise Cycles of Birth, Life and Death becomes more firmly sealed into the heart and mind of the chela after his Teacher's passing. Also, the joy of receiving priceless blessings from his Teacher through the Mantle proves the power of love to transcend all barriers between Earth and Heaven.

> *The power of the guru is transmitted through the mantra to the disciple. That is why the guru at the time of initiation takes on himself the sins of the disciple and suffers so much from physical maladies. It is extremely difficult to be a guru, for he has to take the responsibility for the disciple's sins. He is affected by them. A good disciple, however, helps the teacher. Some disciples make quick progress, and some do it slowly; it depends on the tendencies of the mind acquired by one's past deeds.*
>
> —*Sarada Devi*

SOUL-KNOWING

> *My sheep hear my voice, and I know them, and they follow me.*
>
> —*St. John 10:27*

There is no greater knowing than *soul-knowing*. Through soul-knowing, one recognizes his Teacher. The student has been taught by the Teacher in different lands and times in previous lives. In these lives of the past, the Teacher was known to the student by other names. However, regardless of the place, time or name, the student and the Teacher will immediately recognize one another through soul-knowing. In future lives, when the student and Teacher come together again to resume their work for God, they will once again recognize one another through soul-knowing.

Soul-knowing is a gift of God activated through one's love. If one loves in the spirit of the Commandments of Love, he will experience soul-knowing in all important areas of his life. Decisions based upon soul-knowing always prove inspired, harmonious and happy. A happy and harmonious marriage results when a man and woman are blessed with *soul-knowing* of each other. The choice of a vocation or occupation, when made through soul-knowing, is a wise choice.

Decisions based upon soul-knowing never fail to produce increasing blessings. Decisions made without soul-knowing lead to unhappy associations in marriage, business and other relationships.

Soul-knowing is a priceless gift of God presented to those who have a deep and abiding faith in Him from life to life. In the Teacher-student relationship, soul-knowing is as a sensitive radar providing protection and as a powerful antenna attuned to the Word and Will of God.

In a dream I saw a guru seated with several chelas. Suddenly a cobra started moving toward them. The guru told his chelas to remain motionless and to be without fear. Every chela obeyed as the vicious-looking serpent moved by each one, and finally departed. The dream was revealing to me the importance of a student's obedience and fearlessness. To be disobedient to one's Teacher or to have fear is to be immediately struck dead by the snake, symbolizing the tester or Satan. All students on the Path are thoroughly tested. The disobedient and the fearful experience a spiritual demise, while the obedient and the fearless are preserved, protected, and prepared to receive the Mantle of the Teacher.

To Kiss the Feet of One's Teacher

O Lord Jesus, I take the dust from your feet.
I kiss the dust from your feet.

—*Ann Ree Colton*

When a student kisses the feet of his living Teacher, he is honoring the Spirit of God in his Teacher. To kiss the feet of one's Teacher is an act of veneration, respect, gratitude and humility.

To kiss the feet of one's Teacher is to kiss the Feet of Jesus in Whose Name the Teacher teaches. When a student or devotee kisses the feet of his Teacher, the Teacher knows that he (the Teacher) is filled with the Abiding Presence of Jesus. *"Abide in me, and I in you." (St. John 15:4)* Therefore, the Teacher knows that the devotee is, in reality, kissing the Feet of Jesus. In this, the Teacher receives the kissing of his feet with humility, knowing that it is the Lord Jesus Who is filling him with knowledge and wisdom.

To kiss the feet of one's Teacher is to honor the Heavenly Father, the Divine Mother and Almighty God, for the Teacher is at one with the Creator and the Heavenly Host through the Divine-Marriage Anointing.

To kiss the feet of a servant of God is to be rewarded by God with increasing knowledge and grace through the

Teacher's instruction. By kissing the feet of one's Teacher, the devotee or chela draws closer to the time when he, too, will become a Teacher of God's Word, filled with Divine Grace and Truth. *"God . . . giveth grace to the humble." (1 Peter 5:5)*

When one kisses the feet of his Teacher, he is kissing the feet of all Teachers of Truth, all Gurus, all Healers, all Ministers, Priests and Holy Ones who are serving God with dignity, integrity and steadfastness.

"How beautiful are the feet of them that preach the gospel of peace, and bring the glad tidings of good things." (Romans 10:15) Beautiful are the feet of those who have walked the Path of Virtue for many years and many lives; walking in the footsteps of Jesus; living in the Law and Will of God.

To kiss the feet of one's Teacher is to receive a special blessing from his Teacher.

Whenever a devotee lovingly kisses the feet of his Teacher, the Teacher passes the student's love on to Jesus and to God. In the spirit of Holy Poverty, the Teacher places the student's love on God's Holy Altar. In so doing, the Teacher and the student are bountifully blessed by the Angels, the Saints and the Presences of Light who sanctify and serve the world through the Holy Altars of God.

The lord guru is the root of all siddhis.

If you recognize him as space, you will realize the unborn truth.

If you recognize him as the sun, all-pervading great compassion will arise.

If you recognize him as the moon, you will dispel the anguish of the klesas (veils).

If you recognize him as the ocean, you will acquire supreme, unwavering samadhi.

If you recognize him as a jewel, needs, desires, and hopes are spontaneously fulfilled.

If you recognize him as the captain of a ship, he will convey you to the jewel island of liberation.

If you recognize him as a general, he will quell the attack of the enemies, perverted views.

If you recognize him as a sword, you will cut the bonds of fixation.

If you recognize him as a wheel, you will realize the truth of not dwelling in extremes.

If you recognize him as a lion, you will overpower the wild animals of grasping and fixation.

If you recognize him as a steed, he will carry you to the realm of nirvana.

If you recognize him as a king, all will honor you and make offering.

—Marpa, 1012–1097 A.D.

In order to achieve the Accomplishment, one should depend upon a Guru for the Initiation, Instruction, and Inner Teaching.

It requires a disciple possessing merit to receive the teaching; it requires a man who disregards discomfort and suffering; it requires the courage of fearlessness, the defiance of death!

At times you will think of your Guru. Whenever such yearning arises, visualize Him upon your head and for His blessing pray. Visualize Him sitting in the center of your heart, and forget Him never.

—Milarepa, 1040–1123 A.D.
Disciple of Marpa

. . . Ann Ree Colton

5

THE TEACHER AND THE PASSING

And when he had said this, he breathed on them, and saith unto them, Receive ye the Holy Ghost.

—*St. John 20:22*

There is no greater life in the world than the life of the Teacher. It is the hardest. It is sacrifice, but it is gloryship. To be a Teacher is one of the most sacred things possible.

Every Teacher must stand in the *Synchronized Mantles* of great Souls who have preceded him. What a Living Teacher leaves *lives,* for it is of the Life-Stream.

The best Teachers are those who ask little for themselves and give much selflessly. The Living Teacher carries the Light; he transmits the Light; and he channels the Light. No one can get into the Light without the Teacher.

Before a person can be a Teacher, he must be obedient to the Great Laws. When a Teacher is lawful, he has the Power.

The Teacher must pass on to his students the necessity for self-control, self-responsibility and self-reliance.

There is dogma, doctrine and sound doctrine. *Dogma* is a mechanics resulting from reliance upon repetition. *Doctrine* is the extractions from Scriptures that have survived and lived in the minds of the sages. *Sound Doctrine* is proven spiritual experience and the functioning of the inner consciousness.

Dogma comes from rigidity as to rules. Doctrine stems from veneration; sound doctrine, from reverence. *"But speak thou the things which become sound doctrine." (Titus 2:1)*

The body of the bird is love. And the wings of the bird are truth. The body cannot fly without the wings; neither can the wings survive without the body.

If truth is taken as a vessel of correction without love, it burns and sears rather than enlightens. The enlightened seer is a Teacher as a vessel of love. His inspired truth-words lift or give wings to the receptive mind into illumination and light.

Love-tones in the voice are necessary for the Teacher. Love-attitudes in the stance of his body when he stands before his students is necessary. The Teacher must be aware of the love-thirst in all persons. He must clairsentiently flow into the hearts and emotions of his students.

There is a time when the Teacher must say to his chela or disciple: "Peter, lovest thou me. Peter, lovest thou me. Peter, lovest thou me?" In this time, the disciple moves closer to his Teacher, to become co-atom to him after the third "lovest thou me?" But if there should be some retention of karma in the disciple delaying this union, the disciple will have failed his progression.

The greatest thing a Teacher may pass to his students is the *Esse. The Esse is the Essence of God overcoming absence from God.* The Teacher who passes the Esse and the Ethic to the student is the Teacher having the grand elegance or master elegance of the Archetypal Logos.

The first duty of the Teacher is the Passing. Without the grace of the Esse, there is no Passing.

Men cannot longer be sedimentized or concretized into the sloths of inhibiting formats and formulas. They must be free in the Esse. The Archangels have announced: the Esse has returned; the Holy Spirit in the Esse is alive, revolutionizing a new virginal light for the mind, for the soul, for the heart.

Therapies must be from the origins of the Esse, that in teaching there is healing; in healing, there is revelation and Passing. In the healing as the Opening comes the revealing.

There is no greater gift a Teacher can give to his students than the Esse-Enlightenment through the Passing. The opening of a mind to the reality of the heavenly resources is the first and divine culture, which can be made only by selfless Teachers who as Passers of the Esse are bound to no creed, no dogma, no doctrine supported by total materiality.

Men are sick of false prophets, of declaimers on the Altars. They thirst for the living waters of Truth. They thirst for the light in the purest form of mental chastity vehicled by Truth; there is no greater expression of the mind and soul.

The soul is tortured and hampered and stifled in partial truths. The more perfect way, as spoken of by Paul, is the Apostolic Light, which now indents itself into the soul-effervescence of men.

Godly men are as wise as the serpent and as gentle as the dove; wise as the Seraphim Angels who are the Holy Nagas of the Great Purusha or Unconscious. When the Nagas are gathered together, the mysteries are made plain; the Third Heaven spills itself through the Archetypal Light into the souls and minds of men.

All in the Earth desire in their emotional natures to become recipients of the Love of God. To know their true birthright is their right. Thus, the love-nature and the Ahimsa heart must come forth for *all* men. There must be reverence and consideration for one another so that love may speak its message through the expansion of the emotions.

There must be an understanding of the desires of man as a guiding principle to lead him to God. There can be no fetishes in the spiritualized mind. As long as there are fantasized desires regarding worships, persons or life, men are rocked to and fro, never centered, never happy, never pure.

Jesus gave the true knowledge of the Laws of Prospering. One must research his prospering-vajra techniques if he would cultivate integrity in person, in works and in grace.

The chela should cleanse out; search out; mark and trace his desires, feelings and emotions, that he may be selfless, renunciated, desireless. To be passionless, one must be like Jesus. To be compassionate, one must act like Jesus. To be dispassionate, one must be whole in giving, whole in loving.

The soul knows God. One should draw upon his soul-center Pulsation in the crown of the head to make union with God and His Spirit.

A devotee should learn of the meaning of his *self* through Soul-Pulsation powers. From the power of the Holy Spirit in him come the *Gifts,* and from the Gifts comes the *Passing.* If one is to become a Living Teacher, he must earn the Gifts so as to Pass, and to Open those who are ready.

The Teacher prepares the student to teach. To be a Living Teacher, one must accept instruction in the spirit of holiness. All other teaching falls into intellect. All things of intellect last but one incarnation. Holy teaching lasts forever, for the Eternal.

I accept the Holy Truth fed by the Holy Spirit.

THE GRACE OF LOGOS

> *If any man among you seem to be religious, and bridleth not his tongue, but deceiveth his own heart, this man's religion is vain.*
>
> —*James 1:26*

It is excellent to be in proximity to grace. Having the tongue of grace is to be immortalized in the Archives of

Holy Writ. The tongue of grace has come from mastery of the split tongue of criticizing and judgment.

To be harmless within the harmonics of the Coinciding, one must master the divided tongue, and move beyond harsh hardship-law judgments. Judgment is electrical. As sharp arrows electrified with non-mercy, those who judge become assailants of the grace.

There can be no virtue without charity in speech. This is the crowning virtue of self-expression. He who would be self-cultivated and self-enlightened must in all things speak with charity and with love.

That which was Truth in Jesus' speaking of the Maya realities of sin was a love-vajra for the world. A Truth-tongue absent from accusation is a knowing tongue which exorcises untruth for the sake of Truth.

Jesus, in seeing the evils in the temple, in the hypocrisies, in the cheating, in the evasions and twisting of the Law, spoke plainly against them. He spoke not as self-judging, saying, *"Judge not, that ye be not judged." (St. Matthew 7:1)* Jesus knew the true judgment was with God, yet He discerned darkness. He discerned it as evil standing against the Light, and therefore the cause of suffering. He forgave the sins of those who sought forgiveness. He forgave the sins of the world during His Passion.

Hypocrisy is created from the wolf-pack nature of man. Desiring to appear as a sheep rather than a wolf, one is hypocritical. Man supports his hypocrisy with the help of the wolf-pack instinct in his nature; he uses principle to display what he is not and uses ethic to exploit what he wills by his own willing. Each one on the Path of Initiation must learn the difference between principle offended and ethic exploited.

There is an evil silence, a separative silence between men of hypocritical instincts, saving their words or conversation for times or opportunities to communicate their self-seeing-in-part natures. To explore Truth, one must come face to face with speech as right healing, right logos, right reconciliation.

Jesus warned all who would walk the Path to be sincere. Sincerity is the testing tool against the evils of the divided tongue. *"God is not mocked." (Galatians 6:7)* Neither can His Word be twisted.

The value of Truth-speaking is a logos-grace. It is a sacred jewel ever to be shining, ever to be polished, ever to be framed or centered in the spirit of love.

> *The preacher must propound the truth with unshrinking mind. He must have the power of persuasion rooted in virtue and in strict fidelity to his vows.*
>
> *The preacher must not be prone to carp at others, or to blame other preachers; nor speak scandal, nor propagate bitter words. He must not mention by name other disciples to vituperate them and reproach their demeanor.*
>
> *A preacher must be full of energy and cheerful hope, never tiring and never despairing of final success.*
>
> *He must not take delight in quarrelsome disputations or engage in controversies so as to show the superiority of his talents, but be calm and composed.*
>
> *No hostile feelings shall reside in his heart and he must never abandon the disposition of charity toward all beings.*
>
> *So long as the people do not listen to the words of truth, the preacher knows that he has to dig deeper into their hearts, but when they begin to heed his words he apprehends that they will soon attain enlightenment.*
>
> *—Buddha*

HIGHER SELF-GENESIS TEACHERS

> *Go ye therefore, and teach all nations, baptizing them in the name of the Father, and of the Son, and of the Holy Ghost: Teaching them to observe all things whatsoever I have commanded you: and, lo, I am with you alway, even unto the end of the world. Amen.*
>
> —*St. Matthew 28:19,20*

When a student's motivation for instruction is fixed upon ego-advancement, this reveals to the Teacher the sort of disciple with whom he is working. When a student's motivation is fixed upon a *cause,* the Teacher finds a student who has entered Higher Self-Genesis.

The Higher Self-Genesis disciple is concerned for enlightenment for all of mankind. The Lesser Self-Genesis motivation is concerned for the preservation of the ego and ego-interest.

The most sensitive points in Initiation in the present-day disciple are the crossing over from Lesser Self-Genesis to Higher Self-Genesis. Teachers who come to initiate such ones have attained Higher Self-Genesis. Being the proteges of Omnipresence, these Teachers are few. When a student is engrossed in ego-motivation, he is blind and deaf to the instruction coming from such Teachers.

The Higher Self-Genesis Teacher treads two waters to accomplish his mission: the waters of Maya and the waters of Purusha. The Higher Self-Genesis Teacher is initiated in profundities little-understood by ego-motivation. In the life of such Teachers, their wealth and enrichment pertain to knowledge nourished and inspired by the Cosmos and the Cosmic. It is rare to find a Teacher who has both Cosmos and Cosmic literacy. When this occurs, there is harmony enacted, which will be reaped eventually by all souls in an eternity system.

Lesser-Self-Genesis-itis is a sickness in the modern time. A Lesser Self-Genesis person reacts with resentment toward anyone who tells him what to do or how to do it. A Higher Self-Genesis persons longs for instruction and accepts it gratefully.

A Teacher must be careful that he is not pulled down into the collective thought-expectancies of his listeners, or else he will betray the Word that he represents and is called to give in its whole and pure blessing. Today, they "stone" the Teacher with their indifference and unbelief.

Until the disciple spills out his heart with a whole confidence, the Teacher cannot give a whole healing or instruction. It is necessary for the disciple to know that he is a disciple and that he stands in the sunlight of his Teacher's light. To receive the full benefit of Teacher-to-disciple association, one should give over his heart to the heart of the Teacher.

One of the ways you know a Teacher is by how he looks upon other Teachers and speaks of them. When a Teacher gives true appraisement and testimony as to the good existing in another Teacher or teaching, his own teaching moves forward.

When the Teacher appears and the student does not accept him, the result is that the student swings totally to the left to psychic mysticism or spiritualism; or if he has grace and determines to make union with God, he enters the middle path, which is a death sentence to the little ego and self-aggrandizement. He becomes as a person shackled to a tree on a small island with no other life—with a storm and tornadoes raging upon him. All of the wild winds of his karma push against him. He is confronted with karmas of ages past and of the present. When the ego no longer lives—and desire for self-claim, name or fame has died—then come the beneficent voice and face of the Master; and with the storm subsiding, rescue is at hand. In the middle-path initiations, humility is born; rescue comes; and the Master appears.

Every spiritual Teacher knows the answer to his disciple's suffering, because the true Teacher lives in the causal world, where he is at home with cause, and therefore competent to rearrange the effects of karma.

It is the work of the Teacher to produce a new mind in his disciple. A true, ethical Teacher will not seek to possess the mind of his disciple. He only asks for the heart of the disciple, and the mind thereafter will take care of itself.

The Teacher gives you the method. God gives you the grace.

There are initiated Teachers and uninitiated teachers. The initiated Teacher has *transmission powers.* Some uninitiated teachers are guilty of *psychic rape.* Such teachers try to open centers (chakras) before a person is ready.

One does not and cannot inherit virtue from his parents; he inherits it from his soul. Finding the Teacher is the result of having earned the virtue stemming from instruction.

Willingness to be taught is a virtue. To be teachable is grace.

On finding one's Teacher, it is an automatic process for him to open certain virtue-grace. The first process of learning under a Teacher produces a mystical happiness and uttermost joy. In time, however, more virtue must be added. Then begin the true trials in initiation. From this comes the virtue for the present and for the future.

When one has patience with pain in the body, he earns *great* virtue, which gives the ultimate virtue, or the power of resurrection.

Prayer is the first virtue of spiritual practice. When you remove prayer from the spiritual life, there is no devotion and no channel for the love-current between God and the soul.

Flattery from others is the Achilles heel of spiritual leadership. At all times one must be on guard against excessive praise as to one's self and gifts of the spirit. Genuine appreciation for one's labors is experienced by blessings from Omnipresence which become apparent in every phase of life, physical and spiritual.

Praise must be to God and God alone. However, it is grace-justice when one acknowledges his divine obligation to a true Teacher or channel for God.

One who wears the garment of channelling should be aware at all times that it is a pure garment with a heart supported by gratitude to God as the Source of his spiritual gifts and powers. God will see that it is so, that any one channelling His powers shall be repeatedly searched, even to the point of persecution, to purify His anointed vessel.

He who would be praised for his virtues must learn the hard and painful way, for his virtues are but God in him manifested in the nature of virtue. The whole and complete Spirit of God cannot come into a conceited, vain, puffed-up nature; for where there is erratic, wavering virtue, there is spasmodicity of virtue. There must be basic and root virtues, which are the projections of ultimate good extended from the mercy, charity, harmlessness and peace-essences of God. Whole virtue must be the goal, that one may serve God in holiness.

Underconfidence is a sin and overconfidence is a sin, for they are both projections of self-righteousness.

Saviours enter the world having perfected the virtues. Self-appointed saviours are self-hypnotized—corpulent and fat with egotism. Beware of any man who comes in the name of a teaching who appoints himself a saint or saviour. Be ever alert to see the saviour concealed in the silent, unobtrusive purity and good.

Learning for oneself creates sediments of ego. One must share his learning. He must use learning as a service for God: to help humanity and the souls of men.

One should never exhibit his knowledge or make a display of it. It should be inoffensive.

If the Teacher has one sunny bliss-day a month, it is grace, because the other thirty days he is aware of the griefs, the inertias, the willfulness and the karmas of others which he carries with joy and divine privilege.

As long as the Teacher, who is the mother and the father, knows that his children are slow, unwilling, in debt, the Teacher—as the one who holds the key to the freeing grace—must forbear and be bonded with those who are in bondage, that all might be free in the Light. Every Teacher has a Maya covenant: to break the bonds of karma for those who seek to escape out of the repetition of suffering and ignorance.

Having taken the inward vow, it is the task of the Teacher to remain constant where there is inconstancy; to remain loving where there is unloving; and to remain chaste within his vow of selflessness, which is the integrity-armor of all true Teachers.

One who comes to free the state of Maya has chosen a bed of thorns. He is realistic. Beyond the fantasies of Maya, he knows his own suffering to be that point of tension setting free those who have chosen to wear the Crown of Thorns and follow Him who was crucified. Those who aspire to the Crown of Thorns must first sleep upon the Bed of Thorns, which is a day and night vigil that all men be led out of darkness into light, sorrow into happiness, suffering into health.

The Teacher is always looking for that one who can change the course of the world. Socrates found Plato. Ramakrishna found Vivekananda. John the Baptist found Jesus.

THE GOLDEN VAJRA: THE GRACE OF REPROVING

> *All scripture is given by inspiration of God, and is profitable for doctrine, for reproof, for correction, for instruction in righteousness: That the man of God may be perfect, thoroughly furnished unto all good works.*
>
> *—2 Timothy 3:16,17*

Everyone has a *word* which will resurrect his Virtue or bring it forth—and the Teacher's work is to give him that word. In Sanskrit, this word is called a *Vajra* or lightning bolt. A true Teacher gives the word in timing, that one may be blasted into Illumination.

It is the work of the Teacher to give the *Passing* which comes from the Jesus Passion. It is received by the chela as the "birth word" or the vajra—to move the chela from a jammed-atom situation or condition.

When the chela receives the Vajra as a blessing, birth to a new level of knowing and acting comes. This realized state opens an expanding world on all levels. The wondrous joy of new birth is given. This is the "Way and the Truth and the Life" in its most sensitive state! To resist is to fall back. A true Teacher is known by the use of the birth-word in right timing to the call of the soul in the chela.

The two hands linked together with the right thumb on the little finger of the Left Hand—the Right Hand facing outward, the Left Hand cupped toward the heart, keeping the thumb and forefinger closed—form the *Teacher's Mudra*.

The Right Hand facing straight upward and outward, open palm, is the *Blessing Hand* and also the *Vajra Hand.* When attached to the small finger of the Left Hand with the Right Hand facing outward in the Teacher's Mudra Posture, one attains unswerving love through which he is united with the Informing Principle or Buddhi.

The Teacher's Mudra to be used to give out knowledge or to teach is under the direction of the greater Bodhisattvas who give to the initiate the authorization for its use.

The Teacher's Mudra, used with unswerving love to enter into the gates of knowledge, can be utilized by the uninitiated as a pre-meditation posture. It should be used with reverence, with holy expectancy, accepting the Right Hand as the Vajra Hand or the Law; accepting the cupped receptivity of the Left Hand as the Love-Wisdom which feeds and nourishes the nature of love.

The small finger in the Left Hand should always be pointed toward the heart; the thumb and forefinger closed in the posture of Eternality. The Left Hand should be always as a cup of elixir delicately poised in the Anahata or Heart Center.

When one separates his hands and holds his Right Hand out and facing those whom he would heal, the Right Hand signifies blessing power within the healing, right and just Law of God.

The Mudra of Teaching reveals the perfect marriage of Love and Law. The Vajra is one aspect of Eternal Spirit and the Love-Wisdom is another aspect of Eternal Spirit. There can be no Dharma unless these are united in the one who teaches.

If one is all Vajra in his teaching, he curses rather than cures. If one is all Love in his teaching, he mystifies rather than teaches. If one would teach, he must be equal in both Law and Love.

The Dharma is accompanied by the Vajra: the Correcting Principle. A teacher failing to have the Correcting Principle is working with the pleasure principle. He is seeking only to inflate his own ego. Such teachers are harmful; they stimulate and stir the karmas of their students, but by their own selfishness fix their students into karmic relationships.

A Teacher carrying the Correcting Principle rearranges the karma of his student so that the student may make restitution for his errors, and thus provide for himself a way to reassume the true responsibilities gathered through Initiation. However, a Teacher carrying the Vajra never uses it in excess or exhibits it to humiliate his student or in any manner looks upon it with any form of judgment or satisfaction.

The Vajra sometimes comes from the Teacher as one word, which acts as a self-disillusion electric-blast upon the fantasy forces operating through the disciple or chela. Or the Vajra may come through the Teacher as a sealing-off anesthesia, blocking off the heart channels between the student and the Teacher. Or a Vajra may work through the Teacher through the Divine Supreme. If the student's karma be heavy, some act of the Teacher or choice of the Teacher may set up a roadblock upon the path of the student, that the student may work upon a situation which is antagonistic to his spiritual life. Thus, the Teacher is sometimes, through higher or divine authorization, used to set the student to work upon a neglected issue, possibly in family or finances or certain aspects of lust in the disciple's sentient nature which stand between him and his progress on the Path.

When the student meets the Living Teacher, he must be aware that such Teachers work with the Living God. Living God, or our Father, represents the Life Principle. The Teacher comes first to show the Way. That which is concealed within the Way is the Life; and that which keeps the Way open is the Life made plain or free.

Truth which follows the Way and the Life is the Thunderbolt Vajra. Anyone having true authorization from God as the Living-God power to teach and to educate must also heal. Truth as the Vajra is the surgeon's knife cutting aside the chains and the bonds binding the disciple.

The responsibility of the disciple to his Teacher and to that which is taught through him is the first requisite or requirement in the spiritual life.

The Vajra is a love-gesture from God.

Every test is a showing of the Way. A probationer's life begins with a major Vajra that carries with it many small vajras, which one must face, mark and trace, and successfully confess, that he may be unburdened. In all, he must pass over *twelve* abyss-vajra testings. These will lead him to discipleship initiation and, ultimately, Apostleship. In atom-association, man works with *twelve* zodiacal energies. In each life, he incorporates one or more of the zodiacal prototypal inclinations.

It is the nature of man, while living in the Maya state, to be dissatisfied with the partial. His soul desires, with the holy passion of the Holy Spirit, to be free within all of the potentials of the Image of God in him.

It is unhealthy to seek to crystallize environments or personal association. Man must be a mover, immovable within the Image of God in him. The immovable of God in him as Spirit is called the *Constant*.

The more Coinciding you have, the more Vajra you have, until you are cleaned up.

To him who carries the guardianship of the Dharma is given the responsibility of administering the Vajra with delicacy and love. Therefore, he who has been given the Vajra-power must forgive all and everything—for he is not the Law. God as the Law tempers the greater Vajras and Corrections with mercy.

Man-instrument as a Dharma-channel must lean wholly upon the Mercy of God for his own past sins, lest in his judgment of others he call down upon his own head the lightning blast of the Vajra.

A teacher sitting in the judgment seat has enlarged his own suffering and is hurled from any throne of self-esteem by the Just Law and the Good Law. *Therefore, if thou wouldst be a channel for the Dharma, beware of judgments—judgments which are fire-vehicles for the sustaining of the curse. He who maketh a judgment without mercy and love invokes the Vengeance Angels who stand as the protectors of the Just Law and the Good Law of God. These are the Mercy-Seat Cherubim who guard the good and protect from evil, but who also are affronted when pride and disdain come with judgment. The Angels of the Mercy Seat stand to avenge that one who would sit in the judgment seat.*

To represent the Vajra, one must have been born into this world with the Law.

Jealousy is madness. Competition is fed by jealousy. Jealousy demeans and destroys. Whoever possesses jealousy is also a concealed zealot who would climb regardless of the suffering of others. He who is over-zealous is jealous and works in the sense of competition. He who administers the Vajra must be absent from zealousness concerning any human or spiritual desire for power.

Competition is healthy and righteous when one competes with his own nature. Competition used as a vehicle against any person or thing promises failure and demotion. All persons having exaggerated competition are builders only for themselves. He who delights in the fall of his enemy is inviting his own fall and embarrassment.

The Vajra falls into the life of an initiate to test all of the frailties in temperament, character and ambition. One must go under the waters of the Vajra first through the holy thunders of Baptism and Purification. When one has reached the end of scourging and has no retaliative scars or winces or pride, he is equipped to be a channel for the Vajra or Correcting Principle within the Law of God.

The Ethic in the seeking of union with God; the Ethic within the seeking of life-purification; the Ethic in the use of the mind and the will; the Ethic in the use of love—these are the four doors to initiation on the apprentice level. When one moves beyond the apprentice level, he must be wholesomely united with the Correcting Principle or the Vajra aspect of the Dharma.

If one has retained any form of hypersensitivity regarding the Admonishing and Correcting Principle, and flinches from the Vajra, he is yet an apprentice, and must be taught again and again the Ethic. Finally, when he acknowledges to himself the wisdom of the Vajra and gratefully accepts the surgeon's scalpel freeing him from fantasy infections, he will become a whole initiate in the state of adeptship, whereby he will take up the shepherd's crook, and his sheep shall follow him.

> *Poverty and shame shall be to him that refuseth instruction: but he that regardeth reproof shall be honoured.*
>
> —*Proverbs 13:18*

The Vajra is the discipline and the correction which must go with the spiritual life.

All preparatory steps to instruction are discipline-steps. Without discipline, reverence is fanatic and fantasized.

If the Teacher becomes a Vajra to his student or students, he must bear the bruises of the blows received from his students or chelas who resist the correcting from the

Vajra. In cases of heavy karma, the very presence of a true Teacher is a Vajra to one who resists the Light. Guilt-ridden persons flee from the very one who holds the key to the lifting of their karma.

To give the Vajra or to let the Most High give the Vajra, this the Teacher must decide. The Vajra will inevitably be received whether the Teacher gives it or the Most High.

The Golden Vajra begins with the Golden Coin. The Coin Talisman of spiritual sovereignty has two sides as does the physical coin one spends in physical exchange of monies. On the side of the coin where the face is seen is the Satanic point of the Vajra. In transenergization, one turns over the coin which contains the golden side of the Vajra.

"And he said unto them, Render therefore unto Caesar the things which be Caesar's, and unto God the things which be God's" (St. Luke 20:25) We give 10% and more of our income to Caesar's side of the coin through income tax. Caesar's side is political. Men in the world are presently hypnotized and de-energized in their souls by politics.

All are having to bear the sexual guilt of the whole world which has broken down the morality of the world. Only Christ can lift us and help us.

The Satanic is the dark teacher, and the Christ is the Light or White Teacher. *"Choose you this day whom ye will serve." (Joshua 24:15)*

Jesus is the antidote against evil. The Angels are the antibodies against the effects of evil. To unknot the "hard sayings" of Jesus, one must first encounter the Law.

The reproving comes from the appraisal. The Teacher must give appraisal. A teacher who flatters a student to gain approval is immature emotionally.

The Pointing Angel works through your Teacher to point out your errors.

The Correcting Principle and the Reproving Principle work in different ways, coming from the same source, which is the Law of God. For every Law of God there is a mercy aspect whereby one may fulfill the Law and receive the grace within the Law. The Correcting Principle working as the Law in the life of the disciple rearranges the life of the disciple. The Reproving Aspect of the Law flies like an arrow to the heart and center of the offense nurtured by the disciple from wrong use of Law.

One is in a state of grace and a full functioning of the Law which provides direct and perfect Guidance when he is grateful for rearrangement and flexible within change. One accelerates and increases manifold grace when he accepts reproving.

The first virtue given from acceptance of reproving is obedience to the Law and acceptance of the Law as being the ultimate support of Will, Life, Light and Love.

The person who brings the Rudra Fire has already walked through the Fire. He has been corrected through the Fire—and he brings the power of the Fire to correct those who must also walk through the Fire.

One knows the real character of a person by the way he takes correction.

Those who cannot stand reproving are not even novices. A novice expects reproving. He enters into his novitiate period knowing he will be reproved, and from this reproving will prove his own worth.

When a student looks upon reproving as chastisement, he must become more mature before the seeds of correction fall into his conscience.

The Recording Angels are in charge of reproving. When one shuts away his Recording Angel, Satan begins his work.

A Teacher does not reprove a Judas-Prototype because his encounter with a Judas-Prototype is an *ordained* event in the initiatory processes of becoming Christ-like. One becomes Judas-like because of his darkened heart and coveting mind. One becomes Jesus-like because he thinks only of soul-remembering and soul-union with God.

Every true Initiate knows when it is time for Judas to strike. He plays his part in the drama as an honest server for God.

After the Epiphany Baptism by John, Jesus went into the desert to begin His fiery trial. There, Satan tested Him; and in some other part of Galilee or Judea, Judas began his preparation to be used of Satan.

Jesus, by his refusal to turn stones into bread, began His Ministry as a Son of God. The coveting and lust in the heart of Judas made him a perfect prototype for Satan's use. The Christ in Jesus, giving all power to the Mind of Jesus, gave Him discernment of evil. As good has its cycles, so does evil. This is the story of Judas and Jesus, and evil and good.

All of the testing one receives from a commissioned Satanic Judas-Prototype are thorns seeking to become the nails on the Cross, whereby a Christ may give Ascension to all men in the world.

It is the work of the Initiate to transenergize evil into good. This is the work and the way of the Path.

> *But the path of the just is as the shining light, that shineth more and more unto the perfect day. The way of the wicked is as darkness: they know not at what they stumble.*
>
> *—Proverbs 4:18, 19*

The Masters can speak through a clear mind. They cannot speak through a cluttered mind, a prejudiced mind, a revengeful mind, a bigoted mind.

One who would work with the Great Immortals must have achieved Total Compassion as a grace-blessing from

Jesus. This is the message of Jesus: Compassion; Compassion for the sinner. The only healing for spiritual illiteracy is Compassion.

The Teachers are here to evaluate and to grade their students. A Teacher filled with compassion for those who procrastinate will often harm a student by his acceptance of procrastination in a student. It is the Teacher's obligation to a student who refuses to rise, that he act as a Vajra by example from time to time by direct depth-exploring through Marking and Tracing together with his student.

The Teacher brings the student to rebirth. However, the Teacher must know when the Vajra has taken over where he leaves off, and should never offend the Ethic by pressuring the student beyond his strength of character.

The Teacher is not in the life of the chela to chastise. "Vengeance is mine, saith the Lord." The Teacher knows this, and abides in this law. A Teacher is one who enlightens. The requirement of Enlightenment is that one must reveal. If a Teacher is sincere, his very shining light will screen by picture the Vajra. Without words, the light in the Teacher will persuade, will teach, and will admonish. A chela having a conscience will respond without resistance or rebellion to the shining light of the Teacher.

The true Vajra is in the shining light of the Teacher who comes as a total and whole example of intelligence, of compassion and of selfless love.

To be a Teacher is one of the most awesome and heavy moral responsibilities when one carries the heavier side of the Vajra. You can be a Teacher and pass on enlightenment into shallow phases of morality—but when one becomes a Teacher with the Vajra, there is no higher morality-responsibility than that placed upon the Teacher who passes the Vajra.

The Vajra, the projectile of Holy Truth, can only be effective in its Passing when it comes from a pure and holy, unjudging vehicle. The Teacher must be of a noncondemning and nonjudging mind, that he attain the Passing-Vajra Initiation.

He who lives and practices Truth with love is the life in the Dharma. Truth is the protector never losing its battle against evil. Truth is the inevitable winner in all issues, all concerns, holy and unholy. Let the doors to your temple of Truth be not locked in or else the mighty Vajra of God will fail to fall. The Vajra of God is His Right Spirit righting everything within the Castle or Temple of Worship.

> *Behold, happy is the man whom God correcteth: therefore despise not thou the chastening of the Almighty.*
>
> —*Job 5:17*

. . . Ann Ree Colton

6

THE TEACHER AND REVELATION

Make me, O Father, more each day closer to Thy Image.

Learning

Study to shew thyself approved unto God, a workman that needeth not to be ashamed, rightly dividing the word of truth.

—II Timothy 2:15

Above all, with the first breath in the morning, rejoice in Learning; in knowing that Learning is one of the most precious processes of the mind.

For your growth in learning, earn, work, love, give. Learning is nutriment for the mind, producing strength of character. If it is not used, assimilated, ingested, the result is anemia in consciousness.

The lifeblood of learning is contained through the desire to serve God and to make oneself more capable in the use of the body and the mind. He who refuses to learn is a mere object or sentient vessel supported by animalistic tendencies.

A closed mind is an outrage against Spirit. Learning is yielding to the issues of life with a volatile and vital acceptance of life as a teaching process. An inflexible mind is a waste, violating Nature and Spirit.

Learning is founded upon the Mother Principle. The first learning for the soul began when man was in the virginal, primordial, Prakriti state, called *Eden* in the Bible. All learning begins with Spirit and soul, and proceeds to soul and mind, mind and body, conscience and consciousness.

The central igniting core in man is Spirit. The rays stemming from Spirit function through Prakriti or Supreme Mother. The ego is a product of Prakriti. The power of a free ego is wisdom-knowledge. The free ego maintains itself as an equi-center. When learning has ceased, death has come.

The tools of life are the same in every existence. In each life—while appearing as different or new—Spirit in man, as the ocean, casts up the same shells on the shore, that man may accept or discard from the bosom of life.

Knowledge in each life is a record of soul-experiencing. Wisdom gained from accumulation of lives contains the ultra-energies of Spirit, giving life. When one has loosened the bondage of the mind into free spirit, he knows his ego is but a vehicle of the intellect used from life to life to create for wisdom-consciousness, working for the Godhead or God Within.

Conscience is a vibrational membrane of the higher mind. Every lesson learned through karma is to give more freedom in the use of the conscience. Repentance without conscience is of the intellect.

Telepathy, as a learning vehicle, speaks directly *into* the conscience. Conscience is the vehicle for telepathic receiving and sending.

The subconscious is baptized with fire. And the conscience is baptized with the Holy Spirit.

The conscience is a function of the Comforter or the Spirit of Truth. The Spirit is Electricity, consisting of both fire and light.

Religion gives two-dimensional learning. Metaphysics gives three-dimensional learning. Spiritual physics gives four-dimensional learning. From there on, Omnipresence leads one into the fifth, sixth and seventh dimensions of spirituality, whereby he obtains the twelve dimensions.

The Satanic works through the intellect. The misuse of mental power produces perversion in a coming life.

If a person lives in a state of gratitude all the time, this is his real protection. Gratitude insulates him from the dark.

In the educational system, the use of the intellect has lost its morality. Teachers having intellectual morality are looked upon as idealistic, impractical. Cunning-mind intellect dependency is prevalent in the Self-Genesis Age.

"Me first" is the credo in the accumulative conflicts within the present Mayaic expression. To the Self-Genesis ego, Jesus is a fairy tale.

Learning dependent upon self-preservation is death to the mind and soul. A lasting integrity earned from a past life is little understood by those who take pride in the gain, the fame and the name.

We have an epidemic of spiritual ignorance in this country. To read great books is like being within a great Mind Medallion of conjoined, creative ideas. In the great Mind Medallion, one is in a state of higher mental-body grace. The motives within writings are more important than the writings.

In the learning of the soul, one learns the difference between *existence* and *being*. *Existence* is that man must struggle for morality, but *being* is that man *is* morality. One does not need instruction as to morality if he has *being*. His very being instructs all others as to morality.

Ahimsa is the first morality: Harmlessness to others. *"Behold, I send you forth as sheep in the midst of wolves: be ye therefore wise as serpents, and harmless as doves." (St. Matthew 10:16)*

Heaven is music, and the soul of Heaven is color. The beat of Heaven is the heartbeat of Universal God in all life, in all things.

THE TEN COMMANDMENTS AND THE GURU LINE

The Ten Commandments are the way one masters the Guru disciplines. Every Guru Line has its Ten Commandments. The Ten Commandments are the stairs to the Greater Commandments of Love, the Bhakti Love supporting the Solar, Bodhisattva Line.

The Lunar Light has the Ten Commandments. And the Solar Light has the Greater Commandments of Love.

The Bodhisattva Soul is one who reincarnates into the Maya hates, frustrations and sufferings by deliberation that he may lift all. Jesus is the Most High Bodhisattva for all who seek to move from the Guru Lunar-Line Light.

The Sapphire-Blue Tablets came into this world through Christ Jesus. He is the Lord of Lords of this eternity system. The Father in Him dwells in all who seek to be in the Solar Line of Initiation.

Jehovah, the Race Lord working with the Lunar Guru Light, has initiated men into races, into creed. The future raceless human race before men under Christ is seeking to come to birth, to harmonize within the Unifying Principle: God as One as the Life in All.

The latter part of Self-Genesis moves man toward Cosmos Genesis. Self-Realization will be realized in the latter part of the Self-Genesis era. When Cosmos-Genesis has come, men will be to some degree in the Solar Light.

As mankind advances in Cosmos-Genesis, they will move more and more toward the All-Genesis and the One-Genesis states. For this, the Christ, as Spirit and as the only Begotten

Son of God, entered Jesus and took command of the axis polarity of the Earth.

The twelve Prototypes of men seek to be the thirteenth Prototype or "like" Jesus. All of the Lunar Guru-Line trials are designed to lead man to his Archetypal first-origins through the Solar Light.

The Christ Body can function only in the Solar Light. The Jehovah Body can function only in the Lunar Light.

DHARMA EYE

True enlightenment electrifies.

The Scriptures are made up of individual man's illuminative experience. The great Recording Angels of the Archangel families are responsible for the records of the Scriptures being preserved, recovered and utilized.

Despite the deletion within the New Testament, the etheric contents of this holy portion containing the Ethic and Miracles of Jesus are still intact to the reader and student with the Illuminative Eye, called in the East the *Dharma Eye*.

The Spirit of Truth is in command of the Dharma Eye. To see true beyond the conniving and twisting avidities of misrepresentation, one must have the Dharma Eye to read into the depths of the Scriptures of the present and of the past.

When one protects the Bhakti in the heart, he has the Dharma. His old aggressions must become pure defenses of the Word, which has been tested through the heart and the mind.

One cannot be a disciple until he can defend or prove what he knows or what he says. When this occurs, he has the Bhakti heart and a spiritualized intellect. He can prove all things out of the proof of his own Initiations, and the

Dharma through him is loud, true and pure, standing against the world of evil as Truth. One must protect his Bhakti heart as if it were a defenseless angel who needs the covering of his strength and of his valor.

Niscience has been entrusted with the Western Gate of the Dharma. In Niscience we have the *Versatile Dharma.*

The Dharma cannot enter the world on the heated and frenzied wavelengths of the psychic. He who has the heated psychic cannot present the Dharma. The Dharma must enter into the cool, distilled frequencies of both Bhakti and Jnana. The Dharma is the Atma Wisdom, the Transcendental Purusha.

The Dharma flow in the Western consciousness, supported by the Christ, cools the heated fervors in the psychic nature, producing a dimensional rationale suitable to the converging processes between science and religion. Surfacing Dharma now saturated with the Christ will produce a spirituality never seen before in this earth. Upon the West now rests the yoke of this Dharma.

The Teacher must be excelled by his student or he has failed as a Teacher. But woe unto him who thinks he has exceeded his Teacher or excelled.

MEMORY: THE SOUL-GIFT

Memory is the key to the Eternals.

Memory and conscience are the two most valuable gifts residing within the soul. These must become equal before one might walk with undefilement upon the Path.

Memory is a very wonderful thing. It holds the clue to everything we want to know. Everything we have a right to know is in our memory and can be called forth from the subconscious recollection.

When we stand at the gate of a new initiation, we are the recipients of clues in memory, which often enter in as strangers into the tight little fixed fantasy-paradise we have built in by the preservation of the ego.

Until we are ready to give, memory will approach us with distorted figurines of the imagination. In this time, we can become very cunning so as to cast out these strangers who have entered the gates of our self-assumption.

Memory based upon frivolity, lack of character, becomes sour on the plane of the subconscious. Man alone must take this bitter gold and make it sweet that God may image His true likeness as being the Origin of Himself in man.

The spiritual-life Path requires acceptance of the unknown within oneself so that he may encounter the unknown in the physical world. One moves beyond ordinary deductions in encountering the memories sent forth from the subconscious relating to past lives.

In the cunning mind, one is often exposed to past-lives' memories. The ego, having over-self-esteem, would prefer that these memories of past lives be glamorous and filled with exploits and deeds of grandeur.

Unfortunately, the subconscious, in being relieved of its past-life sediments in memory, releases first the dregs of past-life mistakes and non-virtues. When the recollective-mind memories of a past life make union with the recollection in the present life, restoration and birth have begun. He who accepts these frightening encounters of misdeeds and sin is a brave and courageous initiate-to-be.

It is true that in the memory of past lives one may occasionally come upon a life of good or even a life of grandeur. One must remain cool and undaunted when he enters into the landscapes and scenes of the past. He must remember that God does not deal with the trivial, that His Increase as Spirit takes possession only of that which truly reflects Him.

Memory stemming from ancestry and gene-cultures of the ages is found in whatever House Capricorn possesses. Moon in Capricorn in one's own natal chart signifies this ancestral memory, causing it to be experienced in greater dimensional wisdoms or knowledge as to why races came to the world and also to benefit from gene-knowledge.

When the Moon is in Capricorn for the period of two and one-half days each lunar month, all have extended memories and emphasis placed upon ancestral compulsions or drives. By this, one understands why he incarnated in certain ancestral streams so that he might expand his ego despite negative compulsions coming from the ancestral line or genes.

If one would understand the cycles in sickness or disease, he should learn the therapies of the cycles; for example, when the Moon is in Capricorn, treatment should begin. If there is a tendency to have inherited the disease of cancer through one's family or ancestry, treatment should begin when the Moon is in Capricorn.

Even though this is not understood, the gene cycle shows some form of rejuvenation and receptivity in the cure of ancestral inherited diseases when the Moon is in Capricorn.

The memory of the just is blessed.
—Proverbs 10:7

NEGATIVE NEXUS INTERFLOW

Work as initiation on the Enlightenment scale means self-honesty, self-integrity, self-wisdom.

The negative nexus interflow which comes into a person's conscience as an intrusion affects his direct choice and will. In the rightful states of Initiation or a step forward beyond the dweller action in the family-atom, one may undergo extreme sickness or pain or suffering, which is unidentifiable by medicine.

The initiate must disconnect himself from the negative nexus interflow bombarding his consciousness. This nexus interflow can come from four things: religious bodies; the family-atom; the race; or any group-body having very severe traits of enclosure.

The negative nexus interflow enters only the emotions. The exorcism of this flow can be accomplished only through the emotions, never through the mind.

To mentally seek to master the negative nexus interflow is to enter into great physical distress in the body. The organisms of the body, such as the heart, the liver, the spleen, the lungs, the kidneys, are all negatively vulnerable to the nexus flow. These organs suffer extreme disorientation when there is unabated negative nexus interflow bombardment.

A person can be ill of *nexocity.* Only initiatory knowledge gained by the mastery of the negative nexus interflows can correct the stress-filled rajasic sicknesses.

The nexus interflow occurs in cyclic action to two days of the week, Friday and Saturday. In greater Initiation, the nexus interflow occurs without end until Marking and Tracing identifies and utilizes the current.

Nexus points are links with the dead, links with the angels, links with one's ancestors. A nexus dream means ancestral linkage.

When a parent who has died is contrary to your soul, you should not go to his grave as a form of honoring-ritual—as this strengthens the negativity nexus action. When the parent is *for* your soul and *with* your soul, you should go to his grave or to his ashes-temple to honor him and revere his atoms and the atoms of his physical body which are contributing to the higher aspect of the atomic system.

The *high nexus* is to make a linking with a person from another teaching, where there is no controversy or conceptual bias between the persons involved. This is a form of holy oneness in which the paths cross through the higher harmonics of co-atom association. Teachings having the fruits of grace make this possible. This is the hope for the unity-flow between souls who have mastered religious prejudice and bias.

> *Give me a person with character. It is the most beautiful thing in the world. Character is built by fulfilling the Laws in past lives. It is a rock.*

CONFESSION AND VISUALIZATION TO MASTER THE NEXUS FLOW

> . . . *confess to God.*
> —*Romans 14:11*

> *With the mouth confession is made into salvation.*
> —*Romans 10:10*

There are three Esse or Holy-Spirit Essentials: (1) Marking and Tracing; (2) Transenergization; and (3) the Practice of Confession.

Confession in the state of the Esse consists of confessing for your own sins and asking for forgiveness; confessing the sins of your fathers and your ancestors as far as you can remember. Confess the sins of any person you think has harmed you. Ask for their forgiveness, and forgive them.

Confess the sins of any person who has harmed you, persecuted you, or made trouble for you. Confess the sins of those who seek to stand between you and your choice on the Spiritual Path. Ask their forgiveness, and forgive them. Ask that they be forgiven.

Confess the sins of all world-sinners: national, religious, political.

Do not use judgment or condemn a thing or person you confess for. Let God and His Holy Angels exorcise your sins and the sins of those for whom you confess.

Confession is the secret. Pilgrimage is the answer. Christ confessed for all mankind when He said: *"Father, forgive them; for they know not what they do." (St. Luke 23:34)*

What saves Christ saves you. God in His Omnipresence in timing to the need of man, gives him the way through Christ.

It is through confession for mankind, for one's nation, for his ancestors and for all of those who are in the dark anxieties of suffering, that one in Intentional Suffering changes the current of the negative energy-processes which man by ignorance has established in the world. All men have inherited this frenzied current of guilt-laden anxiety. This current presently expresses the rajasic, creating violence between nations, between men.

The soul cannot establish its light in earth misery, suffering. In this present time, men must return to their consciences. This can happen only when they confess for the sins of their ancestors, for the sins of their nation, for the sins of all persons, inclusive of themselves.

By confession, the conscience comes free. Men through this practice will purify the earth through the spirit of love for one another.

To confess the sins of one's ancestors produces the forgiving spirit. The soul is free to shine in its whole light. The unit of the measures of the earth and the Timing of God become as one.

When you make confession for the sins of your ancestors, you are blessed by the downpouring of grace from the ancestors—and those not yet born and those born will all benefit from the grace. This is a great service. Confession for our ancestors is an everyday situation in the family-atom. One should confess every day for his ancestors.

We have had thousands of fathers and mothers through reincarnation. We are now using the Father and Mother Principle.

It is only through confession for our ancestors' sins that we can truly honor our fathers and mothers of countless lives. It is only by confessing the sins of our ancestors that we become free.

If our fathers and mothers in this life fail to fulfill the Commandments, we confess for them and forgive them so that our sins may be forgiven by our children and so that they will not be karmically bound to the sins of the fathers.

All persons sin, not knowing that sins live.

It is the unknowing that makes one sin, but when there is deliberate, grievous harm by a parent to a child, this sin remains in the samskara action within the genes. Those born to such ancestral lines must make restitution for their ancestry as well as for their own past karmas which attracted them to such parents.

In every Commandment, the spirit for spirit is active, or the Sowing and Reaping Law. To truly be free in the family-atom, one must forgive, confess and make restitution, if necessary, for his ancestral inheritance of sin and of his own karmas.

The abuse of children begins with the family-atom. To manipulate one's child; to reject one's child; to stand between a child and his right to worship; to in any way give offense to his child—is to make ancestral and personal karma.

Souls are free to work through confession which contains no judgment, condemnation or personalized assessment.

All in God's Image are blameless and innocent. Man cannot be free to become a whole person radiating the total soul-light until he becomes one with God through the Commandment of "Love Ye One Another."

When we love, we care enough to desire through visualization processes the good of others. To visualize healing, one must prepare a visualized heart by beginning his visualization with confession. Thus, the certainty of healing becomes evident.

> *It is only in the spirit of restitution that grace can come.*

Natural Grace

> *As every man hath received the gift, even so minister the same one to another, as good stewards of the manifold grace of God.*
>
> —*1 Peter 4:10*

Every one has Natural Grace. We have the Grace of being born expecting to be loved. We have the Grace of being in the earth with new expectations of life.

If we are born in an environment of love and care, this Natural Grace follows us throughout life, and is the modus operandi by and through which we view life. However, if it is our karma to not understand that Natural Grace is the natural right of soul and spirit born in the body, we short-circuit our Natural Grace and fall into unhappy situations.

Natural Grace assures one that he will make right choice throughout life as long as he loves and is grateful. Such gratitude must not be discolored by any form of coveting, for gratitude distorted by expecting more without earning nullifies the flow of Natural Grace.

Natural Grace is present when one has by virtue the return of the gifts of life received on his being born again through reincarnation. Natural Grace is the very first gift of God accompanying the gift of life.

If one is born to parents who love him and share with him the magnanimity of selfless love which by its nature is Natural Grace, one owes to his parents a portion of his heart as long as he lives, for the Natural Grace which brought them together keeps alive the sense of gratitude for having been given birth through the body of some other in the world.

One should use his Natural Grace as respect for parents without thought of claim upon the virtue or good earned by his parents. Only by development of virtue and good in one's own nature does he repay the parent who shares with him his most chief virtue: a trusting love.

A parent not trusting his adult child's efficacy will intrude upon his child's life. Seeking to shape him after his own image, he will use many forms of inducement after placing the child in the position of unrighteous obligation.

A parent having Natural Grace to recognize in his child individualistic qualities as beneficial for the whole rather than for himself as a person, is in a state of virtue.

The Natural Grace one is born with remains with him until the day he dies. If he fails to use his Natural Grace with gratitude, he has disowned his own birthright; he has failed to accept his inheritance of grace.

We have rejected the birthright of being in this nation. We have rejected the birthright of our Natural Grace of our loving our neighbor as ourselves.

> *There can be no wisdom unless there is first goodness.*

THE TEACHER AND REVELATION

> *I will come to visions and revelations of the Lord.*
>
> —*2 Corinthians 12:1*

Teaching is the most divine art of all. And desire to learn—and longing to learn—is also a divine art.

There are teachers who teach from their hate core to the hate core of their listener or student. There are teachers who teach from the love core. There are teachers who teach from the mind core. There are teachers who teach from the will core.

The student must become as a babe at the breast of instruction, taking of the milk of truth with perfect trust in his Teacher. In this, he receives knowledge into his own truth-core of being and experiences the elevated bliss of the mind illumined.

Teachers of the hate core and will core have yet to develop the Bhakti heart, for the whole of truth cannot reside where hate or ego preside. One should beware of teachers nourishing hatred and separateness. Such teachers are dividers, leaving in their wake fractured emotions devastating to the soul.

Self-righteousness is one of the greatest sins; it is a sin of the mind. He who is self-righteous—and yet teaches others to not do what he inwardly craves and lusts to do—is a sinner. Under the estimate of the Recording Angels, such self-righteous teachers are incompetent and unqualified to teach. Thus, self-righteousness is a foul indulgence. The Living Word becomes a burning brand upon the brow of a self-righteous teacher who craves self-aggrandizement.

Adulterous thinking produces the downfall of one who flows his sentiment through the gate of psychic or mental lechery.

A true Teacher knows the suffering a sinner must undergo to be cleansed of sin; he knows one cannot sweep under the rug or seal away the stench of evil. By his own trial for purification, he has suffered, having cleansed the poisonous fumes and toxins of his lower nature.

It is his work to lead one who sins or errs into the Path of Purification. This he cannot do through condemnation or judgment; only through a tender love devoid of unclear sentiment can he free souls entrusted to him. This can be done only through his unceasing communion with the sinless: Jesus, His Angels, His Apostles and His Sheep dwelling within the green pastures of the Living Spirit of God.

Detachment is the ultimate goal and gift of purification.

All Archetypes are Christ-Mind Codes of the Divine. Through the expediency of need and through the versatility of one's innate logos, the initiate breaks open the codes within the Greater Archetypes. An open Archetypal Code is like the blasting of an atom bomb falling into receptive consciousness, exploding as Revelation.

When Revelation is on the Altar, the Mystic Christ is alive. If the teacher does not bear the Archetypal Seed, he is not a revelator. Every Archetypal-Seed Statement is a seed of truth containing power to open the revelatory aspect in the consciousness of the hearer.

Any teaching having a message must have a messenger, a messenger filled with Archetypal Light. Archetypal Light is Revealing Light, banishing ignorance obscuring the soul.

In Niscience, we are opening the Galaxy Consciousness of the Eternal Self.

Jesus took on the conscience of the world when He was crucified. He is the balancer of the world-conscience. Man must experience his conscience within the strength of Jesus to be healed and well. Jesus is the only Avatar ever to take upon Himself the world-conscience.

All of His justified Teachers work within this principle. Their Mantle, through being yoked to Jesus, enables them to take upon themselves the conscience of their students. Through right teaching justified in Jesus within the Father, a student gradually assumes the burdens of his own guilt under the instruction of the Teacher.

The Teacher must trace the *Prototypal Memory-chain* of his student to dissolve karma and to free or liberate one who comes into the orbit of his instruction. The Teacher does this by his own *dreaming*. During dreams, he opens the dream-code germination within the life-force supporting the karmic frustration and suffering of his student. Liberation begins in the life of the student when the Teacher observes the practice of Prototypal-Healing rhythms of Niscience.

The flow of Prototypal Wisdom flows within and upon the heart. To teach with authenticity within the first attribute of spiritual power, one must unite through the heart chakra with the twelve prototypes. These are reflected within his own heart. The chain of self-existence in all life is wholly pictured within the heart chakra or center.

Niscience meditation practice and all accompanying chakra awakening begin at the repository of existence—the heart. Through the Niscience meditation of holding in the light and the use of Angel to Angel Mantrams, one unravels the mysteries of the prototypal cores, thus giving healing and release from karma.

If you can think through the Niscience Archetype, the super-sensible powers of your mind produce obedience to guidance. Divine privilege of Altar-serving can be earned only with devotion or Bhakti love.

God-Realization gives Samadhi articulation. A God-Realized person automatically has Revelation.

There is no greater grace than being a Teacher of the Light.

. . . Jonathan Murro

7

CLAIM YOUR INHERITANCE!

Blessed be the God and Father of our Lord Jesus Christ, which according to his abundant mercy hath begotten us again unto a lively hope by the resurrection of Jesus Christ from the dead, to an inheritance incorruptible, and undefiled, and that fadeth not away, reserved in heaven for you.

—I Peter 1:3, 4

The Teacher as Lawyer

My little children, these things write I unto you, that ye sin not. And if any man sin, we have an advocate with the Father, Jesus Christ the righteous: And he is the propitiation for our sins: and not for ours only, but also for the sins of the whole world.

—I John 2:1, 2

Jesus fulfilled many roles during His Ministry on Earth as Messiah and World Saviour. As the Great Physician, He healed multitudes of suffering persons through His Gift of Miracles. He was also an advocate, counselor, defender. In this important role as Lawyer, Jesus came to prepare the children of God to receive their *Inheritance*.

Many persons in religion are healing-minded but not law-minded. A true Teacher under Christ is a physician and a lawyer, even as His Lord while on Earth was a Physician and a Lawyer.

The majority of individuals in the Hebrew and Christian faiths do not tithe to God nor do they worship Him each Sabbath Day. Many are immoral in their actions. Persons who do not observe the Laws and Commandments of God are not law-minded. In modern times, law-minded individuals in any faith are rare souls.

A great number of religious persons who pride themselves on being law-minded are bigoted and prejudiced, thereby offending the Commandments of Love and the Virtue of Compassion.

An Enlightened Teacher, as a physician, seeks to unite each student with the Healing Power and Miracle-Grace of Jesus. As a lawyer, the Teacher tells each student the requirements for receiving his Inheritance as an *heir* of God.

> *And because ye are sons, God hath sent forth the Spirit of his Son into your hearts, crying, Abba, Father. Wherefore thou art no more a servant, but a son; and if a son, then an heir of God through Christ.*
>
> —*Galatians 4:6, 7*

Every person is being created in the Image of God; therefore, every one is an heir of God. However, one must *claim* his Inheritance. He must go to the Judge and *ask* for his Inheritance. In the Sermon on the Mount, Jesus emphasizes the importance of asking. *"Ask, and it shall be given you . . " (St. Matthew 7:7)*

The Teacher who serves God in Jesus' Name is *obligated* to enumerate to each new student the Laws and Commandments of God. These Scriptural edicts are the requirements for one's beginning to qualify for the receiving of his Inheritance from God.

If a new student has lived an immoral and unrighteous life, the Teacher, as lawyer, will counsel the student to repent with sincerity, honestly confess his sins to God, reverently approach the Judge with a humble and contrite spirit, and offer to make a full and honorable restitution for each witting or unwitting offense against Holy Law. The Teacher will ask the Judge to be merciful to the student—and to bless the student with his Inheritance.

The suffering endured by Jesus during His persecution and Crucifixion created a reserve of *grace* that may be likened to bond money available to sin-laden penitents so that they may remain out of the jail of karmic bondage and placed on probation. The Judge then places the student-probationer in the *custody* of the Living Teacher who, as an Apostle under Christ, becomes totally responsible for the student.

During the probationary period, the student learns the basic principles of the spiritual life as well as the fine points of the Law. Probationary students who respond to their Teacher's instruction immediately begin to claim their Inheritance through the Mercy and Love of their Heavenly Father. In this, healings manifest on all levels; their lives begin to come into order and harmony; joys and prospering increase; soul-gifts appear; and holy-inspirations flow. These and other blessings manifest in their hearts, minds and lives in direct proportion to their gratitude for God's Mercy and their reverent observance of His Holy Laws and Commandments.

Students who prove insincere, ungrateful or offend the Sacred Statutes of Worship, Giving, Morality and Love fail to claim their Inheritance; and, as long as they remain under the custody of the Teacher, the Teacher must pay for their sins due to His covenant with God on their behalf.

The Teacher understands the seriousness of his commitment to God to offer holy instruction to the ungrateful, the unteachable, the incorrigible—and he is willing to pay for the sins of the probationers so that they can continue to be graced with sacred instruction. If the Teacher did not pay for the sins of his students, they would immediately be placed in heavy karmic conditions, afflictions and bondages.

Unresponsive students are eventually removed from the Teacher by the Judge. For the remainder of their present lives and in numerous future incarnations, they will have to *re-earn* the grace of a Living Teacher. Also, they will be required to suffer by themselves in payment for their own sins until they can approach the Judge entirely repentant and contrite, hungering and thirsting for knowledge of God and His Plan.

Some students have an *extended* probationary period, while others have only a *limited* probationary period. The length of time one is permitted to remain near an Enlightened Teacher is determined by the grace earned in past lives. Thus, a student with extended probationary-grace may be unresponsive and ungrateful for instruction, yet he will be permitted to remain with the Teacher for many years until his grace-period concludes.

The Heavenly Father is merciful and patient with His children during the probationary period. During this time, many important lessons are learned by responsive students; the Teacher, in turn, is also rewarded with choice blessings that come through his own Inheritance.

The Living Teacher is in a constant state of Inheritance-Grace. The flowing creations of the Teacher are part of his Inheritance; his closeness to Jesus and the Christ-Mind Gifts, Skills and Revelations give testimony to his receiving the Inheritance as an heir of God and joint-heir with Christ.

The Spirit itself beareth witness with our spirit, that we are the children of God: And if children, then heirs; heirs of God, and joint-heirs with Christ; if so be that we suffer with him, that we may be also glorified together.

—Romans 8:16–18

THE TEACHER AS PHYSICIAN: THE PATH OF MIRACLES

. . . many believed in His name, when they saw the miracles which He did.

—St. John 2:23

• A miracle is a natural process.

• The third action of energy is a miracle.

• A miracle is merely the raising of the consciousness, receiving the abundance of heaven.

• From understanding come virtues. From virtues come spiritual gifts. And from all of these come the miracles.

• No one can perform a miracle without the power of love.

• To produce miracles, one makes union with the Angels, Jesus and our Heavenly Father.

• In the Niscience techniques of healing, miracles occur, which are in reality the Will of God at work.

• All persons with spiritual hearts and minds acknowledge that health responds to selfless prayer and that miracles are worked through undeviating faith.

—Ann Ree Colton

The Path of the Spiritual Life, as recorded in the Holy Bible, is a Path of Miracles: the Miracles of the Hebrew Prophets and the Miracles of Jesus and His Apostles. Since Post-Scriptural times, Miracles have continued to occur through holy personages and faithful worshippers of God.

It is the *expectancy* of a Miracle—and the strong and certain belief in the Power of God to create a Miracle—that provide the suitable atmosphere for a Miracle to manifest. Thus, whenever one prays, meditates and fasts, he should always *expect* Miracles to happen. This holy expectation, combined with a deep faith in God, establishes a linking with the Creator through which lesser and greater Miracles occur.

When one *knows* in his heart and mind that God can create a Miracle at any moment in Time, he lives in a constant state of holy wonder and spiritual alertness.

Whenever a probationer on the Path heeds his Teacher's instruction, Miracles will occur in his life as he applies the principles and ethics of the Lord Jesus. If a student follows this sacred instruction, he will receive God's Blessings as Creation Grace, Providential Grace, Timing Grace and Miracle Grace. All manifestations of Grace that occur *after* one repents, confesses and expresses the desire to make restitution are portions of His Inheritance from God. The Inheritance *increases* over the days, months and years of his studentship and discipleship.

Creation Grace pertains to the opening of the Gifts—first, the lesser Gifts; then the greater Gifts of the Holy Ghost. Each year at Pentecost, the Christ quickens the Gifts of His Disciples and Apostles, that they may experience increasing measures of God's Blessings as Creation Grace.

Providential Grace relates to the opening of the Flow of Supply. The Flow of Supply from God increases as one's spiritual dedications, responsibilities and creations increase.

Timing Grace brings all aspects of a student's life into Timing with his Soul's Covenant and the Solar-System Cycles.

Miracle Grace manifests through Soul-Grace and Divine-Grace. When this occurs, the Path of Virtue becomes the Path of Miracles.

". . . the Son quickeneth whom he will." (St. John 5:21) A Teacher anointed by the Spirit of God and quickened by the Son is under the Mantle of the Miracle-Grace of Christ Jesus. The Mantle of the Teacher is created through his serving in the world as an Apostle of the Lord Jesus.

Miracle-Grace begins to manifest in the life of a new student through the Apostolic Gift of Remission of Sins extended to him by his Teacher. This Gift stills the stormy sea of one's sin-debts so that he can enter into the peace and joy of pure instruction regarding God, His Kingdom and His Eternal Plan.

The remission of sins is a *temporary* grace that continues as long as one remains under the Mantle of his Teacher. The moment one divorces himself from instruction through nonattendance and nonparticipation, he begins to remove himself from the protection of the Teacher's Mantle. Probationers who move farther and farther away from the Word of God and the worship of God experience less and less remission-of-sins grace until their old and new sin-debts present themselves for payment. No longer protected by the Teacher's Mantle, they are engulfed by tidal waves of unpaid karmic debts and swept away from the orbit of instruction offered by God and Jesus through Their servant, the Teacher.

Probationers who remain faithful to God experience the continuous remission of their past sins; and the Teacher places into their hands the tools through which the remitted sins are resolved and healed through restitution.

To be free from the burden of ages-old sin-debts brings an indescribable joy that is known only to the righteous, the honorable, the teachable. This freedom is a testimony to the Miracle-Grace of God pouring upon one through the Mantle of his Teacher under Christ.

> *Whose soever sins ye remit, they are remitted unto them; and whose soever sins ye retain, they are retained.*
>
> —*St. John 20:23*

> *The sins and shortcomings of a soul are viewed by the Master in the same light as a washerwoman regards the dirt on a cloth. He cares for the cloth and not the least for the dirt. His aim is to cleanse the cloth by some means or other; whether by the gentle method of applying the soap or the rough and ready method of beating the cloth against a slab of stone . . . The Master at first tries to purify us by his discourses. If this fails, then he applies the soap of poverty, adversity and disease.*
>
> —*Sawan Singh Ji*

PRAYER TO THE GREAT PHYSICIAN

O Lord Jesus, Great Physician, heal our woes.

O Lord Jesus, Great Physician, heal our ills.

O Lord Jesus, Great Physician, heal our fears.

O Lord Jesus, Great Physician, heal our guilts.

O Lord Jesus, Great Physician, heal our sins.

O Lord Jesus, Great Physician, heal our immaturities.

O Lord Jesus, Great Physician, heal our hypocrisies.

O Lord Jesus, Great Physician, heal our uncertainties.

O Lord Jesus, Great Physician, heal our unbeliefs.

O Lord Jesus, Great Physician, make us whole in body, Thy tender, wise and loving care.

Thank God for Thee and Thy Holy Powers and Skills which are able to free us, heal us, enlighten us. Amen.

Absolution

If the Son therefore shall make you free, ye shall be free indeed.

—*St. John 8:36*

Repentance leads to restitution. Restitution leads to Absolution.

Repentance produces Remission of Sins. Remission of Sins eventually becomes Absolution of Sins. Absolution means Total Freedom.

As long as one is only halfheartedly repentant, he does not experience the Remission-of-Sins Grace that would otherwise bless him through his Teacher. To be disobedient to God's Holy Ordinances or to ignore the instruction of one's Teacher is to refuse the Remission-of-Sins Grace being offered by the Spirit of God. When one is obedient to the Laws and Commandments of God, and welcomes his Teacher's instruction and corrections, he experiences the joys and rewards that accompany Remission-of-Sins Grace.

Remission-of-Sins Grace is a gift of God through an Anointed Apostle of the Lord Jesus. The moment one proves honorable in the sight of God and begins to make restitution for his sin-debts, he experiences the quickenings of his soul's gifts. Each quickening of one's soul-gifts signals the approaching grace of Absolution.

Absolution through Christ is a reality. To be debt-ridden is to be in bondage. Any and all debts are healable and payable through the Christ-quickenings of one's soul-gifts. When these gifts are used in service to God, restitution wipes clean the dark places in the soul's record.

As the desire to make restitution increases, the Sun of Absolution adds its expanding light to one's being until he is cleansed and liberated. The Christed Rays of Light move through the Sun of Absolution into one's heart and mind as mighty anointings of Grace and Truth. These sacred anointings produce the illuminations that make one an Anointed Apostle under the Christ. Thus, repentance leads to restitution; restitution, to Absolution; and Absolution, to Illumination.

Blessed be the Lord who has created such a marvelous Plan—a Plan of hope and optimism, wonder and progression.

If all persons who commit cardinal sins were put immediately into jail, there would not be room enough to imprison all law-offenders. All of the present-day adulteries, abortions, perversions, lyings and cheatings are creating mountains of sin-debts for those who show no remorse and have no desire to change their selfish and immoral ways of life.

"Repent ye: for the Kingdom of Heaven is at hand." (St. Matthew 3:2) The journey toward God-Realization begins with repentance. Union with God occurs in specific stages following repentance. These stages involve many self-discoveries that coincide with one's honorable restitutions. Restitutions not only bring the scales of God's Laws into balance, but produce major enlightenments regarding ethics, principles and virtues.

From the many enlightenments coming through restitution, one experiences the birth to the Spirit. Absolution heralds the birth to the Spirit. To be absolved of one's sins of the present life and past lives opens one to the Great Sun of the Christ Mind. This Sun opens one to the Godhead and the Galaxies.

Absolution attained by any individual is an event of Cosmic and Cosmos significance—for he who earns Absolution walks the Earth with the Light of God on his brow and the Love of God in his heart. Heaven and Earth have made their linking within his being. Cosmos and Earth have made their linking within his being. Through these powerful linkings, one experiences perfect polarization with his Soul's Covenant. At one with his Soul, at one with Christ, at one with God, he serves those who are beginning to desire the freedoms that come through Repentance, Confession, Restitution and Absolution.

Ask God for your Inheritance.
Claim your Inheritance.
Live according to Holy Statutes— and let the blessings increase within the Increase of God.

Part II
Rays and Light-Streams

Master, O Master, I am hearing thine inward call.

—A. R. C.

. . . Ann Ree Colton

8

THE INCREASE OF GOD

God gave the increase.

—1 Corinthians 3:6

God is thrill after thrill! Like gentle zephyrs, His love comes over your soul. Day and night, week after week, year after year, it goes on increasing.

—Yogananda

Proportion through Prayer

The prayer of the upright is His delight.

—Proverbs 15:8

The Increase of God is full of bountiful prospering and health. In sickness or disease, man cannot stand still nor can he be static. The Living God through our Father progresses man in his diseases if he fears, if he doubts. The Increase of God heals in trust and in faith. Faith in God is the medicine for all diseases.

Receptivity to God as the Healer increases health, prospering, bountifulness. This eternity system is polarized to be an increasing, prospering eternity system.

Generations fall away from God, producing a structured negativity through which God cannot reach man. When man concretes himself into negativity through no faith, no trust, he is sentenced to destruction. When one has no faith in God, he serves destructive powers; he is initiated through violence, hatred and envy.

In intervals, God uses His plow of rectification to uproot and expose the evils in His soil of Creation. Such is the present time: all evil must be surfaced and identified, that the true morality come forth and that men may be undefiled in their Cosmos march as Cosmos builders and creators for God.

The Holy Spirit comes as lightning setting fire to consciousness, or it may come as water and drown you; it can come as earth and bury you; it can come as ether and bring you to life in consciousness; and it can come as air and polarize you to different places expressing the Holy Spirit.

The Holy Spirit is in all things the circulation of Light, using the elements to form, to shape, to teach. Holy Spirit seeks to use consciousness-energy to enlarge Space; to build terrains where there are none; to manifest conditions never before existing: to enlarge provisions; and to increase *Being* as consciousness in Earth and in Heaven.

In non-judgment of one's self as to sinning, there is a delicate balance between conscience and works, for works in the spirit of restitution with self-asking for glory is not penance—and conscience is not appeased. Only through works is penance made possible, but works which have any content of self-claim or of resistance as work have no value in the balance of conscience.

All sicknesses are an offense against the *Increase-of-God energies.* Sickness can be healed only through total cleansing of conscience.

The first work in life is prayer—prayer totally devoid of self-asking. Self-asking is imbalanced desire. Desire is the image-maker. If there be wrong desire, the image is distorted on the negative film of creation, producing distortions of health.

The healer-initiate must enter into the sacred sanctum of the one sick. He must teach those who turn to him for health to pray away his sins.

The prayer of a true and pure conscience is first praise of God; secondly, gratitude for life and all of its contents and experience. The third is, a gratified acceptance of one's appointment and direct charge from God as a worker and creator.

Man is a mind-vehicle with superconscious soul-powers. He maintains his life in perfect health and happiness by God-centered determination.

Happiness and health prove God and prove life. One seeks this holy proportion and balance through prayer as the first work for maintenance in this Earth. From prayer come works whereby he manifests new and wondrous things as a citizen of an eternity.

> *When one turns loose of God, everything is out of proportion.*

Holy Fire in the higher etheric body pours down into the lesser etheric body in answer to prayer. Diseases seemingly impossible to heal are healed through the Holy Fire flowing downward into the lesser etheric body. These are the Miracles of Healing. And the person earning this Healing has earned the Grace of the Healing, Holy Fire in other lives.

If it were not for this Holy Fire, one who would seek to be an Intentional Sufferer for the healing of others would die, for he would be faced with his own sins rather than with the sins of another. Prayer then is vital and answerable when there is total releasing of one's own desire as to how the healing can come.

The Angels use this Holy Fire when an Angel-to-Angel Mantram is spoken selflessly, leaving the Healing totally to the discrimination of the Angels.

Let prayer be unceasing. Let it be fervent. Let it be filled with the love of God and faith in God.

The lower mind is like the currents of the ocean, negative and positive, in and out. No matter how one may analyze this process of the inner tide and the outer tide of the mind, he will never succeed in changing because it is part of Universal Current working through gravity. By recognizing that it is always there and will never go away except through transenergizing, one reaches a third current; the soul-mind is in control of this current.

It is through absolute faith in God and one's own transcendent powers, which are the Jesus powers, that one walks on the water of the alternating currents of the lower mind. One must have total faith to move into the third aspect beyond the lower mind.

Everything created comes from the Creation Power of God. When man uses this Creation Power, he has two choices: to use it for negation or for good.

One must pray for a whole faith that he make right choice in his creation. All who make right choice are in the Creative Will of God. All who make wrong choice in pursuit of their self-will have chosen death. Life everlasting is choosing rightly through faith.

> *Thank You, Father, for Your Divine Grace, Your enveloping Joy.*

HEART EVALUATION

> *Where your treasure is, there will your heart be also.*
>
> —*St. Matthew 6:21*

If you offer with an unwilling heart an apple as a gift, giving half of it to your friend, you suffer. Anything given with blessing overcomes suffering. Giving in the name of friendship is service to God.

By sharing and giving, you open the Coinciding—this is the only way. All giving with a selfless heart opens the Coinciding, where beyond suffering one is in direct communication with Omnipresence and the Guiding Principle.

Giving with expectations to gain fixes one into the square of Maya karma, where suffering is inevitable. Maya is a jealous host, making demands for payment for all and everything in her kingdom.

One steps free from karmic restraints and suffering when he lives in the giving heart. The soul is the giver. Until one realizes giving is the way, he will continue to be a failure to himself.

If one chooses to remain in the lower scale of energies which are Mayaic, he is exacted payment for his karmas one by one. He is cheated, defrauded of his birthright. The soul is an expanding vehicle. To cramp its freedom is to suffer.

The heart is the maintenance organ of the body. There is no halfway for the heart, no lukewarm way. The heart is the filterer of Truth and Soul-Essence.

A fantasized heart is devoid of heart-centering. It is yet to have found its center.

The heart is either the organ of unrighteousness or righteousness, two extremes in polarity which toss the soul and its record—exposing one to the elements of life, which are both harsh and pleasurable.

When the self is prevented from being all of itself, it is a destroying vehicle rather than a building vehicle for the body and for the mind. When the self is rightly centered within the heart, one has a righteous heart.

Everything having growth in it and providing the spiritual is of God and works increasingly to bless and to lift.

PROSPERING WITHIN GOD'S INCREASE

God is limitless in His prospering for you.

There is no successful prospering without God's support. He who prospers with a clean conscience is God-prospered. Omnipresence awaits the day when all men of the Earth will be God-prospered.

As long as a man plays the game of energies for self, he is doomed to loss. He who loses touch with God as support in all things of the Earth is signing a contract with death through which he has mortal, corruptible works rather than the immortal.

God gives license to every one of the Earth to make choice. How one makes choice is his account book in the record of prospering. If he makes choices to serve the legitimate and whole need which is supported of God as Creation, he cannot fail.

Man decides; God destines. And only that which God has destined can succeed.

These are the terms by which man lives in the world: man as a creator is on trial; he is an apprentice in a forming eternity system. Man is not perfected, for he is yet to know the full meaning of works and creation.

Presently, what man calls creation, when weighed upon the Scale-of-God Creation, is trivia—the foam on the waves of an inexhaustible ocean. When man involves himself in the depths of the ocean, or the Galaxy-remembrance, he will think with the Hierarchs; and he can say with Jesus, "Let this mountain be moved"—and it will be moved.

Everywhere man looks in the present day he can see destruction; he can see the malice existing on man-to-man levels through death, war, ignorance and poverty. When his exterior sense fails to use what the subconscious or samskaras are saying as conscience, the world suffers in its own identity as a world system.

To look in the face of one's beloved and see his suffering and to know not the Way, is to know one of the cruelest faces of suffering. If one will call out toward the Great Unconscious, which is the existing matrix of the world soul, he will find his answers.

The greatest side of egotism is man's refusal to face his unknowing or ignorance. Beyond this is also a form of ancestral inheritance, pride—a pride stemming from the belief that the valor of his ancestors contains the seed for his preservation. Not understanding the Father Principle, and preferring to accept the paternal tradition in his line, he fails to open himself to the true origin of his birth, which is our Father in Heaven.

Every man is an heir of our Father. This is the true Father of consciousness existence in this Earth. He is a caring Father. He is a Father of Providence and Prospering.

The velocities and increase of Spirit in each soul know where one's own providence can be found. To petition the Father and to pray to Him opens the door to prospering through God, or Spirit Eternal.

Prospering does not concern completely the energy of money. Prospering, when God-supported through the Father, concerns a conscience-free mind, an overflowing soul-knowing, and willingness to reciprocate within the work-service channelling for God.

Were it not for men in the Earth who have attained Ethic in creation, this Earth would write a sorry story at the finality of its creation. It is not so destined for man. Man is destined not only to take part in the creative processes in this Earth; he is destined to lift the veil of its future and to see the fulfillment of its creation as a lifted Earth since Christ.

There is a karmic law that cuts one down financially so that he will learn to earn *honestly.* This law is as certain as the night and the day. The law of adjustment in monies and earning is inevitably active in every money exchange.

Money is one of the gifts. When misused, it abuses wherever it falls. Excess of money without charity underwrites every act of violence.

Mortgages assumed in which the bargaining principle is uppermost and bordering on usury discredit the use of money, and incur debts which become obstacles against the equilibrium in security.

A secure man is intuitively connected with the Prospering Laws of God's Increase. An insecure man regarding money is a debtor against prospering for himself, for his children, and for his ideals.

No person can succeed in any thing of a creative nature unless he has within himself an equal reservoir of self-support to that which will earn through his creation. Each man is his own collateral, his own bank, his own vault of resource and treasure.

Man is by nature divided into three areas of Prospering: health, family, works. These three natures of Prospering, when equal, have arisen as a state of consciousness through practice within the Good Law, the Right Law and the Great Law.

The Good Law supports well-being, health. The Right Law supports responsibility toward all relationships. The Great Law supports spiritual financing, supporting the Word of God.

An equipoled man desiring nothing for himself—having all in body, in responsibility and in soul—knows that he is a contributor to life, to existence and to God. All must seek to be these three: a sound body, a sane mind, a living soul.

Fantasy-claiming, wish-thinking and coveting are samskara heritages from non-creative and evil intent. One who seeks to live as a parasite to any smallest degree is more harmful than an atom bomb set off to destroy.

A true teaching provides one with the knowledge of self-cultivation, self-responsibility and self-illumination. By this, Soul-Realization is accomplished, and a worthy workman is at work in the beautiful sphere of this Earth.

He who supports selfishness lives in ugliness, in non-creation. His atmosphere is acid, contributing to no-life. To rise over selfish fantasy into the serene assurance of God-Providence equalized with craftsmanship and work is the desire of all disciples.

God-Providence cannot work for man unless man works. Why he works, how he works, and what he does with his work—when married to the Providence of God—determine when and where man prospers, enjoys and creates.

Man as an existing soul in this eternity system signed a contract with God to work with God as a creator-apprentice and ultimately as a masterbuilder for God. There is no way anyone in this world can escape work and service for God.

The desire to have the pleasure principle keeps a person in debt all the time.

To be laggard in the payment of debts is to suffer unwillingly. The world is filled with the tamas, unwilling server. This is bondage to the hardship-laws within the necessity pressures of life.

No matter what one does in action as work—work, when motivated by unwillingness, is gross, laden with the immovability of wrong motive, intent and aspiration.

A man who will not pay his debts will not pay his karma. Debt is the same in karmic law whether it pertains to monies or character; the spirit of redemption and restitution is shunned.

He who will not pay his debts is angry against existence or life. There is no way in the karmic law under God that man can escape the paying of his bills and his debts, financial and moral.

The Angels watch over the stewardship laws. God has given to man great treasures. He has given His Angels the laws protecting the treasures and the gifts which He has given to His own in the world. To know the Angels as prospering-protectors is to prosper in grace and in works. *"And in thy majesty ride prosperously because of truth and meekness and righteousness." (Psalm 45:4)*

If you want to die in debt, die in debt.

People who deliberately run up debts and live on the earnings of others are thieves. They are the thief next to Jesus. The Apostle-Saint opening the door for healing for them is Saint Jude. This Apostle is in command of the Twelfth House or the House of Imprisonment and Incarceration.

Such thieves are imprisoned in their own fantasy way of life. To meet one and to be exposed to one is to become poorer, for one takes on this impoverishment in lending monies or having joint association with him in business or in marriage.

Debt-leaners are more dangerous than any incurable communicable disease. Until they come to honesty, they carry the destroying principle to all who would consent to live in their orbit.

Wilful use of the debts-system is a disease more severe than alcoholism.

Debt through the credit card is another drug.

No student should go in business with another student.

It is very important that you do not materialistically advantage yourself with a single person with whom you are associated in the spiritual life.

It is a simple thing for God to send you money.

Travel light. *"Owe no man." (Romans 13:8).* Hasten to leave your offering, your spiritual promises, on the Altar. Go forth and work with diligence to pay off the debt carelessly made in time of blind motive. If your path seems twisted at this time, know that the energy wasted by taking what does not rightfully belong to you will change to the blessing-power of the new Archetypal Light within the family-atom. In the new family-atom, there will be strength, self-confident states of grace and of right having.

Be every whit clean. Be whole in the virtue of a rightful grace—a grace spent in right support as the work of God. God does not employ or engage you in the employ until your debt is free, and your giving is abundant.

When in doubt, do without.

When you depend on someone totally to support you, you depend on their sins as well as on their grace. To be economically independent is necessary for all disciples.

In event of marriage, one should be open in his use of the economies. He should look upon the opportunity to share his earnings in the household and living necessities. This should be an open, honest experience between the two people involved.

Through our living honorably, God's Increase flows.

TITHING AS THE FIRST PRACTICE IN DISCIPLESHIP

The cycle of prospering is through the tithe.

The disciple's first discipline is the regular and continued practice of Tithing. In this discipline, the disciple learns self-control and lays the foundation for order in his physical world, security in his emotional world, and a coordinated knowing or thought in his mental world.

A discipline is a disciple's dedicated practice. The practices in discipleship are in alignment with the four original Fiats and enable the devotee to receive the spiritual powers in discipleship: (1) Tithing is in alignment with the Will Fiat; (2) Prayer and Fasting, the Life Fiat; (3) Contemplation and Meditation, the Light Fiat; and (4) Healing, the Love Fiat. The disciple cannot ethically impart to others or instruct them until he has first incorporated all of the discipleship practices as part of his daily and living experience.

When tithing is fulfilled reverently and sacredly, it is a will-practice in alignment with substance and determines, discriminates and selects how the disciple uses and commands substance so that he will have a well-planned and ordered life. By tithing the disciple shows his gratitude to "Our Father which art in heaven" and aligns himself with the Father, the Source of substance for this eternity.

Effort in man and substance in the Father create the law of supply. Money is but the outer symbol for effort. To have command of substance as of the law of supply, one must have earned it in this life or in some other life. If one has failed to fulfill the fundamental requirements sustaining the law of supply, he must with stronger effort re-dedicate himself, that he may once again open the Source from which he receives his supply.

It is required of all disciples that they prove themselves adequate on every plane or region. Therefore, the disciple must qualify himself on the physical plane that he may in the future command substance. In this, he must prove to himself and to the world that he is self-sustaining and can make a living.

As long as a person is an onlooker or observer to any teaching of spiritual nature, he cannot enter wholly into that being taught and make it a part of himself. When the disciple fulfills his material responsibility—that is, gives his tithe or tenth toward the nurturing of substance and form back to the source from which he receives spiritual truths, instruction and strength—he becomes a participant in that being taught. Thus, to those who are highly evolved, tithing is a privilege fulfilled reverently and sacredly.

Tithing is of the conscience. No one can press us to do what the conscience has yet to tell us. However, tithing must be practiced to receive the joyous benefits and true bountiful results of this practice of Grace, as tithing taps the Grace reservoir in the spiritual worlds and ascertains a continuing flow of supply despite famine and want.

How we use our portions of grace determines what is recorded into the soul's record. If we give only through the demands of karma or pressures placed upon us in environment as of duty, or the doing of what we term the right, this gives peace only to the lesser will and lesser mind's action. If we give with the intent to gain or receive, we fall short of earning Grace. Such expectations expressed through the cunning mind will invite disciplines through hardships and lack. When we tithe toward good works to benefit and ennoble mankind and to aid its rise, we fulfill the Grace of the ages, of the soul, of the now.

The secret of a prosperity blest by the spiritual worlds is tithing. There is no lasting prosperity without tithing. He who fulfills not this practice cheats only himself, for it is an infallible law that we receive only that which we give.

Hierarchy works in ten labors. Ten per cent of man's gross and total income tithed back to the Lord and the Lord's work is the only means and way of man's reproducing the energy within the law of supply, of keeping open the freeing and wellspring of the ten Hierarchy archetypal energies. The substance or image degree of the Great Archetypes received from Hierarchy and the Father give to man the supply of foods, grains. etc. When man returns his tenth through selfless channels to the Lord's work, he multiplies his seed or supply for the next harvest, thereby preventing famines, depressions, recessions and heavy taxation. In this, the unending thread of renewal in substance is sealed not away. Thus, when man tithes, he fulfills the first step and practice in discipleship and also frees the Melchizedek powers of future protection for substance and supply. (Genesis 14:18–20)

When the disciple is in a certain stage of evolvement, he may be required to experience the withdrawal of substance so that he may use on a higher spiral power, authority and substance in a broader range of stewardship. He prepares in this dry period to revalue the Source of substance and supply and to cleanse out all remnants of self-claiming or any fragment of self-esteem or self-omnipotence.

A disciple who is fulfilling the practice of tithing may have a dry time financially or a door to close on supply for one or more of the following reasons: (1) faulty stewardship in this life or in other lives; (2) lack of gratitude in this life or other lives to the Source of supply; (3) a poverty vow in former lives of religious piety; (4) a covenant in this life with the Higher Self for non-possessiveness. Until the dry time has concluded, he will be without, but on its ending he will have through change of values the opportunity to use his stewardship for the serving of all. Continued tithing in spite of this restriction in supply will create a talisman; and each tithe, as a small seed planted one at a time, will become the means of return to the fully qualified stewardship.

The good works of former lives known as soul-grace will aid the disciple in the time of crisis, peril or dire need. And in time of desperate trial, sorrow, anguish, suffering, he will receive a mysterious second wind or a latent sixth sense; and though it may seem he will not survive, he shall receive his sustenance day by day and from often unknown sources receive his helps.

The *Widow's Mite Disciple* is the disciple who gives his all without prudence and with this receives all. Through desperation and need he opens the channel for the receiving of the all. (St. Mark 12:41-44)

The *Merchant Man Disciple* sells all he has to gain the goodly pearl. He gives of himself, of his time, and of his physical means such as he has. (St. Matthew 13:45-47)

Nicodemus, in the night, gathered knowledge directly in the auric glow of the Jesus One. (St. John 3:1,2) There is the *Silent Giver* or *Nicodemus Disciple,* who unknown to others, silently gathers knowledge from the Teacher; and though his karma requires him to remain behind the scenes, he fulfills his part by aiding regularly and rhythmically. In crisis, the Nicodemus Disciple openly defends his Teacher and dares public opinion and wrath. (St. John 7:50)

Joseph of Arimathaea gave to Jesus his own costly and sacred burial tomb. (St. Matthew 27:57-60) The *Joseph of Arimathea Disciple* renders timely and invaluable service, for this disciple has the courage to face the opinions of others and show loyalty to his Teacher even unto death.

The *Martha Disciple* is the hospitable disciple who welcomes and serves her Teacher.

"Then took Mary a pound of ointment of spikenard, very costly, and anointed the feet of Jesus, and wiped his feet with her hair: and the house was filled with the odour of the ointment." (St. John 12:3) Mary of Bethany used her most precious ointment to anoint her Lord. The *Mary of Bethany Disciple* is the disciple who renders service as part of her giving.

The *Peter Disciple* is the what-is-in-it-for-me disciple. *"Then answered Peter and said unto him, Behold, we have forsaken all, and followed thee; what shall we have therefore?" (St. Matthew 19:27)*

The *Jacob Disciple* is the disciple who would bargain with the Lord or make terms before he will serve Him. *"And Jacob vowed a vow, saying, If God will be with me, and will keep me in this way that I go, and will give me bread to eat, and raiment to put on, So that I come again to my father's house in peace; then shall the Lord be my God: And this stone, which I have set for a pillar, shall be God's house: and of all that thou shalt give me I will surely give the tenth unto thee." (Genesis 28:20–22)*

There is also the *Ananias Disciple* who withholds part of his tithe, feeling poor in the spirit of material things. His result in karma is death to his spiritual life. And he must await a longer and extended cycle before the opportunity for a spiritual life returns. (Acts 5:1–11)

The *Worship of Things Disciple* is the disciple who makes "things" or possessions his god. Wealth has been earned through effort in this life or effort in former lives. On acquiring money or wealth, if there is lack of continued effort as to its right spending or expression, such possessions become an obstacle in the seeking of light or eternal life. (St. Mark 10:17–24)

The *Stone Into Bread Disciple* is the disciple who immediately after fulfilling certain spiritual practices expects the downpouring of physical wealth without effort. He is an unconscious worshipper of phenomena and is yet to understand the initiation and ethical formula of Jesus who refused to change a stone into bread. *"And Jesus being full of the Holy Ghost returned from Jordan, and was led by the Spirit into the wilderness, Being forty days tempted of the devil. And in those days he did eat nothing: and when they were ended, he afterwards hungered. And the devil said unto him, If thou be the Son of God, command this stone that it be made bread. And Jesus answered him, saying, It is written, That man shall not live by bread alone, but by every word of God." (St. Luke 4:1–4)* The Stone Into Bread Disciple, in wrong expectancy, expects by some miraculous event his sustenance to single him out and come to him. Such a disciple is confused in thinking that a spiritual life offers a wealthy substance of financial supply and is yet to understand that all things experienced on the physical plane must be earned through effort on the physical plane.

The *Judas Disciple* is an irresponsible student with a critical mind. He is often a covetous and parasitical student, failing to build the essential or love body between student and Teacher. Being primarily a taker, he is incapable of understanding the Law of Giving and Receiving, the first step in ethics between the student and his source of instruction. His attitude of non-cooperation reflects on the other students and endangers the material structure upholding the means by which instruction is given.

When not of a charitable intent and pure dedication as to devotion, an irresponsible student, multiplied by two, creates an infection in a group-body. Such students inhibit their own means of receiving instruction and block their entry into the freeing of that which seeks to come forth. In reality, these students are of the Judas Ray and come to overthrow the Christ Spirit's penetration and command of the group-body. If the parasitical minority in the group increases into the majority, the result is that the ring-pass-not is shattered and the Dweller may enter the group and destroy its initial purpose. The Peter Disciple and Judas Disciple make a negation-note through which the Dweller is built in a group-body.

Only the heart can tell the student where his spiritual home is, and he can by "the very work's sake" working in his own life know this. Wherever a student finds his spiritual home, the practice of tithing should begin. When he is nourished at the table where the Lord's work is represented and fulfills not his part in gratitude, that which he partakes of as spiritual food shall perish in him and shall benefit nothing except a momentary and fleeting experience. To truly build a spiritual life, effort must be extended in which service and sacrifice of some nature or of equal degree are fulfilled.

A student on the cross-walk between vortice-pools of worship has an inclination to scatter his energies and to divide his interests in serving. Should the student through a feeling of intellectual magnanimity or divided loyalties continue to disburse or divide his gifts to the Lord's work, he is like a man who plants his seeds in distant fields to one another and reaps not the full harvest of his labors. In this, he reaps the grace out of charity rather than tithing.

The true works of charity and the practice of tithing are separate functions or actions. To give to charity is to keep open the humane heart of man's humanity to man. To tithe is to support and to sustain the physical structure housing and symbolizing the spiritual flame of the heart's need in worship of God.

Tithing should be fulfilled regardless of debts or obligations. Our first debt is to the Lord's work. Thus, if we re-budget our debts and fulfill the tithe dedication as a first debt to the Lord, knowing "your Father knoweth what things ye have need of," our tithes are then the living catalyst to enable us to transubstantiate or change one energy to another. The burdens of indebtedness are relieved first in the consciousness. The freeing of supply begins to circulate and debts will be honestly met and paid. And we find the means to overcome the necessity to make debts, inclusive of human karmic ones on other levels.

To the one who has a block regarding tithing, there inevitably comes the lesson of lack. It is best to begin tithing immediately—and not to use human judgment as to wait the convenience of a better time. Until the would-be disciple sets up a regular practice of dedicated tithing, he is a drifting student caught in the crosswalk between vortice-pools.

We concern ourselves when we have physical debts because we are off the budget of spiritual sustaining. When we truly tithe, we earn the means of sustaining our lives, and more than "just bread alone," therefore freeing ourselves to experience spiritually without fear of lack or want.

The moment a person starts tithing, he is a selected vehicle that God may use. The other side of tithing is the giving of one's self. This expands his tithe, providing the grace of prospering—spiritual and physical.

The tithe is the greatest thing to bring one into Timing.

Students show their sense of responsibility to God's Altar by tithing. Without the tithe there is no religiosity. The steel structure in the tithe-supported Altar speaks loudly and clearly that faith supports the *Word* given on the Altar. The integrity of the tithe supports the *True* in the *Word.*

He who wavers in his tithe has no faith and integrity toward life and all of its promises. If man keep not his promises to God, how may he expect anyone to honor him and his word?

Tithing is moral security; it is Word security. The Word will have its way. The Word is the Great Vibration.

Churches must return to the dispensing of the true Agape or Holy Charity; the dispensing of the Word through the Bread of the Christ. The tithe supports the Holy Charity within the Word.

In the beginning is the Vibration, the Word, the Spirit, which becomes the Christ as the Bread. The Christ within the Vibration or Spirit of God is the Continuum Sacrament. The "word made flesh" is the Omnipresence among men.

The Word in its four aspects is a Continuum Salvation in the presence of the true and only Saviour, the Christ. In the beginning was the Will—Spirit. The Life of the Spirit became the Light in the Christ. And the Light in the Christ became the flesh and the light. These four lines of John contain the key to man's total religiosity.

A Church's deficit in funds is due to people not being taught *properly* the Law of Tithing; and in some instances, not at all.

To be a parasite in one life is to become a poverty-person in another.

What one needs is Soul-Prospering rather than ego-prospering. The only way to balance ego-prospering is to share one's beliefs. Sharing one's belief is fulfilled through tithing. Tithing is the first prerogative for the way that one may be instructed by the living teaching through a living system, through a Living Teacher or Teachers.

In a marriage, tithing assures and insures that the husband and wife will grow and prosper equal and more to their financial necessities.

MANTRAM FOR TITHING

My hands reach forth
To gather the harvest
Of my Golden Medallion,
The Grace and Fulfillment
Of my Works in Light.

I receive the Mighty Protection
And Shield
Of my past labors of Love,
That I serve
And become strong.

MANTRAM TO BLESS YOUR PROSPERING

To be said while folding one's tithe or offering and giving it to God:

I am a responsible one.
I work in the Will of God
until my day is done.
Whatever I give, I give into the fund of
prospering
in the Will of God.

INHERITANCE AND SUCCESSION

The real Inheritance is what one inherits from the Teacher.

The highest point of Inheritance is *Succession:* one Teacher passing his Mantle to another. As Saint Paul said, *"I planted, Apollos watered" (1 Corinthians 3:6);* and as Elijah passed his Mantle to Elisha, so is passed the true Inheritance which is inevitable as an heir to God.

Jesus and the Father gave us Heaven as a whole Inheritance. The Teacher gives to you the toll-fare and the toll-way by which you find and inhabit the Inheritance.

One is led by his Teacher into brief excursions whereby he receives a glimpse of divine-energy functioning in precision and perfection. If the disciple is co-atom to his Teacher, he is preparing for the day when he will become a guide to celestial realities.

Every true Teacher must set up an enterprise in the life of his disciple, always recognizing that Succession is a great Law, and that what he passes to his disciple is a reverent repository of grace, truth and wisdom, which when devoid of devotion and dedication is useless in the gross etheric and earth worlds.

Gifts, when donated without foresight, become hindrances, harming rather than blessing. The true donor gives that which fits the one receiving. To give to a disciple a gift not suitable to his range and capacity offends the Law of Succession.

The seer, prophet and Living Teacher, by the nature of the Line and Law of Succession, must pass on to the one who is to inherit his Mantle. As a father must pass on the gene and ancestral traits to his son through the line of descension, so must the Teacher, by the Gift of Prophecy in him and Dimensional Powers supported by the Grace of the Teacher's Initiation, pass on to his disciple the ascending grace-powers of Teaching and Prophecy.

If by grace the disciple encounters and incorporates the grace-side of ancestry, and then by grace melds it with his discipleship grace under the Living Teacher, he is ready to receive the Immutable Ephod or Breastplate of prototypal powers. This Breastplate enables him to wear the Jewels of the Ancestral Valor. Such grace builds the shield against vulnerability to the dark.

Ascending Grace united with Ancestral Descendant Grace is the structure upon which one remains in the State-of-Grace Insulation, withstanding the trials of discipleship.

On the Path of Initiation, one is weighed for his Ancestral-Grace collateral. By this he purchases a continuum of very-special grace which protects him from the offenses or from the full measure of the blows thrown against the Ephod of his dedication.

The twelve jewels on the ephod as worn in the ancient time by the priests represent the twelve hierarchy powers of the soul, which one must earn or gain that he become a guardian over the Dharma and a warrior against the evils in the world.

> *Each saint has his mission in life and comes with a definite instrument of instruction. As soon as he completes his job, he retires from this world and goes back into the spiritual ocean from which he sprang, leaving the work of further reorientation to his successor. Even if the predecessor has to do something for his followers, he does it through the living successor to whom he entrusted the work on retirement; and only the latter, as a brother-in-faith or Gurbhai may help his brethren on the physical plane.*
>
> —*Kirpal Singh*

. . . Ann Ree Colton

9

THE TEACHER AND THE MASTERS

I am insulated within the Mantle of Jesus. I will to will in God within the instruction of Christ Jesus, the Lord. Abba, Father. Amen. Amen. Amen.

Earth Teachers and Supreme Consciousness

This is the infinite birthright of each soul: To make union with the Eternal Spirit as the One in the All, and thus achieve God-Realization.

It is the goal of the initiate to live in the world and to live in the spiritual world equally. The Jesus Path is a Master and Mastering Path. To follow Him and to walk with Him is to be always present with His instruction. All masters or gurus—even though some may be unaware of His true meaning—are under Him.

Let Jesus be the door. Let the Great Sages and Gurus of the Path echo or reflect His words, that one may enter into the true life, light, love and will instruction, safely reaching God-Bliss and Heaven. Such Bliss is the Way, the Truth and the Life.

All true Teachers in the physical world point the way to the *use* of the Ethic—the first step on the way to will-initiation. All true Teachers reveal the Ethic, yet leave the student free to make choice in the use of will. Only the highest of Gurus, Jesus, has given the full requirement in the use of will—that is, all must turn to the Will of the Father. The Gates of Initiation are many and there are many Masters protecting these Gates. The door to will-initiation is protected by Jesus, whose heart-atom points the way to a selfless and total love-alignment with the Will of the Father.

When one enters the Path or Way to Initiation, he begins by reverence, devotion and serving. Then comes the way of the purifying techniques for the auric cleansing. Through knowledge interiorly given, one is shown by the greater Gate-keepers of the soul, the Bodhisattvas, how to direct the akasic indwelling fires within the etheric soul-portals of the etheric body and thus cleanse out each day the debris of a misused will.

Every negative thought must be erased; every vow or promise must be kept; every scripture containing truth must be observed; every act must be a consecrated act before a true initiate comes into the adept powers of the will. These are manifesting powers of the Spirit. All initiates strive and work joyfully toward this fulfillment in being, in creation.

All free-to-serve initiates have paid the full price of initiation and thus have paved the way for leadership and service to the souls of mankind. Through rightful disciplines and acceptance by the inner guidance directing the higher will, spiritual power is ascertained.

Until the disciple has made perfect alignment with his Higher Self, his spiritual Earth-Teacher imparts instruction to him and interprets each phase in the disciple's evolvement, aiding him in the resolving of his karma. Alignment with the Higher Self enables the chela to enter into the highest of all instructions. Through the Great Immortals and the powers of Mediation, he makes alignment with the Higher Worlds and the World Teacher, Jesus. When he has made alignment with the Jesus One, he aligns himself with the Archetypal Worlds and the Light of the Christ—and receives of the Eternals.

Certain Earth-Teachers assist in giving birth to spiritual powers; powers lying latent in the souls of all persons; powers uniquely distinct yet forming a part of the *All* or Supreme Consciousness.

Earth-Teachers initiating souls in groups are ripe channels united with the Guru nucleus-chain of Teachers in the inner planes. A group supported by a channeling Teacher is made up of souls representing all of the seven Light-Streams.

The work of the Teacher is to keep and maintain the converging individualistic streams of soul-potential and power; to recognize individually the soul powers and capacity in each student or disciple on the Path; to free each soul to his elan and so give aid in cutting to perfection the diamond facets of each soul.

Only in one person in a million souls can such ripe Teachers be found. Sent in timing to the coinciding progression of advanced souls, the Teacher appears in timing to a world climax or need. Channeling Teachers come not as servants to their chelas, but as those who carry the flame for the Greater Light opening the budding font of certain souls in the world.

The Teacher comes as one without a second or duplicate, adding to knowledge; extending knowledge while giving approachable techniques to Light in preparation for centuries to come.

Souls in a group supporting in reciprocity the power of the group leader-soul add their powers to the power of their Teacher; these become builder egos contributing to the new era or age. All prayer and meditation techniques in a group-body when converged are the tools or skills of combined souls not to be found in singular or separate self-developing attributes of one soul.

Separatist persons cannot be assimilated into a group-soul environment. All persons drawn to soul-group environments are first tried, tested and gauged by the central or master tone congealing or coagulating the vortice-power of the group.

Rejection of separatist non-blending persons is regulated by the repository selector Angels overdwelling the group. The Supra-Guru nuclei within the spiritual worlds overdwell the group also as discriminating determiners to call, to send, and to utilize all functions in the spiritual life as well as in the physical life of souls etherically encased within a builder soul-group.

Group ethics, group interrelationships are merged and fused on soul levels. All individualizing karmic or personalized relationships are at intervals worked out in certain phases of initiatory combined trials. Recognition of such combined initiation is kept alive by alerts from the group leader-soul Teacher.

Through the combined soul-resources, trials are transcended into combined spiritual group-soul power through which world service is rendered to many souls less evolved, or yet to be called. Souls assimilated into combined group instruction, however, should not think themselves to be beyond the resolving of their own separate karmas. It is necessary that each person build his own ground beneath his feet by self-responsibility as to his physical placement in the world. Nor can one shift the burden of his own individual day-by-day practicality onto the weight of the group. It is only by the mature accepting of responsibility by each soul in a group that the group can as an outer form in the eye of the world survive or be recognized.

Weakness or over-reliance upon supports from the physical aspects of strength of any one individual in the group extracts automatically such persons from a group body.

The sustaining chela body is made up of soul power, not physical power. Soul power, however, must of itself be framed in material strengths, for souls working for world-good must also be supported by strengths stemming from the physical as well as the soul.

All of the victories held as grace-survival in physical circumstances enable a person to be uniquely selected for a specific group work. Thus, the techniques of a group-life build a powerful animating body through which God can do His Will in a very special, splendid way.

> *When you are bitter, take the Sacrament; then the gall in your hates will turn to the sweetness of joy.*

THE RETURN OF THE PRIMORDIAL

CHELA—Student or disciple.

ESSE—The grace atmosphere or pure heavenly substance.

HIERARCHS—The great Constellation Over-Lords or Fathers.

MASTER-TEACHER—A pure, true, living Teacher; an Adept.

MANU—The Law-Giver supporting Karmic Law in the system of Maya.

PRIMORDIAL—The Pre-Edenic Light or Pure Purusha (Soul) substance.

SAT-GURU—Jesus: The Door.

With trust, devotion and acceptance of the Path of Discipline, the soul-thread between the Teacher and his chela grows steadier until the trust-love becomes no longer a tug on the chela's heart, but a firm, reassuring, balancing cable-tow. The chela looks to his Teacher not as a separate entity, but as a soul-presence living in a rare atmosphere which he has yet to attain.

Heart-rhythms of the Master-Teacher provide heart-rhythms for the chela. The heart-rhythms have been mastered by the Master-Teacher through the Hierarchy-heart overdwelling the soul of the Master-Teacher. The stepping stones of the rise are always extension into superconsciousness which is of the Infinite, and therefore limitless.

Each day bears the record of effort. Any lingering tamas-inertia is an irritant to extension. Or if there be any rajasic activities, the electricities therefrom produce a cloud, a lightning and a thunder. Only where sattvic-poise and sattvic-calm exist can the Master's quickened regularities be experienced.

The Master-Teacher has walked far beyond the microcosmics of Maya cyclic change. His walk is upon the two seas of the microcosmic and the macrocosmic. He would lead you on this walk into dimensions beyond sense into the Divine.

There are gurus who will never attain mastership. They indirectly serve the Master-Teachers. There are Master-Teachers who are the channelled *servers* for the Masters. The true Masters walk the course of the Hierarch. These are the Old Ones, the Elect, whose works of the Primordial Days still exist in their natures. Only the adept has communication with those who are Star-charted. Only those who have made union with their own direct star can reach or touch the hem of their Splendored Garment made of the finest gossamer light of the Eternals.

The chain of the White Gurus is a network of interrelating velocities. Time, Space, motion, gravity-mastery are of the Essence. *The Esse* is the charted way. Only the Sat-

Guru Master knows the steer-code, the guide-star to *Esse.* To live in the Esse is to be a utilizer of Maya forces and charges.

Dimensions extended beyond Maya-fixity are of the *Esse freedom.* He who lived in the body of Jesus lives in the Esse. The Master over all Masters is Jesus.

The one who sired Jesus is from Sirius; this was Joseph. He is the Master-builder for the dimensional *Ark* of the Essence; in former times, he was that one called Noah. In the present, he is the *Noah* for those who prepare the way for the deluge of the darkened storm now entering the world of Maya-irritation. Maya-irritation is as a gas bag of helium moving toward currents beyond controllable compass. Earth-Maya cataclysms are close at hand. The thunder of warning has long since sounded. Suffering sent onto the face of the waters is close to the reaping time. Cleansing must come, that men of Earth may return to renewal of the Primordial Light. Those who carry the seed of light to repopulate the Earth will be kept sacred or secretly safe.

Pollution of sin now requires renewal of the Primordial forces, that the strong Adamic light or first beginnings may once more emerge. The Demiurge must always come before the *emergence* of Primordiality.

The Primordial One, or Ancient of Days, works with the Hierarch-hearts of the Inward Hierarch-Masters, who are the crowned Kings or Sons of Man over the children of men.

The Manu works with the Ancient of Days as the Law-giver through the Sons of Man. He who comes to accent the Law is under the Manu, the Law-giver.

The Son of Man, Jesus, came to relax the suffering-octave enforcing the Law. He transposes sentient suffering to the suffering of *conscience.* Suffering then must be overcome not from outward, external helps, but eventually from within the self. From this comes joy *beyond* suffering. For life in truth is joy. Only Truth moves the conscience into right Law stemming from the Manu firmness within the Law.

We are radiant beings in a radiating universe.

THE DHARMA AND THE MASTER

> *The Causal Mind is the non-contesting higher mind where peace reigns, where innocence omnisciently dwells.*

The word *support* in the Rishi, the Christ, or Divine White-Line of teaching is called *Dharma.* Dharma-supports are established through merit-strength or grace earned on the physical plane by selfless works, sacrifice and giving; on the emotional plane, by processes in the use of love earned by union with the Love of God; on the physical plane, by use of energy-power extracted from Nature-energy; on the spiritual plane, by use of mind-strength and God-Realization, seeing with the Causal Mind God as the Creator.

The opening of the door to the Causal Mind is the ultimate goal for all on the Path. The Causal Mind is an unblemished mirror-vehicle for the Archetypal thoughts of the Christ Spirit.

The Buddhi Principle acting within the Causal Mind is the Informing Principle, giving to the one who enters into full Bliss-Meditation the freeing of the Dharma-supports. Therefore, to free Dharma and thus live a life wholly for God, one discovers and earns through Bliss-Meditation the wondrous peace and power within the Causal Mind.

Bliss-Meditation does not mean a trance state or an out-of-consciousness experience. Full awareness of the objective or outer consciousness must be a quiescent, detached observing instrument during Bliss-Meditation experience.

The Master prepares each of his students for the more extended states of meditation with a planned process in the approaches to meditation. The Master's process is to first instill into the disciple or student a philosophical dharma or support. This philosophy is based upon the universal cosmic unity of all life in the One or God.

Secondly, the Master works to free his disciple to some extent from karmic-memory, guilt-laden patterns of the past and in the present life, for the Master knows that guilt-laden memories are magnetic and kinetically electric, drawing the disciple to reproduce his past mistakes. It is unwise to dwell upon one's own unworth, as one can be fixed to the unbelief in his own worth as an instrument for God. The realization of one's own soul-worth is liberation. The Master works with his disciple to achieve this. However, the Master does not remove his disciple from the self-responsibility of an honest attitude as to wrongdoing of the past and present.

The Master endeavors to set up a finer vibratory course in which the student is supported by the Mercy of God. Upon the screen of the conscience there will be projected the need and compulsion to rectify the wrong deeds, attitudes and actions of the past.

The finer vibrations in the supernal rearrangement of karma move the disciple beyond pain and suffering. If one fails to remain in alignment with God and neglects his practices of light, he returns instantly to old karmic regressive thoughts and actions.

In the beginning when one is a novice, he is aware of only one source of Mediation. As time progresses, he becomes aware that he is initiated by many Great Souls watching over his destiny.

All Great Teachers represent the Omnipresence. They are the schoolmasters of the soul and the spirit. They are the protectors of truth, justice and mercy. With the exception of the Angels, all have lived in the Earth and have known the struggle of human life. Each has been tested by the forces of Maya and has attained mastery in his own right. They live in the World of Light. Their life is one of uttermost dedication to lift men toward the great Light—the Christ.

The *Living Teacher* is a *born Guru*—that is, he is born with the knowing of the Dharma or instruction.

The *Angels* reinforce your world with light, with vitality, and with regeneration.

The *Saints* come forth in Mediation to free your gifts of the spirit.

The *Illuminati* are the genius Risen Dead whose instruction enters into your telepathic stream of consciousness to lead you to recover your soul-talents from past lives and to produce new talents in this life.

The *Masters* initiate you into the processes of the mind and the will.

The clumsy experimentation now being used in psychology, psychiatry and the psychic sciences will come under the Ethic of living and pure Teachers or *born Gurus* who have come in timing to teach directly under the Master-tutelage.

The Masters have scanned the horizons of the soul, and into this world there will come the two or three who will drive the chariots of the Dharma of instruction. Niscience is the opening of the door to these Archetypal-sent Teachers. Niscience is speaking now to the world.

On becoming a Teacher, an enlightened one does not seek to give to the less evolved the responsible transcendental Atma-wisdoms. He prays therefore to be stationed always in a realistic point of evaluation in that which he gives, and particularly in that which he judges or weighs.

Thus, he cannot judge one who has not the capacity to learn or to believe. Yet he does not lose sight of the contributing factor as individualized expressions of life and consciousness.

All Teachers pray for holy discrimination rather than personalized discrimination, for that which works through a true Teacher discriminates how and where the Dharma falls. One having access to the flow of the Clear Light or Dharma should give freely within the holy rain of the Dharma; the discriminating Esse within the Dharma will search out and find those who have earned their unique receptivity to the Dharma.

If one be not in the Christ, the responsibility for the ignorance of others weighs heavily upon the conscience and soul of one who seeks to teach. If the Teacher is in the Christ, the burden of ignorance and separateness is taken over by the Christ. In the Christ, one gives of his Logos as it falls into his own illuminative processes. That which he is, he gives. *"Such as I have, give I thee: In the name of Jesus Christ." (Acts 3:6)*

Every Teacher undergoes a virtue-struggle within himself and his own nature. On becoming enlightened, he becomes the virtue for which he has struggled. The virtue he has freely received through grace, he freely gives.

Virtue received by grace is that which he has earned through his own self-denial. It is the virtue-grace in the Teacher that commands him and compels him to teach. And that which he teaches by virtue-grace acts as a baptism, initiator and enlightener to him who is teachable.

MANTRAMIC STATEMENT

My Dharma-supports are:

Observance of study and non-claiming works;

Observance of love as a devotee of God;

Observance of fearlessness in facing the unknown;

Observance of faith in the use of mind-creations through the Christ Mind in me;

Observance of mind-strength through God-Realization mantrams.

TEACHING THE BUDDHI ATOM-LIGHT

All true Teachers have opened their Buddhi mental atoms, which unite them with the Divine Informing Principle.

There is no greater vocation than the teaching of the spiritual sciences. Teaching—when true, when realistically expressed in the spirit of dedication with ethic—is a work sacred under God. A Teacher must know with an informed knowing. He must have the open consciousness or the ever-ready knowing.

Not all are called to teach the spiritual sciences. The harvest is indeed white and the laborers are few as said by the Supreme Teacher, Jesus.

The true philosophy supporting a chosen Teacher begins with the Masters who stand at the gates of instruction, sifting and selecting the aspirants of the spiritual life. To seek to share the overflow of one's instruction under the Masters is to accelerate one's own karma and to be confronted by the karma of those whom he would instruct. Until one can unite with the cause within the karmic laws of those he would instruct, he will be caught into bewildering forces, emotional and mental. Thus, to desire to teach, one must come under the supervision of the Divine Companions or Master Presences who lend or share their Buddhi light supporting the thought and mind exploration of their students.

One earns the grace of mind and soul expansion through devotion to the Masters; through service to God; through willingness to revere the disciplines necessary to the spiritual life; through past-life association with the Masters; through reverent dedication in the present life; through willingness to be corrected; and through strength of character earned in former lives and in the present life.

As a mother pelican takes from her breast the feathers to make the nest for her young, so does the Master share his Buddhi atom-light with his apprentice, until the student—through the process of exploring, testing and challenging—produces his own Buddhi Light.

The Buddhi atom-light supports of the Master enable the student to be informed as to the karmic laws and enable the one receiving instruction to move from astral-tumult thinking into causal consciousness (higher mind), which cancels out certain karmic patterns. Such processes place the student and aspirant of the spiritual life on the outer fringe of his karma and enable him to observe and evaluate the karmic laws. One becomes a spiritual philosopher when he has qualified to open the Buddhi Informing Principle.

No one can teach of the inner life and its developments until he has experienced it completely and fully within his own life's expression. A Teacher under the Masters can be heard, recognized and followed because he provides the true answers to spiritual Ethic and instruction. To do this, he must have constant access to the Buddhi or Informing Principle.

Through demotion of egoism; through the slaying of all ambition to exalt the personal self; through continued service without claim for fame or rewards; through practices of devotion, study and meditation; through reverence for all life: one builds the treasure of Buddhi atom-light awareness, which inevitably overflows into the minds, hearts and souls of others in the world. From this comes a Teacher, a free and liberated soul having command of his life, asking only that he have no other life save to share and to give of his Buddhi Light.

> *For him who has faith in his guru and in the instructions, the experiences and realizations are bound to happen.*
>
> —*Milarepa*

THE REPOSITORIUM

When the repositorium of your soul's motive is clear, it produces in the outward life the true Ethic of Jesus by which Christ may reveal God. One receives God-Realization only when he makes his motive pure. The master repositorium of the Higher Self is infinite purity.

Saint Francis fed the repositorium of the bread to the birds and the beasts. The crumbs of his bread were inexhaustible. Jesus fed this inexhaustible bread to His multitude who were to become reincarnating witnesses for the Holy Spirit throughout the ages. This living bread becomes the strength of our bodies, that they may take on the appearance of the Christ.

To be converted, changed or transformed at the hand of a Saint or a Bodhisattva is to be led by the hand of Jesus to the Father.

Seeking leads one to weigh his motives. Each day motive must be searched and weighed, that the true disciple may free soul-power action into the life of all. Power without purity is an object of hateful fire, pressuring all, considering none. To seek to rise on the shallow promises of men is to receive only the glaze. Fantasy-minded souls must bathe themselves in Truth. To do this, one must be truthful, reliable, constant, loyal.

The master pledge must be taken for self-mastery before one is called to serve the great Maha-Devas and Masters.

This pledge is the vow of purity and chastity. All pure souls bringing the peace-bliss of Devata grace live this pledge in every breath. These carry not the chastening force. They carry the love-armour of Light.

Such souls are the strong; they are detached from ambition for self, firm in that which is true and rightful. They are the heart-initiates, the Gurus of the inoffensive way. Their grace for the world is peace, love, kindness, joy.

Jesus, the Door Keeper of Kindness, is the Initiator of the heart-initiate. Inwardly and outwardly, study His beginning and His end, that you may realize that life under His hand is the way of releasing love, and that the way to render service on His Path is sacrifice plus service for God.

THE TEACHER IN THE WORLD AND THE MASTER

No one truly desires all truth or comes rightfully under the tutelage of truth until falsity is as dry ashes in the mouth, heart and mind. All of the striving, thrusting futilities must have been tried before a disciple is truly a disciple, willing, obedient and receptive to the Teacher of all, Christ.

How much waste and non-creativity must run their course, only the soul decides. When the pupil is ready, the Guardian Angel sends a Teacher representing the Christ.

Christlike Teachers are often unheard and unseen by the spiritually ignorant; and even in the presence of the calloused beginner on the Path the signals, signs and tokens of what makes or represents a Teacher are ignored or obscured. Teachers of the Path in Heaven are many; Teachers in Earth on the Path as lamps for the ready are few. *"The harvest truly is plenteous, but the labourers are few." (St. Matthew 9:37)*

The greatest enemies or foes against receiving one's Teacher are intellect, egotism, inertia. The Teacher in Earth must have been a Teacher in many lives to teach in the hour or the moment of coinciding karmas of the many ready for the first steps upon the Path.

During the bright side of an Archetypal Time, thousands of ego-souls are reaching toward the light of the Anointing Ones, sometimes knowingly with their whole hearts, sometimes only in part. Teachers more often appear to those who have sought in vain to ease their souls; to souls burdened by a thirst to know; to souls submerged in clouds of unknowing who are approaching readiness, having earned the right to be instructed.

To the ready the teaching is ready; to the uninitiated the Teacher stands assisting in the rise and fall over the abysses of expanding in learning and discerning.

No two ego-souls respond in the same manner to instruction and initiation. A true Teacher knows that there can be no static way toward the Light. Individual spiritual enlightenment and progress on the Path are definite yet selectively different and unique according to the soul's tenure or support of the universal-within. One thing, however, is inviolate: a Teacher given of God to a disciple on the Path is a gift of God, not to be looked upon as an accident, a convenience, or as an escape-way through which one can unload or step aside from his responsible phases in advancement toward the Light.

A Teacher does *not live* his disciple's life. He teaches his student to resolve each problem. Through telepathic directives, he velocitizes the atmosphere through which the disciple learns discrimination and discernment. One thing an initiate first learns on coming under his Teacher is that an initiate under a Teacher is at all times obedient to a Teacher's guidance, and he is more than willing to observe the rhythmic steps to remain in alignment. He keeps the vitalities of spiritual life free through rendering service to the Teacher and the Master, and therefore to God. He knows that he cannot return to life as it was before being initiated, having rejected the physical demands and expressions of the physical world which will invariably reject him if he seeks to return and live as having lived before.

All Teachers and Masters initiate their proteges through wisdom-timing to the karma and grace of the disciple, keeping open the flow of inductive directives. Through the higher unconscious, the initiate is aware of the Master, though not always immediately aware of what the message says or to what extent or length he must go in what is expected of him in his serving or mission. Trust, reliance on the Teacher, plus self-reliance make a perfect instrument for the works of light under a Teacher and Master.

Practical helps to discern what is being revealed during accelerated periods of initiation are: Keep a diary of sentences entering the mind beyond the ordinary aspect of thinking. Weigh and assess objectively one's own shortcomings interfering with the transmission flow between the disciple and the Teacher or Master. Watch impersonally the dream-flow at night. Temper all intense dissatisfaction with the physical, emotional or the mental life. Seek to remain receptive through a balanced calm and contentment. An endeavor should also be made to have some active facet of creation to keep open the circuits of communing and receiving, and certain methods of physical discipline such as yoga, mild exercise, walking, rhythmic dancing, and swimming.

One meets the Teacher or Master consciously throughout the complete day if he is linked in his heart and his soul to the Master. One also receives special and significant instruction during meditation. In the night's sleep, the Teacher and Master appear with freedom to the soul alert. A mantram spoken before sleep is an invitation to receive an actual visitation from one's Teacher or Master.

One must mute out the arrogant, skeptical wavelengths of the intellect. He must face the mirror of his emotions, and he must season his body to the expectation of dwelling physically, mentally and spiritually within the diamond-like thought wavelengths of a true Teacher or Master.

THE APPEARING MASTERS AND THE INITIATORY SCHOOLS

In the Master Initiatory Schools, the school finds the student rather than the student finding the school. The school suitable for each one appears in perfect timing. The appearance of the Master or a representative of a Master opens the door to instruction.

The appearing Masters do not make themselves known to the timid, the doubtful or the vacillating. All probationers of the higher life must expect discipline and character tests to occur when one is blessed to have received the first overdwelling of the Master.

What is an initiatory school? An initiatory school consists of a nucleus of advanced egos headed by a Teacher, a Guru or a Master. Students, when ready, find themselves drawn irresistibly to an initiatory vortex of philosophy and spiritual instruction.

What is expected of the student in his relationship to such a school? The student must first of all be loyal to the Teacher. In being loyal to the Teacher, he is loyal to his best good and therefore more competent to use his instruction with ethic.

Are all initiated in the same schools? Is there more than one initiatory school? There are countless initiatory schools in the inner planes.

The inner schools most frequently visited and active are situated in the First Heaven. These are called *the Hall of Learning.* One experiences this instruction first during sleep in night-flight and in dreams. Also, one can be instructed telepathically by the Masters working with these schools during the day. If the student-initiate has mastered the art of daytime release of his etheric body, he can receive instruction during the day from the inner schools. This more often occurs after the student has mastered going *inside* in his meditation practices.

In the initiatory school of the night, one meets the Master in total freedom. In the daytime appearance of the Master, he can be seen only by an initiate who has known in many lives the technique of *seeing*. However, he can be *felt* with a form of ultra-sensitivity by one who is being prepared for the higher aspects of initiation. He can also be heard by such students with a form of *clear inner hearing*.

In the school of Shamballa, or the Hall of Wisdom, initiation into hierarchy powers is experienced by the initiate. Here, in the planes of the Second Heaven, called *the Spheres of Light,* initiates become Teachers, Teachers become Gurus, Gurus become Masters, Masters become Bodhisattvas. The Hall of Wisdom school in the white light of akasia unites and flows into the seven initiatory polarity points in the Earth where the overdwelling Master uses the earth-atoms in his higher etheric body, appearing to the key initiate residing in the polarity point.

The seven polarity points of initiations under direction of a polarity Teacher are magnetic white-fire pools of instruction. There are only seven such polarity Masters working with the world at a time. These do not relate to the twelve vortice-pools of worship. It is unusual grace when a worship vortice-pool and a magnetic white-fire vortice of an appearing Master correlate.

In Niscience one finds this grace. The thirteenth Archetype in the Third Heaven and the thirteenth vortice-pool of Niscience are synchronized with a master vortice-pool. Thus, the Niscience instruction for the world is an interflow power for initiation under a Guru-chain headed by Masters having earth-appearing bodies.

Jesus, Master of the Masters, Lord under the Lord of All, needs a worship-vortice through which He may work with the masses. He also needs a body or nucleus of specialized souls to work with individually. In all worship bodies where the Masters synchronize their labors uniquely with Jesus, a very wonderful message can be given to the world.

It is needful to worship; it is also needful to work toward higher initiation that one may truly serve in the world. All initiates will remain in the lesser instruction until they understand that Jesus is the Archstone upholding the building of spirituality. Since Jesus, the Masters can do a mighty work, and the greater things *men are to do* are made possible through synchronization and mediation.

MASTER SYMBOLS

Symbols are living Archetypal particles of light that never change in the inner consciousness. The higher unconscious is familiar with symbols. One is constantly absorbing symbolic nuances into his outer consciousness.

All persons constantly use symbols in their expression. All thinking and feeling are dependent upon symbolic life. The emotions are especially dependent upon the energy symbols emanate. The mind depends upon the meanings within symbols. Symbols are stabilizing reassurances from birth to life, from life to death, and from death to birth.

Symbols are the vocabulary in dream life. In the life between death and rebirth, the language used is the language of symbols. God has given man symbols, that he might extend his powers of concentration and use the energies of his mind to create, and that he might move over the limitation of language, race and place.

There are seven great master symbols centered within seven great Master Archetypes. When one penetrates the master symbol in a Master Archetype, he opens 144,000 symbols. These are released into his consciousness. From this he gathers an amazing inner vocabulary of the mind.

All great Teachers use the symbolic language in allegory and in parable. All Masters use the myth stories to communicate to their disciples. It is true that one can recognize his Master or Teacher by the quality of the myth parables he communicates to his disciples. Such myths are given to one on the Path in sacred allegorical form, or sometimes they are given in parabolic form. They always carry a kernel of memory held over from a past life by which one may recognize his Master. A familiar or endearing parable or allegory is told to the initiate in a specific way. From life to life there is a sacred tie between the Master and the disciple. This is a tie which is never severed. In each life the Master seeks to bring the disciple into harmony with his eternal being.

CO-ATOM TO JESUS

To be *co-atom* to any person, one must be on the same wavelength of energy emanating from a sacred atom; to be co-atom to Jesus, one must have an open circuit or a degree of light in his mental atoms to the mental atoms of his Teacher or Master. In this way, he is telepathically communicable to the mind and thoughts of his Master and Teacher, and thus receives a continued flow of instruction.

One can develop his own capacity in co-atom association through meditation and through thoughts of oneness with all life as given of God. When two persons have instant recognition of one another, and absolute congeniality, they are co-atom to one another. This can occur only when one has been with the other person in many lives where relationships have proved to be harmonious.

When God prepares to use a person for a greater work, He first sends to the one chosen a Teacher or Master; secondly, He sends to him a co-atom person in the world, that the work may be consummated and fulfilled.

Each Prototypal Zodiacal House is divided into thirty degrees. Each ten of these degrees represents the three *Gunas.* The first decan of a Prototypal Zodiacal House relates to *tamas;* the second decan relates to *rajas;* the third, to *sattva.* In prototypal mastery, Jesus stands in the center as the Hierarchy Blueprint, which all men must eventually reach in this Earth system.

In mastering the Prototypal Initiations, one on the Path must incorporate more than one prototype. To gain the Hierarchy mastery within his own consciousness, he may at one point of initiation be working with a tamasic Pisces, a rajasic Scorpio, etc.

The tamasic electricity is black. The rajasic electricity is red. The sattvic electricity is white. Jesus in the center as the Hierarchy Blueprint for the initiate represents the white or sattvic electricities. Through co-atom alignment with Jesus, the initiate masters the thirty-six prototypal associations.

To do this he must become as a musician or a painter using the three Guna forces of transenergization. For instance, when a Teacher as a center of a group-body is called to initiate many persons having varied degrees of zodiacal evolvement, he must struggle, one by one, with the dark tamasic nature of each zodiacal prototype represented to him.

As the Teacher evolves, he finds himself struggling for the soul of each one on whatever level he finds them. It is his work, however, to remain centered in the sattvic through Jesus, never in any manner personally involving himself with the struggle of the student being initiated. It is his work to see each prototype as one who is coming to birth through soul and soul-powers.

The Prototypal Initiatory trials are trials of water, blood, fire and Holy Spirit. The Teacher, to sustain his equilibrium, must discern what trial is being experienced by his student, and give encouragement and enlightenment on that particular theme of initiation. There will never be a physical Teacher who will teach wholly to a sattvic initiatory group. Every Teacher who lives in the "Follow Me" principle of Jesus must accept the fact that he is teaching the spiritually ignorant, the sinful, the willful. Jesus came not to save the righteous but to save the sinners. ". . . *for I am not come to call the righteous, but sinners to repentance." (St. Matthew 9:13)*

Two co-atom Teachers know each other in a depth of knowing that others in the world do not know. They share with one another an incessant and ingenious knowing in a form of autobiographical light. This conjoined knowing or quiescence between souls becomes a teaching vessel containing integrities long pursued as virtue.

John the Baptist and Jesus were co-atom. On the death of John the Baptist, John the Beloved became co-atom to Jesus.

Elijah and Elisha were co-atom souls.

In the beginning phases of co-atom association and attainment, one draws upon the gross co-atom association between Esau and Jacob, who, in the timing of their souls, laid down the pattern for the climb toward Initiation.

Every person has some other person who is acting as co-atom to him in Earth. He is either an antagonist or a blessing. The co-atom association has its negative or positive. As Judas was the negative nemesis for Jesus, so in every life of the initiate, in the earlier stages of Initiation, he encounters his nemesis in the shape of a person acting as his downfall or as his assailant on the Path.

In the Post-Easter tide, one must expect to meet the low co-atom nemesis assailant as to his beliefs, his trust and his faith in God. This lasts until Wesak or the first full Moon in Taurus in which the Preacher is acclaimed in the Heaven Worlds as being ripe, ready or qualified to pass the instruction for the Path. Let every initiate be aware in the Post-Easter cycle that his very soul is in balance between the dark and the light. The very terrain or footholds of the Path are trembling yet with the afterflow of the Crucifixion energies.

Jesus, on proving Himself to His disciples through Apparition and Ascension Powers, appears after Easter as an etheric apparition in the lives of all would-be initiates. As Jesus proved to the disciples the reality of His deathlessness, the disciple in this time must prove again that Jesus is deathless and that all men are deathless. Thus, he is challenged by a co-atom person or persons on the low scale of atom association.

THE TELEPATHIC DISCIPLE AND THE COSMOS DISCIPLE

One becomes aware through direct evidence that he is a mediating and meditation vehicle through the use of the Cosmos and Cosmic energies. The initiate is animated by the knowledge that he has the power to participate in the process of shaping, reproving and pointing the way prophetically to certain events which would not ordinarily be acted upon by the gravity sense of direction and willing. He is then for all time approaching Telepathic Discipleship. In this, he is in accord with the Caring Principle or Guidance Principle which has taken hold of his desires, his will and his life goals.

When one uses Mediation and proves that some thing or some one has responded constructively in an ingenious and totally uncontrived way, he has arrived at the first stages of becoming a Telepathic Disciple, and is thereafter a better vessel under the Guiding Spirit of God.

All Telepathic Disciples are centered within the Telepathic Matrix on the functional, physical and spiritual levels. They have access to the mind-banks gathered from soul-cultures built by the interflow between the Greater Minds of the Elect who mentally and spiritually direct and influence the human spirit.

God as Spirit projects His Spirit as Omnipresence. Omnipresence is manifested through God-willed minds. The true telepathic filigree supporting the Great Intelligible Unconscious, or Purusha, is inhabited by the countless mind or mental hierarchy-nature vitalities of Great Souls who have lived in the Earth as *Knowers.*

The Greater Telepathies are open to the Telepathic Disciple especially when he is close to becoming a Cosmos Disciple and therefore a direct revealer of Archetypal Light. The Greater Telepathies are those that keep alight the Light-chain of ideas, passing them onto enlightened souls with hierarchy-nature minds. A Telepathic Disciple has mastered the sensitivities of the senses on the gravity level and is ready to be a vehicle for the Cosmos-Universal Power of Passing.

A Cosmos-Disciple life always occurs during the latter years of the earth-life. One enters Telepathic Disciple apprenticeship as he approaches his mid-forties. One enters Cosmos Discipleship when he has entered into his latter wisdom-years.

All true sages, prophets and adepts earn longevity, that they may use what has been learned through the telepathic initiations, and finally flower to fruit within the Cosmos Disciple hierarchy-nature mind.

Male initiates who experience Telepathic Disciple apprenticeship undergo the fiery trials beginning in their 42nd year, ending in their 49th year.

Every Telepathic Disciple works directly with one or more Cosmos Disciples. The union of minds between these souls is necessary to produce manifestation of the Dharma.

There are few Telepathic Disciples or Cosmos Disciples in the world. The Spirit of God has willed it so. Such Disciples know themselves to be what they are, who they are, and where they are going. They cannot be deterred from their Way or the Path.

Many, many lives of total dedication have enabled them to walk in the Way and to leave their marking-and-tracing steles for the world. On this hangs the hope for the prophets and for what they see as a vision for the future as to the spiritual destiny of mankind.

THE WORD AND THE THREE CURRENTS

God is the Word. The Word contains three Currents. These three Currents are opened to the initiate in different stages of initiation.

Through meditation, one unites with the *Light Current* of the Word and becomes illumined. Through life-force mastering, one masters and unites with the life-stream or *Life Current* and becomes a healer. Through the *Sound-Current* Initiation, one unites with the Holy Ghost or Spirit of Truth and sees and *knows* the past, the present and future, and thus becomes a prophet.

The Light Current, the Life-Stream Current and the Sound Current become one when one has made union with the composite Masters who now work with the true initiates aligned with the Greater Archetypes. The Masters come to keep men in the *Word* or the Light Current, the Life Current and the Sound Current.

The *Venerable One* is a Bodhisattva Master-Saint. He is centered within the hub or center of the Great-Soul Medallion of the White Line of Masters.

The Archetypal Masters are presently overdwelling the light, life and the souls of those who are called to teach, to heal and to reveal what the Greater Archetypes are saying to men of the Earth.

All New-Era Teachers will be influenced by these three Master Currents of the Word. They must master these Currents. Some will express but one, and in rare instances of the advanced souls, all three Currents—Light, Life and

Sound—will be manifested to and for the good of the Word in the world.

Christ is the Initiator into the Light Current. The Father in Heaven is the Initiator into the Life-Stream Current. God is the Initiator into the Holy Ghost or Sound Current.

Jesus is the door through which one is opened to the three Currents in the Word. He quickens whatever phase or aspect of the Currents is ready to come forth. All Masters work with Jesus, the Sat-Guru of Initiation and of Love.

All disciples and initiates since Jesus enter the door through Jesus. Jesus overdwells the Masters.

The Masters are the gates and Jesus is the door to the three Currents in the Word. The Masters' instruction and initiating powers enable the disciple to blend the flow of the three Currents in the Word—the Light, the Life and the Sound.

The System of Niscience is founded upon the Light Current, the Life Current and the Sound Current within the Word of God. The initiate under the Niscience Archetype is seeking to blend all three Currents. When one becomes co-atom to Jesus, all three Currents become active in the Niscience Archetypal statements and in the mantra-supported mantrams which are a part of the Niscience daily practices for discipleship.

Every practice given in the White Papers and in the revelatory books by Ann Ree Colton under the Niscience Archetype is within the plan of the Masters, that the unique students and the disciples of Niscience will unite these three Currents with their soul powers and potentials, and thus enable them to serve in the world through the Word.

FOUR ASPECTS OF THE SOUND CURRENT

The Sound Current containing the Will, Life, Light and Love of God, known as the Word, can be heard in four major ways.

The Name is spoken of in the White Line of the Masters leading to the Sat-Guru, or Christ. This Name is called the NAM, the NAD (the audible Life Stream). Through the Jesus logos in the John gospel, the Name is spoken of as the Word.

In Niscience, the Sound Current supports and inspires all of the aspects of the ministry and ministering. The Currents of the Word are expressed in logos speaking, in mantrams, in mantras, and in healing angel-to-angel mantrams. All Archetypal statements in the White Paper material and in the books by Ann Ree Colton, the Founder of the System of Niscience, have been received within the Sound Current of the Word through the Archetypal Tones and the Archetypal Light. Jonathan Murro, Co-Founder of Niscience, has also been initiated into these Currents and is presently giving to the world the overflow of his own God-Realization experiences within the grace of the Sound Current.

The Niscience System is alive with the Word of the *Name* or Infinite Spirit sounding through the Holy Ghost action within the Word. This Sound-Current action is producing a spiritual System suitable for the new era of terrestrial and interterrestrial blending and fusing.

As a philosophical, healing, meditative, devotional and dedicative vehicle, Niscience is alive with the Omnipresence of God. God-Realization is the ultimate goal for all being instructed and manifesting the teaching of the Word through Niscience.

I. One of the Sanskrit terms for four of the initiatory experiences of the Sound Current is VAIKHARI, meaning God or *Eternal Tone,* or the invisible made visible through Light and vision in the third eye while in the state of meditation. This Sound-Current aspect of Light can be experienced when some outer tone as a mantra or mantram is released into the Mouth-of-God Center located at the base of the skull. This occurs as a refrain of sounds in the inner ear. The use of the master mantras is given to the disciple by the Teacher in intervals of illumination and sensitivity development. This is necessarily a slow process refining and shaping the outer life, and also giving the inner life greater degrees of expansion. The Sound Current of the Will of God is experienced in the crown of the head as a drawing upward into greater degrees of wisdom and knowing.

II. MADHYAMA. This is the *Heart-Tone*—the Sound Current of Love playing upon the nervous system. It is experienced through and during meditation in the heart chakra or center. The nervous system of the body in the Rishi teaching is considered to be the spiritual heart. Inasmuch as the heart is the headquarters for the nervous system, the mantras of the Sound Current are experienced through the highest aspect of feeling—bliss. The inner ear of the heart opens through the Love Current of the Word, and one hears the voice of his Maha-Guru, or sometimes the voice of Jesus, his Sat-Guru, through His sayings, or the voice of encouragement through his own divine soul-power of the Higher Self. The heart is the receptive vehicle for the Sound Current. It is vital that the heart tone be mastered to penetrate and master all planes of existing life in Earth and in Heaven. One always goes first to the door of the heart and the heart tones to become a balanced vehicle of spiritualized union and harmony for God.

In heart-chakra centering, one speaks his mantram or mantra, visualizing the light in the deep devotion of love for God. He then listens beyond the breath and heartbeat sounds. He next unites with the great sound mantra-power within the Word. Love becomes the tongue of God speaking through and to his devotion.

III. PASYANTI (Mind Tone). This aspect of the Sound Current cannot be heard with the physical ear. Pasyanti means *mind seen,* or clairvoyantly seeing a sound within the vibration of the mental light-waves produced by the finest soul sounds. The sound also comes from the purest light-waves of the mind, rather than being heard by the outer sense-vibrations of the ear.

All spiritual experiences are supported by the great Sound-Current music or Cosmic music impossible to be reproduced to the sense levels of the ear. However, one does sometimes transpose to the ear-sense some of the mental waves of Pasyanti sounds by hearing mentally certain NAD tones, such as: the flow of a waterfall, ocean sounds, a bell, a vina, a bee, the wind, the conch-shell tone, the song of a nightingale, the roar of thunder, the beating of drums, the lightning blast, joy sounds of laughter in children; in dreams or waking, a phone ringing or doorbell's sounding, or one's name may be called. The Pasyanti-sound stems from the Light aspect of the Sound Current within the mind. When these are experienced, one is very close to the prophetic powers of revelation.

IV. PARA. Para is the Infinite Spirit as the silent vibration or the vibrationless sound of God. This is experienced as absorption. One realizes the PARA sounds as God-Realization or union with God, or bliss-oneness with God. One absorbs rather than acts or reacts to the Para sound. There is no duality in Para, only the Word, the One, the Nam—God.

The after-results of the Para aspect of the Sound Current are Will as action in all planes: Life as health in the cell aspects of existence; Light as superconsciousness in all dimensions and kingdoms of the mind; Love as harmony, purity and peace in all expressions of creating, begetting and desiring. The Para state of union within the Sound Current or Word produces SAMADHI or total oneness with God.

Another distinctive feature of the Yoga of the Sound Current is the unique and pervasive emphasis it lays on the need at every step for a competent living Master. The Guru in the Surat Shabd Yoga is not only a being who explains to us the real nature of existence, instructs us in the true values of life and tells us of the sadhanas (meditation practices) to be practiced for inner attainment, he is all this and more. He is the inner guide as well, leading the soul from plane to plane to its ultimate destination, a guide without whose aid the soul would mistake the intermediate stages for the final goal and would encounter barriers which it would be unable to surmount. The Master links us to the holy Word, and without him there could be little hope of salvation.

—Kirpal Singh

. . . Jonathan Murro

10

THE GIFT OF ATONEMENT

> *A man is a* faithful and prudent servant *(Matthew 24:45) when he is quick to atone for all his offences, interiorly by contrition, exteriorly by confessing them and making reparation.*
>
> —*Saint Francis of Assisi*

Three Prayers to Activate Grace

> *And all things, whatsoever ye shall ask in prayer, believing, ye shall receive.*
>
> —*St. Matthew 21:22*

The Heavenly Father and the Divine Mother are *Perfect Parents.* They desire the very best for each of Their children. *"It is your Father's good pleasure to give you the kingdom." (St. Luke 12:32)*

When one leaves the Prodigal-Son way of life, and turns wholeheartedly to God, there are three prayers that will begin to activate Grace in his life. This Grace is part of his Spiritual-Birthright Inheritance as an heir of God.

The first Prayer to activate Grace is the Prayer for a Living Teacher. This Prayer is the key to all future Inheritances of Grace.

I. Heavenly Father and Divine Mother, as Thy child I pray for a Living Teacher to guide me in the ways of Righteousness and Truth, that I may fulfill God's Will and Plan. In Jesus' Name. Amen.

When one prays for a Living Teacher, he is revealing to God his yearning for spiritual knowledge and instruction. Sincerity inspires a truth-seeker to reverently heed his Teacher's instruction, for he knows that his Teacher has been sent by God in answer to his prayer.

The second Prayer to activate Grace is the Prayer to Come Into Timing with God's Plan of Universal Creation. This Prayer opens the way to the joys, discoveries and Grace-Inheritances that come to those who are in Timing with their Souls' Covenant, the Solar-System Cycles, and all other mighty Rhythms of Universal Creation. Everything in God's Universe *is* in Timing. When one prays to be in Timing with God's Creation of the Cosmos, his life comes into order, harmony and fulfillment, for he is at one with the order and harmony of the Time-Cycles of the Moon, the Sun, the Planets, the Stars and the Galaxies.

II. Dear Lord, I pray to do all things in Perfect Timing according to my Soul's Covenant and Thy Divine Image. In Jesus' Name. Amen.

The third Prayer to activate Grace is the Prayer to be Free From All Debts. This Prayer has far-reaching consequences in the present life and in all future lives, for the Liberating Powers of the Lord Christ are set into motion in one's present life and in coming lives.

III. Almighty God, I pray to be free from all debts, that I may be free to serve Thee and my fellow man.

Let all be for Thy Good and Thy Glory. I ask these things as an heir of Thy Spirit. In Jesus' Holy Name. Amen.

One's Living Teacher, anointed by the Christ, is a genius of Timing and understands the Principles that unite one with God's Providential Grace. Thus, he who prays for a Living Teacher will learn the Great Laws of God that govern Timing and Prosperity through which come Inheritances of Grace-Gifts and Grace-Freedoms.

"And of his fulness have all we received, and grace for grace." (St. John 1:16) As one proves obedient to God and His Laws, the Creator, through His Mediators, adds Grace to whatever Grace one earns. Grace is ever-expanding through union with God and His Increase. Grace increases from life to life if one lives according to the Laws of Righteousness and the Commandments of Love.

Union with God has been likened to a Ladder. As one progresses, he ascends to higher rungs of the Ladder of God's Grace.

Grace moves in flows and tides. God's Grace flows through the Universe even as blood courses through the body of man. To learn of Grace, one should learn of Cycles, for the Cycles of God seek to move one into greater and faster flows of Grace.

Each increase of Grace is always accompanied by an increase of responsibility. Thus, to remain in a state of increasing Grace, one must expect increasing responsibilities. He who accepts this truth grows in Grace and matures spiritually through added responsibilities determined by the Wisdom and Love of God.

God knows which of His children feel a responsibility for the Covenant and the Dharma. Those who accept this responsibility unite with the Creator and His increasing Grace.

Well done, thou good and faithful servant: Thou hast been faithful over a few things, I will make thee ruler over many things: enter thou into the joy of thy lord.

—*St. Matthew 25:21*

THE WORD OF GOD AND CYCLES

And his name is called the Word of God.

—*Revelation 19:13*

The Word of God is speaking clearly through the Cycles of the Planets, the Cycles of the Sun and the Moon, the Cycles of the Stars and the Galaxies. The more one learns of these Cycles, the more he may open his heart to the Word of God.

The *Intelligence* of God within His Word is the Intelligence that established each Cycle in the Solar System and in the Greater Universe. To revere the Intelligence of God within His Cycles, is to revere His Word creating the Solar System and the Cosmos.

The Cosmos consists of countless Stars and Galaxies fulfilling their synchronized Cycles. The Solar System—with its Sun, Planets and Moons—has Cycles that occur in perfect harmony with all other Stars in the Galaxy.

The Word of God consists of energy, sound and wisdom that resound within and through each Star and Galaxy. The Word of God can be heard in reverent stillness; therefore, all enlightened Teachers teach their students the importance of Sacramental Meditation. *"Be still, and know that I am God." (Psalm 46:10)*

Cyclic Meditation dedicated to God attunes one's ears to the Word of God. Study of the Scriptures unites him with the Intelligence of God within His Revealed Word. Sacramental Meditation combined with Scriptural study prepares one to become a spokesman for the Revealed Word and a revelator of the Unrevealed Word.

The Unrevealed Word is the Unmanifested Word of God. Revelators and Prophets anointed by God's Spirit are the first to hear and learn the truths emerging from the Mind of God to the mind of man. In this, the Unrevealed Word becomes the Revealed Word—and mankind begins the next stages of growth and understanding within the Eternal Plan of God.

God speaks to His Prophets, His Anointed ones. He has spoken to them in the past; He is speaking to them today; and He will speak to them in the future. His Prophets are the Word-Revealers, the Truth-Discoverers.

The New-Era Prophets and Revelators will open to mankind increasing knowledge of the Cycles of the Sun, the Moon, the Planets, the Stars and the Galaxies—for these Cycles *are* the Word of God creating His Universe through Divine Love and Perfect Wisdom.

> Listen, O devotee, to thy Teacher, for thy Teacher would open thine ears to the Word of God.
>
> Revere each Celestial Cycle, for each Cycle is part of the mighty Word of God. Each Cycle is a resplendent Truth. He who communes with God hears His Word revealing the Truth within the Cycles of Creation.
>
> "As ye sow, so shall ye reap" is a truth regarding Cycles. Let this Truth be thy key to thine understanding of the Cycles of thy Soul. The Cycles of thy Soul are one with the Cycles of the Moon.
>
> The Cycles of the Moon begin the opening of thine ears to the Word of God. Bless and praise the Lord for the Cycles of Night and Day, the Cycles of the New Moon and Full Moon, the Cycles of Perigee and Apogee, the Cycles of the Four Seasons—and thine ear will begin its

opening to the Wisdom and Truth within the Word of God.

The Word of God shall live forever.

Samskaras: Marking and Tracing

> *When the forces of the world beat you down and rob you of your dignity, self-worth and spiritual inheritances, the Teacher, as the Good Samaritan, comes forth to rescue you, to place raiment upon your bruised and naked body, and to find you shelter in the house of your soul.*

Samskaras is a Sanskrit word relating to the positive and negative tendencies that one inherits from his previous lives. Samskaras are also tendencies, reflexes, traits and attitudes inherited from one's parents and ancestors.

Observing a little child is a study in samskaras. Observing a student new to the spiritual life is a study in samskaras.

Marking and Tracing, as a spiritual science, begins by observing *oneself* and identifying one's positive samskaras and negative samskaras. If he is a carbon copy of his parents' attitudes, motives and desires, he should weigh and measure their influences on his own feeling and thinking worlds. He should retain the good, reverent and moral samskaras, and avoid the selfish, irreverent and immoral samskaras.

To become a skillful Marker and Tracer, one must know the difference between right and wrong, good and evil, virtue and vice. He gains this knowledge from the Sacred Scriptures and from his Living Teacher. He also gains this knowledge through an innate knowing in his Soul. The more honest one is in his appraisal of the negative and positive samskaras he has inherited from past lives, parents and ancestors, the more quickly he progresses on the Path of Truth.

Negative samskaras are hindrances to spiritual progress. Any tendency to ignore or not comply with any Commandment of God denotes negative samskaras that have become ingrained ways of thinking and feeling. Such persons may be likened to little children who are selfish, possessive, temperamental and do not know that they have these negative traits. The same is true of a person who is naturally greedy, prideful, lazy; these negative traits are their way of life—and they have no desire to change.

Some children grow out of their negatively-inherited samskaras; many do not evolve beyond their childhood hostilities, fears, covetousness. If a child's parents are emotionally immature and spiritually retarded, the child will be the victim of his own negative samskaras as well as the negative samskaras of his parents. Such children become the criminals and the misfits in society. However, if a child inherits positive samskaras from his own past lives, his natural virtue will protect him from being influenced by any parental immaturities or negativities.

Virtuous parents provide a wholesome atmosphere for their children. As good examples, these parents inspire their children in the ways of righteousness and truth. However, if a child with virtuous parents retains many negative samskaras from his previous lives, the child may remain unteachable and irreverent throughout his life.

An earnest devotee is one who is constantly alert to the negative and positive samskaras in his nature. As soon as the Lord calls attention to a negative samskara, the devotee works to overcome the negative trait or tendency. A devotee remains oblivious to his negative samskaras *until the Lord discloses them.* These disclosures may occur in dreams, during prayer and meditation, or they may be revealed by one's Teacher. The Creator may work through many different ways in order to awaken His devotees to the *truth* about the negative samskaras blocking or delaying their progress on the Path.

A devotee can close his eyes and ears to the Voice of the Lord revealing his negative samskaras; or he can express gratitude for each disclosure, regardless of how painful it might be to his pride and self-esteem. Humility combined with honesty assure one's rapid progress toward God-Realization through the overcoming of negative samskaras as they are revealed by the Creator.

As one overcomes the negative samskaras inherited from past lives, parents and ancestors, he becomes more spiritually enlightened through union with the Quickening Spirit of God. The *quickening* of his positive samskaras increases over the years until he is graced with beautiful virtues and jeweled soul-gifts. In this, he becomes a servant of the Lord at one with His Quickening Spirit.

To be one with the Quickening Spirit of God is to work in the Vineyard of the Christ as one who *quickens* the holy attitudes, virtues and soul-gifts of others. As a Teacher of Truth, the Voice of the Lord speaks through his words, revealing the negative and positive samskaras of devotees, nations, the world.

To come nigh a Teacher of Truth empowered with the Grace of God is to be exposed increasingly to one's own shortcomings, weaknesses and resistances. If one has the courage to remain near a Teacher of Truth, he will experience mighty victories in the soul's record. And during the remainder of this life and in all future lives, he will express the virtues and soul-gifts quickened by the Spirit of God through his Teacher's instruction and mediation.

Many devotees remain unenlightened and unquickened spiritually because they fail to respond to the Voice of God blessing them through their Teacher's instruction.

As one reaches his winter years, he may yield increasingly to the negative samskaras of his parents and ancestors—or he may come closer to the Christ through virtue and grace.

Thus, devotees on the Path should be doubly alert in their mature years so that they may move higher on the Path of Virtue rather than fall ignobly from the Path due to ancestrally-inherited meanness, critical-mindedness and separativeness.

Procrastination and unpunctuality are *always* the signs of negative samskaras inherited from one's past lives, parents and ancestors. These negative traits are symptoms of a soul-sickness caused by many deviations from the Laws of God.

The Plan of God is based on the Principles of Progress and Increase. The Spirit of God is forever seeking to free each of His children from their many bondages. To Jesus, God entrusted the responsibility of freeing each of His children into lives of Grace and Love. Thus, as soon as one calls on the Name of Jesus, repents, confesses, and makes restitution, he experiences increasing freedoms. The Grace of God becomes his daily bread. The Love of God comforts, heals and enlightens him.

Through God's Grace, one remains free from the problems and troubles caused by negative ancestral samskaras—and he learns of *Ancestral Grace* and its powerful blessings in his life and being. The Christ, the Lord of Grace, has much to reveal to the devotee-initiate regarding Ancestral Grace as part of the "whole armour of God" (Ephesians 6:11) necessary for the State of Expanding Grace called *Illumination.*

Through Grace-Increases, one experiences his Spiritual-Birthright Inheritances as a child of God. The Lord Jesus came to qualify ready and willing souls to inherit their portions of Grace as ordained by the Creator. As long as one permits himself to be bound hand and foot by negative ancestral samskaras, he fails to qualify for his Spiritual-Birthright Inheritances.

To turn to Jesus in the right spirit of love and humility, to sin no more, to heed the instruction of one's Living Teacher, and to live according to God's Holy Ordinances qualify one to taste of God's Glory through Grace-Inheritances that prosper all areas of his life and being. In this, one unites with the Cosmos Principles of Progress and Increase; his future as a Christed one is assured for the remainder of this life and future lives. This is the Plan and Promise of God for those who love the Truth and who earn the freedoms that come through the Truth.

The truth shall make you free.

—St. John 8:32

POINTS OF DESTINY

It is good for me that I have been afflicted; that I might learn thy statutes.

—Psalm 119:71

The Soul's Covenant determines the Points of Destiny throughout one's lifetime. These Points of Destiny keep one on the course ordained by God for the soul in its Journey of Eternal Life.

Man, through wrong choice and misuse of free will, may temporarily stray from the soul's course; however, through the Points of Destiny, he *always* returns to the Plan of God for him as destined in the Divine Image and the Soul's Covenant.

Illness, sickness, afflictions and all other crises in one's life are Points of Destiny. These keep one from becoming totally absorbed in selfishness or the pleasure principle.

Because of the Soul's Covenant, healings occur—so that one may resume his life. If he should pass away, the Soul's Covenant sees that he reincarnates wherever necessary to gain important lessons. Thus, through healings and through reincarnation, the Soul's Covenant with God is accomplished through Points of Destiny. Each Point of Destiny is a return to the Soul's covenanted course, thereby assuring the creation of the individual in the Image of God.

As much as you do for God, God will do more for you.
As much as you do for Jesus, He will do more for you.
As much as you do for your Teacher, your Teacher will do more for you.
To do anything for God, Jesus and your Teacher will always be exceeded *by them in Their blessings for you.*

VAJRA-GRACE: CORRECTION AND REPROVING

Correction is grievous unto him that forsaketh the way: and he that hateth reproof shall die.

—*Proverbs 15:10*

The Lord Jesus, a Teacher of Love, "made a scourge of small cords" (St. John 2:13-16) and drove the moneychangers out of God's Holy Temple. Jesus used the *vajra* or rod of reproving whenever necessary. The Bible contains a number of references to Jesus reproving His disciples, the scribes and Pharisees, sinful generations, priests and others.

That is the vajra side of love. Each "cord" in the scourge used by Jesus to drive out the money-changers represented a different phase of the vajra falling upon the evils of mankind.

—*Ann Ree Colton*

As a guardian of the Dharma, a Teacher of God's Word must protect the Holy Temple against those who would profane the sanctity of the sanctuary: the corrupt, the immoral and the self-deceived who have no intention of repenting for their sins. Even as Jesus' love for God inspired Him to drive the moneychangers from the temple, so does a true Teacher's love for God inspire him to protect with his life the sacred environment of God's Altar and Sanctuary.

Many students of the higher life cannot comprehend the vajra side of love. Every time a student accepts a timely vajra from his Living Teacher, he has saved himself hundreds or thousands of lives of painful lessons.

Vajra-grace may manifest through dream-warnings, conscience, apprehensions, soul-reprovings, the Teacher's admonitions, Saintly corrections, and in a number of other ways through the Mediators, Beings and Presences of Heaven.

Every Angel, Saint, Being and Presence in Heaven represents a degree of vajra-grace. To be reproved by one's Living Teacher is *mild* compared with the vajra-power of the Angels, Archangels and other powerful Mediators.

Hebrew legend believes that the Archangel Gabriel destroyed the vice-ridden cities of Sodom and Gomorrah. Every Archangel has mighty reproving powers that are directed toward great masses of people in entire races, religions and nations. Angel and Archangel reprovings are grace for the world and for the individual.

Zacharias was reproved by Gabriel with loss of speech when he doubted the Archangel's prophecy that he was to have a son, John the Baptist. (St. Luke 1:19, 20) After the birth of his son, Zacharias' power of speech was restored, for he accepted the lesson within Gabriel's reproof. (St. Luke 1:57-64)

The reproving or vajra one receives from his Teacher is to *exorcise* some negative attitude or trait. A student who resents being reproved retains the same faults from life to life. Such students negate the Reproving and Correcting

Principle blessing them through the Teacher's holy concern and inspired instruction.

Students who brood cannot take any kind of vajra from the Teacher. Students who *know* that the Spirit of God is blessing, reproving, correcting and quickening them through the Teacher's instruction move rapidly on the Path toward God-Realization.

Those who receive the Teacher's reprovings as blessings from God recognize the *truth* within each reproving or chastening. They know that vajra-grace leads to Soul-Grace and their eventually receiving the Crown of Enlightenment through love for Law, love for Truth.

How perfect Thou art, O Lord—
Perfect in Thy reprovings,
Perfect in Thy Love.

RESTITUTION AND ANCESTRAL SINS

> *I the Lord thy God am a jealous God, visiting the iniquity of the fathers upon the children unto the third and fourth generation of them that hate me.*
>
> —*Exodus 20:5*

If one's father, mother, grandparent, great-grandparent or other ancestor passes from the world unrepentant for their sins, they place themselves in a prison of karma in the afterlife. Each unexpiated sin becomes a bar in this prison of their own making. Prayers in which a devotee of the higher life *confesses* the sins of his parents and ancestors release the tremendous power of Healing Grace through the Mercy and Love of God for the living and the dead.

A deceased parent or ancestor feels and knows when someone in the family line is praying for him because of the *sudden relief* from the heavy pressure of his conscience for leaving the world in an unrepentant state. When acts of atonement by the devotee follow his prayers of confession for his ancestors' sins, the burden of the sins begins to be *lifted* from his ancestors in the lower regions of the dead. Prayers and acts of atonement by the living for deceased ancestors produce blessings for the ancestors through the *lessening* of their sin-burdens; blessings for the devotee who is no longer affected or influenced by the ancestors' sins passed through the genes and the chromosomes; and blessings for the children of the devotee and his children's children, who will be born *free* from karmic problems caused by their ancestors' sins. Thus, *many* generations are affected by earnest prayers of confession and acts of rectification by the living for the ancestral dead.

There are numerous ways that the living can make amends for parents and ancestors who die unrepentant. These include:

1. Restitution-Prayers.

2. Restitution-Fasts.

3. Restitution-Offerings.

4. Restitution-Pilgrimages.

A devotee should make *specific* declarations and dedications to God regarding the purpose and intent of a restitution-prayer, fast, offering or pilgrimage. This communion with the Creator will manifest miraculous blessings for the living and the dead—and for future generations in the ancestral line. One should not underestimate the power of a simple prayer or act of atonement. The *atoms* of his faith and love in a simple prayer or act of atonement will be *exploded* by God and the Christ and will shower perpetual blessings upon all ancestors past, all relatives present, and all generations future. If a microscopic atom exploded by man can produce millions of tons of energy, how much more will an atom of faith and love produce when exploded through reverent prayers and acts of restitution! This restitution-energy is used by the Creator and His Son to free one's ancestors from their prisons of karma and sin so that they can be born in coming lives with a fresh start on the Path of Virtue.

Blessed is he who experiences the Freeing Grace that comes through his prayers, fasts, offerings and pilgrimages of restitution—for in freeing his ancestors, he becomes free; and in becoming free, his children will receive inheritances of freedom of body, heart, mind, soul and spirit.

"For thy mercy is great above the heavens." (Psalm 108:4) The Mercy of God is beyond Time and Space. The Mercy of God is activated by prayers of confession and restitution and by righteous works of rectification.

> O World, be healed of the callousness of those who permit their parents and ancestors to wallow in sin-prisons in the afterlife. Let the living free the dead through their prayers, fasts, offerings, and pilgrimages of Atonement.
>
> O Blood, be free.
>
> O Genes and Chromosomes, be free.
>
> O Soul-Record, be free.
>
> Let all be free.
>
> Past generations, present generations and future generations, be free.
>
> O Mercy of God, thank Thee for the Gift of Atonement.
>
> O Lord Jesus, Lamb of God, thank Thee for Thy Mediation and for Thy Covenant to liberate all souls, to enlighten all hearts and minds.

O Image of God, do Thy perfect work so that sin will be no more—and Grace shall shine as an Eternal Sun forevermore.

Thank Thee, Father, for Thy Holy Image. Because of Thy Image, there is always Hope; there is always the promise of Redemption; there is always the opportunity for the sinner to become a Saint.

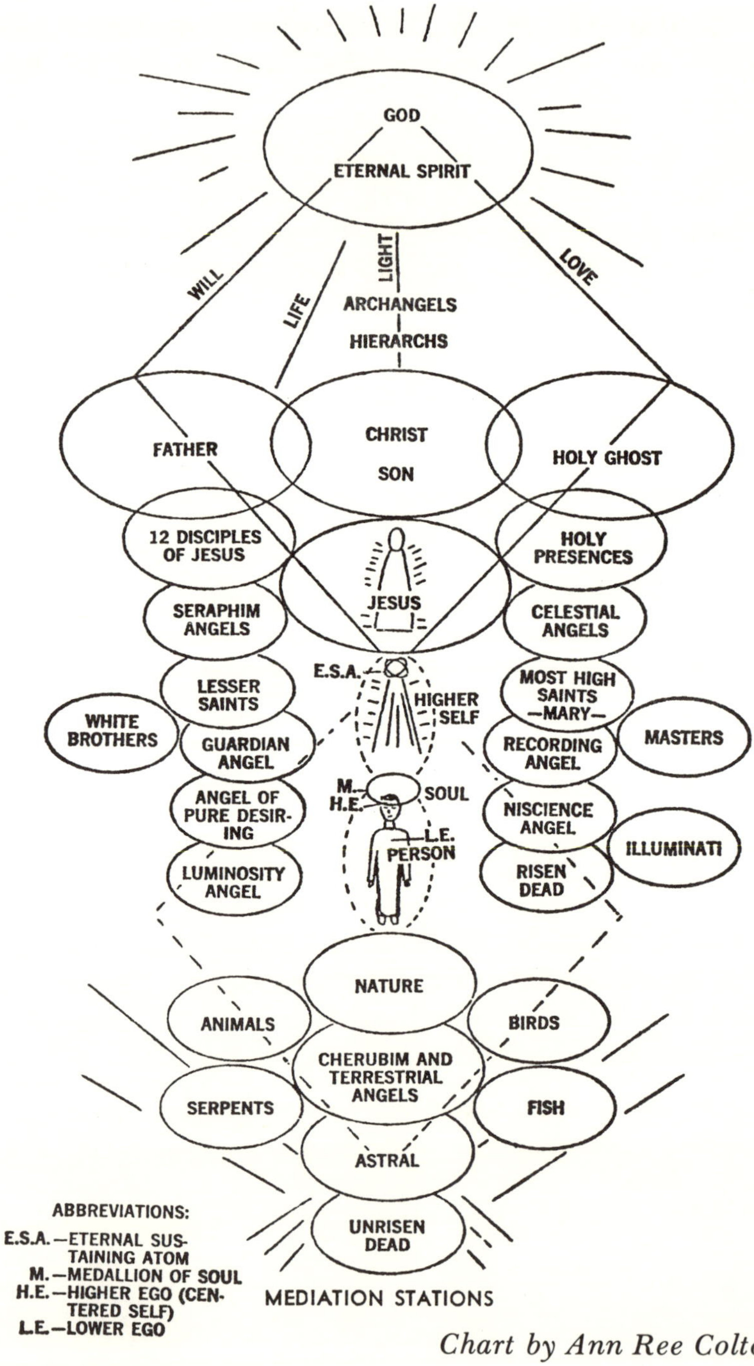

Chart by Ann Ree Colton

. . . Ann Ree Colton

11

THE SEVEN LIGHT-STREAMS

Hierarchy Rays and the Light-Streams

Since ancient times, men have known of the zodiac within the human body. The present physical body, lesser etheric body, emotional body, and mental body are unable to receive the direct Rays from Hierarchy. The planets step down or subdue the Hierarchy Rays. The Light-Streams are received as softer tones upon the emotions and thoughts of men.

Twelve Zodiacal Constellations are around this Earth or eternity system. A great Hierarch is centered within each of the twelve Zodiacal Constellations: Aries, Taurus, Gemini, Cancer, Leo, Virgo, Libra, Scorpio, Sagittarius, Capricorn, Aquarius, Pisces.

The Hierarchs within the Zodiacal Constellations send five Constellation Rays to shape the body or form of man. They send seven Constellation Rays to mold the temperament and consciousness of man. These seven Constellation Rays are absorbed by seven planets around the Earth: Mars, Neptune, Uranus, Jupiter, Pluto, Mercury, Venus. After the seven planets have absorbed the seven Constellation Rays, the Constellation Rays are transposed to man as seven *Light-Streams*. The Light-Streams are as follows:

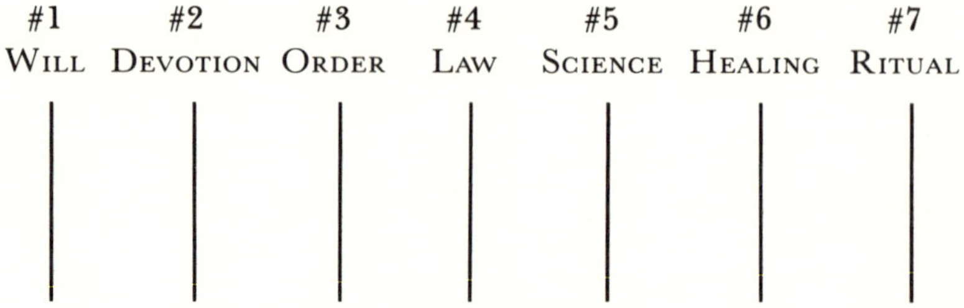

LIGHT-STREAM IDENTIFICATION: LOWER AND HIGHER VALUES

The Lord Jesus and the Greater Beings of Mediation do not dwell in other planets outside the Earth. Their dwelling place is in the spiritual worlds or higher worlds encompassing this Earth. Even as man extracts certain energies from the Sun and uses them for power, so do the Spiritual Intelligences extract the greater degrees of light from the higher energies of the seven planets, utilizing the higher energies as channels for mediative telepathy.

Previous to the time of Jesus, the majority of persons in the world responded to the coarse or crude energies of the planets or the lower values of the seven Light-Streams. Since the coming of Jesus, all persons have the opportunity to respond to the higher values of the Light-Streams. As men evolve, they become more receptive to the higher values of the seven Light-Streams. In this, they become less contented with primitive associations and limitations and try to express themselves individually and creatively. In the present age, men are involved in intensified aggressions, conflicts and tumults because they are beginning to dissolve their crystallized inertias so that they might prepare to respond to the higher values of the Light-Streams.

1 WILL — Master M

△ Dedicated Creation, Spiritual Authority, Self-Mastery.
▽ Tyrannical, Ruthless, Aggressive, Forceful.

Symbols: Owl, Bowknot, Grain of Rice, Unicorn, Diamond, Archetypal Tree, Hourglass, Wedding Ring, Crystal Staff, Book.

2 DEVOTION — Venerable One

△ Pure Reverence, Chaste Emotions, Fidelity, Loyalty.

▽ Exaggerated Self-centeredness, Ecstatic Passivity, Excessive Pride, Fanaticism.

Symbols: White Staff, Pink Rose, White Dove in Rosy Light, Ruby, Acorn, Grain of Corn.

3 ORDER — Master Serapis, Maha Chohan

△ Selfless Governing, Perfect Stewardship, Flawless Organization.

▽ Martial Leadership, Ambition, Delight in Competition, Distrust, Betrayal.

Symbols: Solomon's Seal, 3 Interlinked Loops, Amber Stone, Amber Staff, Dove in Amber Light, Star of David, Stalk of Millet, All-Seeing Eye, Dome.

4 LAW — Master K.H.

△ Non-Judging, Impersonal Justice, Peacemaker, Selfless Sacrifice.

▽ Negative Catalyst, Opposition, Self-Appointed Agitator, Malicious, Prejudice, Antagonist.

Symbols: Jewelled Throne, Hippocrates' Symbol, Red Rose, Emerald, Grain of Rye, Indigo Blue Light, Dove in Neptunian Green Light, Surgeon's Bowl and Towel.

5 SCIENCE — Master Hilarion

△ Science for Humanity and God, Science for Peace, Impartiality.

▽ Calculated Isolation, Science for War, Curiosity, Suspicion.

Symbols: White Butterfly, Symbol of Uranus, Sapphire, Dove in Sapphire Light, Grain of Oats.

6 HEALING Jesus

△ The #6 Light-Stream contains higher values only; there are no negative values on this Light-Stream. It is the Light-Stream of Absolute Healing. Persons who have access to the #6 Light-Stream may become Healers of the improbables and the impossibles. The Lord Jesus and the Ministering Angels channel their mediative light through the #6 Light-Stream. To be the recipient of the miraculous healing sent to the world through this Light-Stream, one must have absolute faith. When a person has absolute faith in any channel of healing, be it a medical doctor, an herb, or a spiritual source of healing, he is healed through his unwavering faith. *"According to your faith be it unto you." (St. Matthew 9:29)* When there is temporary relief or partial healing rather than absolute healing, this is due to a wavering faith and a need for greater reverence.

Symbols: Gold Ring, Door, Healing Hand, Sandal, Christ Child, Shepherd's Staff, Seamless Garment, Fish, Loaf of Bread, Table with White Cloth, Dove in Violet Light, Cross, Crown of Thorns, Small Boat with White Sails, Open Tomb, Lily.

7 RITUAL Master R

△ The Eternity Ritual Correlated to the Eternal Ritual, Pure Formulas for Worship Correlating to the Ethics of Jesus, True Ritual Correlating to the Higher Worlds.

▽ Crystallized Ritual, Hypocrisy, Bigotry, Agnosticism, Atheism, Idolatry, Black Magic, Religious Persecution, Superstition.

Symbols: Grain of Wheat, White Rose, African Violet, Scales, Pyramid, Obelisk, Eagle, Phoenix Bird, Amethyst Stone, Dove in Amethyst Light, Key, Grapes.

Because God has given man the range of free will—that is, the right to choose the high or the low—one may choose the low not only for ages but for complete eternities. And one who turns continually towards the high shall eventually be at one with that which destines the course of his skills for God.

Each person who now lives on Earth lived in other eternity systems before this Earth or eternity system was ever created. The degrees of light one has earned in other eternity systems previous to this one determine the predominating point of light within his Eternal Inner Light. This predominating point of light, located in the crown of the head and centered within the pulsation of the soul, determines the particular Light-Stream to which one correlates. The predominating point of light is the compass, guidepost or *motif au fait* for one's consciousness in this eternity system. Regardless of how many lives a person experiences on this Earth, all of these lives will be colored by the motif au fait established in former eternities.

If one entered this Earth with *will* as the strongest emphasis, he would respond to the lower and/or higher values of the #1 or Will Light-Stream. If he uses the will emphasis in its lower aspects only, he is then unable to respond to the higher values of the Light-Stream; thus, he is ruthless, dominating, forceful, demanding. From such persons come the cruel and callous leaders who disrupt humanity and the world.

If a person alternates between the lower and higher values of the #1 Light-Stream, he is unpredictable. In some of his lives, he may express undependability; in other lives, he may express dependability. However, in each life he may show periods of indecision and also periods of leadership and authority.

When one expresses an uninterrupted rapport with the higher values of the #1 Light-Stream, he has attained mastery over himself and enters the world to meet the need of the world. He is an ethical leader who uses unbiased authority.

When a person continues to vacillate between inverted and creative thinking, he fluctuates between the lower and higher values of his Light-Stream. Thus, he sometimes expresses the higher values and sometimes the lower values of his Light-Stream. A person who wavers back and forth between the lower and higher values of his correlating Light-Stream may be a benefactor to the world but may fail in his love relatings and personal responsibilities.

When one has continually sacrificed for the good of others, he establishes a rapport with the higher values of his correlating Light-Stream and also has access to the higher values of all other Light-Streams. However, his own identifying Light-Stream always remains the central theme of his expression.

The identifying Light-Stream of the renowned Dr. Albert Schweitzer is the #2 or Devotion Light-Stream. Dr. Schweitzer had access to the #6 or Healing Light-Stream; he had access to the #3 or Order Light-Stream to bring order to some of the primitive people of Africa. He also had access to the higher values of the #1 Light-Stream, as he was a genius of the organ and interpreter of Bach. (All great music correlates to the #1 Light-Stream.) Therefore, it can be seen that while a person may have his basic compulsion rooted in one Light-Stream, by the conquest of the lesser self he is enabled to become communicable to the combined telepathic intelligence of some of the other Light-Streams.

The identifying Light-Stream of the great composer, Beethoven, who concentrated his efforts solely upon music, was the #1 or Will Light-Stream. Beethoven, being telepathic to the higher values of the #1 Light-Stream, tapped certain tones of the higher worlds and therefore interpreted the Music of the Spheres to man. His great symphonies, which were drawn forth from his telepathic rapport with the higher worlds, aid men in all walks of life to rise above their negations so that they may be initiated to the higher worlds.

The identifying Light-Stream of Judas Iscariot, the disciple of Jesus, was the #3 or Order Light-Stream. His life is an example of an orderly mind overly analytical. During his association with Jesus, he weighted himself to the lower values of the Light-Stream by adhering to racial expectations. When Judas discovered that Jesus' government was of the spiritual or higher worlds and not for the preserving and saving of the race, Judas fell to the lowest value of the #3 Light-Stream or the "30" pieces of silver, which is betrayal of God and His Will for man. The #3 Light-Stream affects governments, organizations and institutions. The lowest value of the #3 Light-Stream relates to any person who violates trust and betrays an institution, government or organization, thereby upsetting the order of his community and society. He is thus a faulty and incompetent steward.

Descriptive Examples of Lower Values:

One who expresses the lower values of the #1 Light-Stream is quick to anger, violent, and devoid of compassion.

When a person, through fanaticism, devotes himself to selfish causes or to pursuits of oppression, he remains in the lower values of the #2 Light-Stream.

When a person abuses his government, despoils the honor of his government, or violates the archetype or blueprint of his government, he is expressing the lower values of the #3 Light-Stream.

When a person is continually quarrelsome, deliberately malicious, and seeks to become the agitator in his environment for the sake of sensation, he remains gravity-bound to the lower values of the #4 Light-Stream.

When a person enters into irreverent research or sadistic experimentation upon any inanimate or animate thing, he seals away the higher values of true science and remains cynical, bitter and materialistic. By thinking himself to be all-sufficient, he sustains the lower values of the #5 Light-Stream.

When a person is agnostic, doubtful, atheistic, and believes that the physical life is the only life, he is shut away from the #6 Light-Stream, and fails to receive the healing grace as given from the Lord of Love.

When a person depends upon superstition, or seeks to use the procedure of ritual to further his material gain, he invokes the denizens of dark and destruction; he enters into black magic and remains in the lower values of the #7 Light-Stream.

Children and the Light-Streams

Through close association and study, the Light-Stream values of a child may become apparent, for the childhood years reveal certain distinct or outstanding traits of temperament and character.

A strong-willed child, often stubborn and unruly, resenting parental disciplines, is expressing a lower value of the #1 Light-Stream. Such a child resents punishment and chastisement, and holds for a complete life a bitter resentment against parental supervision and care. A child, expressing a higher value of the #1 Light-Stream, enters physical life with very little need of discipline. The parents may approach such a child with logic and reason. All children of the #1 Light-Stream, regardless of whether they are expressing lower or higher values, mature early, and while yet young are prone to venture for themselves, to make choice of a vocation early in life, and to assume responsibility of some nature in their tender years.

If a child indicates a tendency toward dreaminess, or an over-fertile imagination, the child is correlated to the #2 Light-Stream. Such a child should be trained by his parents in drama, color, poetry, and especially taught to channel his emotions into the pure and the beautiful.

A child, expressing the #3 Light-Stream, is neat and orderly in his person. He respects authorities in institutions, and benefits by regimentation in education. A child who expresses the lower values of this Light-Stream can become ill due to disorderly environments.

A child, expressing the lower values of the #4 Light-Stream, is a nervous, irritable and agitated member of the family group. When expressing the higher values of the #4 Light-Stream, the child is the peacemaker, the diplomat or the blending one in the family.

A child correlated to the #5 Light-Stream enters physical life with an inquiring mind and, between the ninth and twelfth years of age, shows some indication of a scientific trend. If a child expresses the lower values of the #5 Light-Stream, he is a nuisance in his environment; he is a meddling, curious, and destructive child.

Regardless of their evolvement and Light-Stream values, all children, until the age of fourteen, respond to the #6 Light-Stream. Thus, children are more receptive to the Ministering Angels' helps than those with incredulous hearts who have reached more mature years.

Children expressing the lower values of the #7 Light-Stream show an inclination in their pre-adolescent years to gang up with other children and eventually become members of juvenile combines; they can become miniature outlaws in society. Children who express the higher values of the #7 Light-Stream benefit by direct adult association and by a particularized training as to their individuality.

THE ARCHETYPAL UNITY IN THE SEVEN LIGHT-STREAMS

Each Light-Stream has a collectivity of virtues.

Everyone follows the same root-disciplines regardless of what Path he is on. These root-disciplines were sealed in as the *Law* in the very beginning of this eternity system. The Path contains the history of this struggle, and the victory novena-steps in mastering self and the forces which work to build a vehicle or center for the soul.

Every defeat contains a victory on the Path. Every victory or acceptance produces discipline-virtue, that the Light on the Path may become more illuminative, more revealing. With each victory come enlightenment, strength and soul-power.

The most gratifying reward of being a Nisciene comes from Knowing or Niscience. Such Knowing comes as a Light in the midst of peril, a time of danger and stress, thrusting against the soul and the most precious and vital gift of life: the Mind.

Mind is sacred. Mind is divine. This divinity must be kept alive by Knowing and by Reincarnation. *Realization* is our heritage. This heritage, when nescient, is ignorant or tamasic.

The seven Light-Stream energies are Will, Devotion, Order, Law, Science, Healing, Ritual. When the dependencies rely only upon the senses and the intellect, the misuse of the seven Light-Stream energies creates the unrealized state.

I. The will is presently used arrogantly by nescient man. *Niscient* man knows the Will to be his maker and creative privilege. To abuse it, one becomes an irritation to the devotional theme of the soul. The soul is tempered to devote itself to God in all environments and in all worlds.

II. When faith is whole through devotion, Will is in a state of perfection. As a Universal product to organization, a Number Two Light-Stream Nisciene knows Universal order to be the Constant of God as Spirit in action.

III. To abuse order or seek to upset the rhythmic, is to harm the sacredness of the Self. A total life without order is a wasted, useless life out of affinity with God, and therefore godless.

IV. Amorality-lawlessness makes a life of criminality and isolates a person from all God-Realized association and associates. Law is the Love of God correcting, shaping, refining. Obedience to the Law of God surmounts the karmic particularizing intricacies of discipline so painful and humiliating to the ego. Law-perfected mastery of the karmic states provides adeptship and God-sent experience as authority over the evil and the state of darkness.

V. In the present time, factual science stands as a cold, materialistic truth-limiting experience. Science, the inhibitor of the transcendental, is on trial. Its benefits claiming to contain the only answer to life, biological and psychological, presently act as Maya regulators. Religions seeking to remain in decaying modes and methods of realization press and oppress the Holy Spirit. Science, when united with Will rooted in Devotion, will grow out of its materialistic soil into energized process with God as the One. The spiritualized mind now reaches deeper into the well-springs of Truth, and step-by-step intuition and skill shall merge. God does not cease in His revelation to him who is Niscient.

VI. God, the Absolute, is reached only through total faith. *Who cannot trust is a failure in life.* Beyond science is grace. Trust and faith act as grace earned through absolute faith in God. A faith beyond peril is imperishable, producing life as miraculous, life as bliss. There is a karmicless way, the way of love as faith. Healing beyond karmic need for restitution comes through selfless love. A simplified, glorified heart seeks this love to be co-atom to Jesus and embodied as a God-Realized soul.

VII. Synthesis, synchronization and the utilization of all Seven Light-Stream values sound the tone-sound of one's own Light-stream as a value in and through the Way of Ritual. This is *Archetypal Unity* within the highest empathy. As a life-soul united, as a Divine Soul within the *Will, Devotion, Discipline, Law, Science, Absolute Healing and Ritual,* one stands in Universal Religion. When he synthesizes and synchronizes all of the essences within the Seven Light-Stream values, he teaches all; he heals all; and he attains to God-Realization.

THE OPEN VALUES AND THE LIGHT-STREAMS

The Maya-energy restraints and enforcements within the Light-Streams are presently loosened and lifted, thereby giving access to all values in the seven Light-Streams. Advanced Initiation through the interflow between values produces accelerated states of initiation, giving opportunity to understand one's self and placement in soul, in life. The open-values freedoms, when working with one's own Light-Stream, are guidance-vehicles through both grace and karma to use the expanding values of other Light-Streams. One finds himself in a world of the first energies. This cross-play and interplay of energy provide the transcendental Omnipresence Light.

For example, if one is born to the Second Light-Stream, and through initiation opens the #2 value and #5 value, he is both devotional and scientific. Thus, he undergoes extreme testing as to the reality of his inner experience. The scientific side of his nature, when overemphasized, undergoes a loyalty, fidelity testing as to what God is. He feels the mystic path to be psychic and, therefore, an experience to be avoided. The fifth-value initiate desires to experience finger, eye, taste and smell in the proving of all things devotional.

The time one remains in a tossing ambivalence of doubt and faith can be set aright only by an absolutely pure, former use of his own Second Light-Stream. Pure devotion is founded upon an unwavering faith. If this is present, the fifth-value experience will produce a ritual for devotion. In this freedom, he will not only explore his devotion processes, but he will gather knowledge plus guidance to light his way for all value-freedoms within Cyclic Law.

The only sure and true way to open the Coinciding Principle and to make it a positive instrument for proving all things is by the union between these two values—the second and fifth.

One opens the Coinciding by entering into the free-value experience. Each experience is a mathematical process and comes in cyclic balance to give birth to the Universal or the Cosmos Knowledge.

It is the goal for and through value-freedom to finally reach all of the Seventh Light-Stream powers. All in the Earth who do this have explored and energized their knowledge through value-freedoms in the seven Light-Streams.

	1	*2*	*3*	*4*	*5*	*6*	*7*
1	1	1	1	1	1	1	1
2	2	2	2	2	2	2	2
3	3	3	3	3	3	3	3
4	4	4	4	4	4	4	4
5	5	5	5	5	5	5	5
6	6	6	6	6	6	6	6
7	7	7	7	7	7	7	7

When the Maya energies are relaxed, one is free to cross over into expanses of values as needed in Satsanga or Search for Truth.

Light-Streams	1	2	3	4	5	6	7
Tones	C	D	E	F	G	A	B

There are four octaves of seven, making twenty-eight tones in the spectrum of planetary sound. Four octaves relate to the four bodies.

Values of Light-Stream B ____
A ____
G ____
F ____
E ____
D ____
C ____

Niscience as the Synchronized Vehicle for the Seven Light-Streams

Niscience is the true select school blessed by the Masters. Niscience synchronizes all seven Light-Streams. Niscience, as a God-Realization Initiatory School, combines all of the Rays and Light-Streams' proclivities.

Schools in the West using but one Ray work individually upon the psychic and occult nature of man. Such schools are presently magnified to those who lean in the direction of self-power.

Niscience is not an intermediary school; it is a school designed to fulfill the worship nature, the learning nature and the activity principle. A synchronized system such as Niscience is an interflow school attracting those who are ready to enter into the true Initiation on the Higher Self-Genesis level.

A school based upon the First Ray or First Light-Stream is an occult power school, being absent from the Christ Initiation. The karmic results for individuals are sometimes drastic and dangerous. If there is an overload of the Undersoul, the result is psychic paranoia and sometimes psychic hysteria, causing disorientation in relationships and in action. The mental body, when caught into occult-power procedures, endangers the stability of the mind, especially when one has emotional immaturity.

Using the power of the will as a chief function results in unprepared astral situations. Such persons are the victims of being overcredulous as to their own right to authority or in the use of their wills over others. A truly synchronized person has been initiated by delicate and refined states in the use of the will within the Will of God.

Those who live steadily and firmly as synchronized vehicles within the Jesus Ethic are repelled by the occult life. Their need for devotion in worship and for rationality in the development of their mental potential through right instruction makes them honest workmen, fellow craftsmen with the Lord Jesus.

The occult person is by nature nonreligious. He is more inclined to seek a fraternity rather than a worship body. If he seeks a power school for self-enlargement through the use of the will, he will inevitably invite the forces of darkness in his own nature and the demonic entities of the lower subtle worlds.

A synchronized spiritual person incorporates all of the Rays or Light-Streams as experienced through the System of Niscience, which has been given as the divine formula for the New Age Illumination. The Great Immortals within the inner planes, overdirecting the seven Light-Streams so that men may enter into their spiritual inheritance, are presently working very closely to those who have the Jesus recollection and the early Christian recollections.

Christ, as the Son of God, is supreme over the Hierarchy System. The Hierarchy System works directly with the Father in Heaven. The Father in Heaven works directly with Jesus to form and to shape, to build and to mold, and to make man into the Image of the Father and of Hierarchy.

Jesus is a Hierarch with our Father in this eternity system in which we dwell. The seven Light-Streams presently represent the Gates to the Door where Jesus stands.

In the Niscience System, the synchronized blended function of the seven Light-Streams emphasizes the twelve-chakras Initiations. The occult schools working under one Ray or one Light-Stream function through one chakra, which an occult student must master. In Niscience, all chakras are synchronized through the Christ.

A Guru or Teacher representing a singular or one Light-Stream school has perfected the particular chakra as related to the Light-Stream of that school. Thus, his training to his students, if it be on the Number One Ray or Light Stream, emphasizes the use of the Will. A Second-Chakra Guru under the Second Light-Stream would emphasize Devotion; the Third, Organization; the Fourth, Building; the Fifth, Science; the Sixth, Healing; or the Seventh, Method or Ritual. A person is attracted to a singular Light-Stream school because he has not yet reached the atom-evolvement state of Synchronization.

In Niscience, the synchronized processes of all Light-Streams function within the total Light-Stream Initiatory cycles and rhythms. It is required of the Nisciene that he become aware that he is working with Cosmos, with Heaven and the Earth as a *Universal* Being and a Unit of Measure within the Christ. To do this, he is initiated to become co-atom to Jesus.

None other save Jesus holds the Door to the Will of God, the Life of God, the Light of God and the Love of God. Individualistic schools work on the astral planes. The Synchronized school works in the dimensions of the Jesus Kingdom or the Third Heaven where the Creative Fiat of God is manifested through the Greater Archetypes.

Niscience is a Synchronized Initiatory School working with the twelve chakras, the seven Light-Streams, the seven Rays and the twelves Hierarchs through the Mediation of Jesus. We work with the Lord Jesus and Hierarchy to make the man of the future.

In this era of seeking to bring polarity into its true equilibrium of the Sattvic, every man must incorporate into himself the Second Light-Stream, and every woman must incorporate the Seventh Light-Stream into her nature.

In the present time, with the synthesizing of the Seventh Light-Stream, the occult use of power and of ego-metaphysics is ending. The Maha Chohan works directly to lift the walled-in enclosure veils formerly sealing in the process of Initiation.

The coming of Jesus and His lifting powers set these dispersement activities into the world. Thus, the sheep seem to be without a sheepfold; they are scattered, confused. Most of all, the energies of the Self-Genesis state in consciousness are expressing a separateness as to group, cliques. In the religious side of this mass psychical phenomenon, this fragmentation is sifting the goats from the sheep, the Judas from the Christ.

The long-supporting columns upholding old and pseudo catechisms are being shaken, uprooted. They are ineffective, sterile, anemic. Jesus prophesied this time. The prophet of the present recognizes its wisdom, for man must enter a New Era or Genesis time with rightful dislodgement of the old.

The condensation of the Light-Streams in this period is producing many new facets or aspects of God. Among these, the scientist and the devotee are seeking to become one.

The synchronizing between all Light-Streams throws the weight of the Path upon the Seventh Light-Stream. All values within each Light-Stream now are expressing within the Seventh Light-Stream.

The return and renewal of religiosity in science, in education, in organization of the family-atom energies, now come under the Coordination Principle between the Masters, the Archangels and all of the Beings representing Omnipresence.

Men as individuals are to revolutionize their religious attitudes; their wills, hearts, disciplines, minds and gifts. This impulse began at the ending of the Second World War and will conclude when men find themselves in another Moving Archetype 3000 years from the present time.

The work of man in the Light-Stream Ethic is to blend, to heal, to correlate, to fuse his soul-powers for the upliftment of the human race. Although the latter days of an era of this nature are dark, somber and painful, the pressure of this commingling will accelerate all men of the masses to take hold of the swift currents of mind and soul.

The Path is *now.* The Bindu for all paths acting through the seven values is the Seventh Light-Stream. On each value of the Master Path, a virtue is being expressed.

All in the Niscience System are presently expressing the Seventh Light-Stream values. They are in the Grand Archetypal Symphony of all harmonious resounding in attunement as blended souls seeking their true station on this master stair of greater evolvement.

The Master R, who was Joseph, the father of Jesus, presently heads the Seventh Light-Stream; the Master M, the first or will value; Brhaspati, the second value, devotion; the Maha Chohan, the third Light-Stream value; the Master K. H., who was St. Francis, the fourth value; the Master Hilarion, or Saint Paul, the fifth value, the Lord Jesus, the sixth value, healing; the Master R, the seventh and crowning value. All of these now act as one great unison in Reciprocal Maintenance for those whose souls go forth within the Christ.

All souls on the Number One Light-Stream in spiritual Initiation are expressing the Seventh Light-Stream and its seven values. Those who are expressing the lower values of the Number One Light-Stream do not have access to the seven values of the Number Seven Light-Stream. They have one-value expression which relates to will, and discipline through will and will-power. Such persons must undergo the grind of the rajasic fiery trials, that they may claim the higher values of the Seventh Light-Stream.

12

HEALERS AND THE LIGHT-STREAMS

Those who have been martyred for the sake of God always come back to the world with supernatural powers.

Intentional Suffering and Healing

Whoever learns, must suffer.
And in our sleep,
pain, which cannot forget,
falls drop by drop upon the heart;
and in our own despair
against our will,
comes wisdom to us,
through the awful grace of God.
—Aeschylus

Let not the fierce sun dry one tear of pain
Before thyself hast wiped it from the sufferer's eye.
—H. P. Blavatsky

The *Fountain* is the center for the Living Waters of God. There are three flows of the Fountain. The first or larger flow is for the washing away of the physical-body sins; cleansing for the body. The second flow is for the washing away of the tears, that one may bear the suffering caused by his sins. The third flow is for the "cup of cold water in

My Name," whereby one is a disciple of the Lord Jesus and a healer of the suffering of others.

Suffering is used to bring us back to virtue. The virtue obtained from suffering is empathy which may enlarge all capacities of the soul and send us as a vehicle of light to heal and to serve. Blind suffering or suffering failing to manifest virtue is a curse.

Wherever we suffer, we have experimented beyond the range of ethic.

Crises are the way we grow, but one should not create his own crises.

Gratitude is the answer to get out of the sealed tomb. Gratitude stimulates all the virtues.

Anyone who is living for self alone is heading for suffering. As long as a person utilizes the third element of life, which is love—and that love must be selfless, rendering some form of giving or service to someone or something—there is hope. But if one is absent from the love for a dog, a flower, a child, a person, a creation or some form of creative sacrifice, he will ultimately find himself faced with a total helpless situation of body, mind and soul.

God gives to each one a time limit to prove himself. If he fails to find the creative side of sacrifice in his own nature, he will fall into the path of desolation.

Suffering is not only of physical health. Suffering may be the suffering to open an idea of an illuminative nature.

Suffering may be through being persecuted for one's being. Suffering may be imposed by subtle tyranny by unbelieving and hostile persons against one's faith.

Suffering may involve one's own accumulated guilts as experienced in the Undersoul.

Suffering may be from wrong desire through frustration of will.

Suffering may be through inherited deformities and afflictions.

Suffering may be caused by unclarified karmas.

Suffering may be caused by the stubborn nescience will or resisting will to the Will of God.

Suffering may be imposed upon one through mass and collective ignorance and neglect.

The most afflicted by suffering in the physical world are children having nescient parents, neglectful institutions of education and bodily care.

The suffering by world-karmas may be caused by neglect of the soil, whereby starvation is enforced upon the multitudes or masses of peoples.

One must be totally dispassionate as an aware Intentional Sufferer. The Intentional Sufferer undergoes the struggle and suffering for the one for whom he mediates. It must be understood at all times by the one mediating that the one he mediates for is completely unaware that he must struggle for his freedom from pain and suffering.

In Intentional Suffering, the healer must constantly send hopeful and optimistic suggestible transfusions into the one whom he would heal. The healer must be in himself unburdened. Although he undergoes Intentional Suffering and substitutes the desire to battle to live for the one whom he would heal, he must of himself remain dispassionately at an ethical distance from the one for whom he mediates.

All suffering is first tamasic, chronic, caused by the most nescient state of ignorance. All rajasic suffering is caused by manipulation, force, anger, violence, hatred, selfishness, envy, separation. Only when suffering has reached the promise of sattvic wisdom can one become an anointed healer and receive the Passing Power of resurrection through the Christ.

In every sickness there is a revelation. In every pain there is a Marking and Tracing. When the initiate moves out of the ego-level of pain, he then becomes aware of the part he plays in Intentional Suffering through the revelatory aspect of suffering and pain.

The Time-Cycle for such suffering is three years. Following the Cyclical Law of Resurrection, it is inevitable in Intentional Suffering that one must suffer to give birth to significant knowledge.

All pain is birth. All suffering contains revelation.

When one learns to understand the cyclic sovereignty of the *three,* he becomes more sensitized as to what the message is within the suffering. Everything giving birth works with the cycle three in microcosmic as well as macrocosmic. Everything living to obtain consciousness follows by its nature and life or whatever it may be, the cyclic three. For example, food gathered in the harvest is first *sattvic;* food readied and prepared for eating is *rajasic;* food in its third aspect of *tamasic* represents putrients rather than nutrients to the body and to fertilization.

In sickness, a fever reveals itself first as tamas; accelerating into temperatures as to rajasic; healing as sattvic.

In night memory of sleep, there are three sessions of the subconscious in sleep, beginning with tamas, the body yielding the physical; the second is the astral and subliminal chimeras, rajasic excitation and contesting in dreams; the third is the sattvic side of dream ultimate, which is revelatory, participating, ministering, and the mastery of the unit-measures of consciousness through dreams.

In the waking state, the life of man is divided into three thirty-three portions of life. If man should live less than these, he must experience them after-death in certain levels. If a person lives one hundred years, these additional units of measure in Time are used through grace, as all persons passing the eightieth year are interlocked with the interior after-death worlds whereby their life in the Earth is colored and sensitized by greater knowing and revelation.

When an Intentional Sufferer has reached a state of vibratory knowledge, he widens the circumference in the touching aspect in healing. He reaches groups of persons—

vital issues in community suffering, in mass suffering, in accumulative illiteracies aspects of unknowing. He widens his reach of Intentional Suffering for all of these and more; thus, he becomes both a direct server for the healing needs and a world-server to bring to balance the imbalanced karmas in the world. Accompanying his circulating efficiencies in healing are many co-atom yoked souls who are on the same wavelengths with his soul-power and oscillation. Mediation becomes a powerful anointing and healing vehicle for mass deficiencies in the human race.

To be co-atom on the initiatory wavelengths of union as an Intentional Sufferer is to be conjoined as co-atom to Jesus, and thus be a part of His Passion with the Power to *Pass* the healing light which contains the Spirit of Truth or the great Esse of the Holy Spirit. This is the ultimate healing power for all who would serve the Christ.

There is no suffering singular or en masse that cannot be reached by the Spirit of God. The Father dwelling in all souls of the Earth has imaged and made all forms and shapes. To Him the initiate turns through Jesus so that the Spirit of God may manifest in health, in peace, in life.

Sickness is initiation through the life-force. How one uses his life-force is how he learns of the Spirit of God and of the Power of God.

In the twinkling of the eye, one may be healed through Jesus and the Father. When one *knowingly* receives such a healing, he has experienced God-Realization through Jesus and the Father.

> *Take, my brethren, the prophets, who have spoken in the name of the Lord, for an example of suffering affliction, and of patience.*
>
> —*James 5:10*

BRHASPATI

The Venerable One, or Brhaspati, is the synchronizer of the seven Rays and the seven Light-Streams. Working with Brhaspati are other Maha-Devas who are the synchronizers of the whole or twelve Rays. All will eventually come into the use of these twelve Rays. The Maha-Devas are the Great Rishis.

Brhaspati is a Rishi, a Great Immortal and a Maha-Deva. He works with the Archetype of Niscience. The Rishis are direct transmitters for the Hierarchy.

Jesus as a Hierarch and the Father as a Hierarch overdwell the Rishis. The Great Immortals or Masters conjoin with the Rishis.

Eventually, all initiates under Christ Jesus will come under the twelve Rays of Hierarchy and become perfected prototypes in this Earth, using the twelve chakras with the thirteenth power of the Christ, which is a Son-of-God likeness.

Brhaspati is the Lord of Prayer. Prayer in the Sanskrit language means preparation.

A Telepathic Disciple is always one who is a shield and protector for a Cosmos Disciple. The Telepathic Disciple runs interference for the Cosmos Disciple on the physical plane and bears the blows of the world so that the Cosmos Disciple may do his work.

Each time a Cosmos Disciple moves up into the inner world or passes from the physical plane, a Telepathic Disciple takes his place. And he, in turn, attracts to him the Telepathic Disciple who will shield him from the crude blows of Maya.

The Cosmos Dharma must teach of the Rishis and the Hierarchs.

Brhaspati, as Father Jupiter, is preparing all initiates who are *the meek* for their birth in the Jupiter Matrix in the next eternity day. The Jupiter Matrix will function as a Cosmos-center of consciousness. Only those who are of uttermost purity and meekness, as was Jesus, will be the future progeny of the Jupiter Matrix, which will come after our Solar System enters into its Silent Day preparing for the birth to come.

Probationary demands are placed upon the one being initiated the moment he steps into the Path under the Masters. These occur as trials, as tests, through which self-awareness and God-Realization become one. The initiate who meets these probationary trials with the dimensional acceptance becomes a true initiate and, eventually, an adept on the Path, rendering a unique service to the human race.

Probationary trials are never ended for one who would serve the Masters. One moves from alternate phases of trial between strength and weakness, that he may gain body-strength, mind-strength, a self-controlled vehicle through which the immense power of the Intelligible Spirit can function in the physical and mental world.

> *I shall be strong enough with the help of my instruction to meet the adverse challenges on the initiatory path of probation. How childish my fears—all shadows of the unreal, which cannot defeat or delay my upward rise on the path of instruction.*

THE THIRD LIGHT-STREAM HEALER

The Third Light-Stream works with the grains.

The Third Light-Stream Initiate heals through the use of energy. He radiates light and life for the one ill or sick. He transenergizes the fever into calm. In this period and time, he transposes the lower negative-mind forces through exorcising powers. His reach of mediation draws upon the Deva or Shining-Spirit essences to heal mind-restlessness, to reorganize mental thought-forms, and to overcome mind abuse. His reach is rajasic for those who are in psychotic states of delirium or dissension.

The Third Light-Stream in its lower values is the divider, the separator; it is the 30. The four higher aspects of the Third Light-Stream relate to the organized discernment of Truth.

Judas represents the lowest action in the Third Light-Stream. His enmity of Jesus the Lord sought to destroy the hope of the soul for which Jesus stands. Those using the low values of the Third Light-Stream are betrayers and act as adversaries to the Initiate on the Path. The Third Light-Stream negative person is a divider, a dissenter, an agnostic. He represents the Judas negativity and is a challenger against anyone having faith in God.

The United-States-of-America Archetype is ruled by the Third Light-Stream. It is the work of the Western Initiate in the United States of America to bring service and creation equally forth under the influence of the Will of God, the Creator of all.

When a Third Light-Stream nation, such as the United States, uses the lower or Judas values of the Light-Stream, it betrays itself if it is not honorable and does not have integrity.

The higher Third Light-Stream person has mastered the lower octaves of Third Light-Stream energy and is used by Omnipresence as a healer of agnosticism. He heals through order, through writing, through right speech, through service to God as an organizer of soul-record powers. The rajasic energies especially are stilled into Sattvic peace by one using the mediative healing powers.

The Third Light-Stream healer is a healer of tamas-inclined children. He also is a healer of animals.

The Angel power of the Third Light-Stream comes down from Archangel Uriel, who is the Guardian over the Hierarchy powers of transubstantiation of substances.

All mediative healers work with their own Light-Stream as the basic root power. In this time, all mediative healers are also working with the Seventh Light-Stream. Their own initial Light-Stream is experienced as a value on the Seventh Light-Stream which is functioning in the life and soul expression of all Niscienes. For example: a Third Light-Stream person uses all of the power impulse of the Seventh Light-Stream as well as his own Light-Stream.

The Third Light-Stream healer has acute telepathic powers. When he works mediatively, his thoughts act as visitation, giving to the sick mind-strength and right resolution.

Earth chaos comes and goes so that the axis pole of the Earth may adjust souls in the world into initiatory processes whereby they are enlightened. Mind chaos exposes men to the destroying principle, for it is necessary that all in the Earth grow mentally, and ultimately express the Spirit of Truth.

The mental life in man is immortal. There is no death to the high mental aspects of the mind, for the mind as a vehicle of conscience must be ever circulated in the divine ecstasies of knowing, learning, creating.

The Number Three Light-Stream provides judgment, selectivity, discernment and discrimination. The Organizing Principle within the Third Light-Stream action works without ceasing to discard that which is neither useful nor necessary. No man can blame any other man when he is brought to judgment for his errors, for his negations. It is the Third Light-Stream action to cleanse, to purify, to adjust—not through the outer, but through the inner side of the value working to bring ultimate perfection, identity and rightness.

Mind of man is God in man. Mind concerned with chaos is organized by the Third Light-Stream action. The Organizing Principle supports the morality of the Cosmos and the individuality of soul experience in the Maya gravity-world.

Presently in Lesser Self-Genesis evolvement, men of the Earth are losing touch with their heritage. The fantasy that causes one to think he can do it all or to have it all for himself shuts away this major construction action in his life. When the lesser mind finally bows down to obedience to the Great Laws which balance all expression of the soul and the body, then comes peace of mind. This peace comes by knowing that one is a chaos-maker in need of discipline, order, and acceptance of life as perfection in God and His mighty Will for man.

> *Again, the kingdom of heaven is like unto a merchant man, seeking goodly pearls: Who, when he had found one pearl of great price, went and sold all that he had, and bought it.*
>
> —*St. Matthew 13:45, 46*

In the disciple's culturing by the Omnipresence, he must incorporate the intricacies of the Third Light-Stream. As Apostles for God, those energized by the Third Light-Stream have the merchant's disciplines through which they view and act upon in life and in work.

Simon Zelotes, who was the ancient Egyptian Teacher initiating Moses in his early life in Egypt, works with the Third Light-Stream Initiate. His work emphasizes quality or to qualify oneself as to possessions, as makers and as energy utilizers.

Mental energy manifested into physical substance requires knowledge concerning true and accurate visualization; true and right motive as a creator; also true and rightful selection of objects and particles as related to the delicate balance in the use of the molecular system, of rightful design arrangement and perfection as to functioning. All Third Light-Stream Initiates must seek to *sell all* that they may process and possess the skills of rightful manifestation.

Under the influences of the Third Light-Stream, one dreams the blueprint and gives birth to new arrangements of forming and shaping. On mental, etheric, emotional and physical levels, the mastery of the Third Light-Stream enables the doer to become a wielder of the fate over the many in science, industry, or wherever the energy of man fits the plan of the need and care of man. This action is never ceasing.

All inventors with vision fixed upon concern for the welfare of man work within the Third Light-Stream energies. Their insight determines how men in mass will earn, how they will be healed, will know God as the One in all, the Providence. Whatever is made for man and by man is of the Spirit of God.

The Being overdwelling the Third Light-Stream, representing the Father Principle, is the Maha Chohan. He comes close to mankind during a Kali-Yuga time for the duration of 3000 years so that man may produce the grace of his recorded works and thus carry over this record into the next Moving Archetype. The Maha Chohan now works in the Kali-Yuga time or the latter days to move men forward into the Christ-Dharma Knowing on Earth.

In the Third Light-Stream, the works and the *Word* as one are God made flesh in man. Man is tested by and through the Third Light-Stream action in the nature of life's experience. One learns the why of the mystery of things possessed, of ideas possessed, of associations tested, when he enters into Third Light-Stream Initiation.

One identifies Third Light-Stream persons by what they aspire to do for others; how one fulfills this desire and what motive is in his dedications or his creative ingeniousness.

The Initiate representing the Third Light-Stream must above all observe a state of reverence or respect for the venerable sages of discrimination. He must avoid any form of overzealousness. He must research his motivation impulses. He must firmly keep his word within the Spirit of Truth. Of all Light-Streams, the Third carries the danger of ego-blindness, or of thinking oneself as the doer rather than "the Father who doeth the works."

The Third Light-Stream represents speech and the voice. So is the grace of the goodly merchant also known through the Third Light-Stream. To sell all to gain the grace and truth in Christ is the goal.

The tithe system through which the Holy Word prevails on the Altar is under the influence of the Third Light-Stream. Melchizedek powers of the priesthood are sustained as service to God that the Word be made flesh through the Sacrament of the Holy Spirit in the Communion and Eucharist.

Self-Genesis development is deeply under the Third Light-Stream testings and initiations. Lesser Self-Genesis is more often suggestible to the Judas aspect of the Third Light-Stream. Higher Self-Genesis seeks to be a novice in the Holy Merchandise of the Word of God. The giving spirit so necessary to life sustaining, when using the highest side of the Third Light-Stream energies, enables one to move freely toward all other Light-Streams and thus fulfill man of mind and man of God in Earth.

THE FOURTH LIGHT-STREAM HEALER

If one is called by his soul to be a healer and knows his vocation and covenant to be a true and ethical holy concern for the well-being of all persons, he comes under the initiatory processes within the Fourth Light-Stream. If he has impurity on any level in his own nature, he must undergo the Temple Initiatory Anatomy-Disciplines, which contain the knowledge of the Life Force through sex, through marriage, through the family-atom, through life as a novice in association, through religiosity-worships, and through every form of Marking and Tracing—reaching continually toward perfection in body, in mind, in soul.

Men, through their prototypal, human natures, are soul-united with those having lived in the world who worked with the healing of the masses. Such great healers were Saint Francis, Hippocrates and the Apostle, Saint Luke.

The Initiate of the present time, working with the Life Fiat or the Healing Principle, is under the tutelage of Sanat Kumara and the Omnipresences functioning through the Fourth Light-Stream. Sanat Kumara is a Time-Emissary working directly in the Father Principle with the Father. Sanat Kumara works especially with Fourth Light-Stream souls. He initiates all healers in the use of Time and Timing. He is the Ancient of Days. His work is to teach Hierarchy-Initiates how to reverse sickness.

In the healing ministry of Mediation, each healing mediator functions through his own Light-Stream, using the value he is destined to use in this present incarnation. If he is a Fourth Light-Stream Initiate and uses the fourth value, he is by nature of his soul-impulse a healer above all other vocations. He is automated to Healing.

If one is a Number One Light-Stream Initiate, using the fourth value, he seeks to will away sickness through positive visualization and obedience to the Will of God. If he is a Second Light-Stream Initiate, he uses the fourth value of his Light-Stream as a devotee. He heals as a Bhakti presence through love.

As one advances in the Science of Spiritual Healing, he should know himself to be a mediator drawing forth from his own nature the Omnipresence of God. God uses him as a channel of will, love, discipline, order, truth, grace and works.

All Initiates seek to become versatile in the use of *all values* of the Light-Streams. The mediative powers initiate one in and through the mastery of the values: (1) Will; (2) Devotion; (3) Organization and Discipline; Consciousness; (4) Law; Building; Healing of physical conditions and body ailments; (5) Science; (6) Transcendental Healing through the Jesus Ethic; Esse; (7) Ritual; Master Polarity through Ritual.

MEDIATIVE HEALING IN THE FIFTH LIGHT-STREAM AND ITS VALUE

Niscience has been maturing since 1952, having grown and expanded into a cultured and realistic way of life—a life expressing equally the exterior experience and the soul inner-experience. The basic Niscience principles fulfilling the Jesus Ethic have magnified and enlarged our comprehension as to its being in time with the birth of soul-expansion for the Human Race.

The mediative-healing techniques, the creative results of research through marking, tracing and transenergization, the cyclic energy enlightenments received through illumination and intuition—none of these would have been possible by any one person. Only through a soul-mastery, agreement and covenant in unison was this made possible.

The combined soul-revelatory energies gleaned through Unit contacts, Altar-serving and Esse-movement are divinely processed to research and utilize the Scriptural and individual soul-contributions accumulated throughout the ages or centuries past. Through this, a needful present is served and a future of enlightenment anticipated.

In Niscience, we discern the spiritual and mind crisis of the present. We seek to make clear our mind divinities, to make clean our undersoul distortions, and to make purposeful our life within a *Living Teaching* or *Dharma*.

All Scriptures of the past relate to the *Science of Practice.* All Scriptures of the past point the way or the method to reach perfection as laid down by procedures stemming from Wisdom-related souls, hearts and minds. *Nothing lives Scripturally unless it contains lasting truth based upon the Spirit of Truth.* The Scriptures are therefore preserved from era to era or from one Moving Archetype to another.

It is the law of Scripture that Scripture must be passed to a worthy receptacle. The foremost gift of Passing for Scripture is the *Word* heard and unheard which must be compounded into writing through the pen of the soul-infected scribe, initiate or prophet.

The Fifth Light-Stream represents the scribe-apostle. Saint Paul of Tarsus was one of these. His Epistles in the New Testament of this era's Moving Archetypal Bible were composed directly through his *Archetonal Grace* or of hearing the Word and of speaking it so that it lives now in a soul-vernacular so close and intimate that in reading or speaking his words Soul-Realization is made possible; communication becomes healing of spiritual ignorance.

Saint Paul was a scientist-adept. He speaks now in and through the Fifth Light-Stream as healer for the rebel of the lower mind, for the agnostic, for the resister to the Holy Spirit. We live in an agnostic, rajasic age coming to birth to energies of the mind.

To unite with the value or the full measure of the Fifth Light-Stream is to come under Saint Paul. Read his life; listen to this ministering; become aware of his Intentional Suffering. He knew the Christ as no one else knew Him.

Holding the Light in the Niscience practice for healing opens one to the scientific healing practice of Mediation. *Make this practice your healing way, your ministering. Be in the body and out of the body through Mediation. Be present as being present with the sick and homeless. Be happy; be provident in Mediation.*

NUMBER SIX LIGHT-STREAM OR ABSOLUTE HEALING

The Sixth Light-Stream is available to the Initiate when he observes the Ethic of Jesus: *Love ye one another.* The Sixth Light-Stream love is of the Soul. All who are recipients of these energies prepare to be Mediative Hierarchy Healers.

The Jesus Path of Intentional Suffering is experienced by the Initiate who has passed the fiery trials providing flawless humility. The more one uses the Love Ethic of Jesus, the more he becomes co-atom to Jesus, and thus automatically functions within the Sixth Light-Stream of Absolute God.

In Niscience, one is shown the two aspects of God: *God Absolute* and *God Conditioned.* God Conditioned is our Father. God Absolute is Eternal Spirit pervading all—all Earths, all Galaxies, all Souls. In God-Absolute Healing, one becomes a mediator within Eternal Spirit moving beyond the relativities of karma. In Conditioned God, one functions in the relativities of Maya, subjected to cycles and timing as to when a healing occurs or where it comes. In Conditioned-God Healing, one must be Self-Realized. In Absolute God, one is God-Realized beyond karmas. It is *all grace* to be healed in Absolute God.

The Sixth Light-Stream begins its work through service for God through Jesus, who is the Mediator of the Sixth Light-Stream; through devotion to God as worship. Compassion and mercy must come from Conditioned God; compassion from Jesus, the Lord of Love.

Absolute healers are rare. They exist in the Bodhisattva line and in the line of the Saints. Jesus is foremost as the Absolute Healer. All healing through Conditioned God is Mediation and occurs as Omnipresence Mediation. Spirit of God as Mediation is mercy and grace.

All absolute healing comes as Samadhi union with God as Spirit. A healer who has earned the small miracles of healing is subjected to the gravity reflexes within karma. A healer who has opened all of the values of the Light-Streams and has made prolonged Samadhi Realizations within the Spirit of God is a son of God and is through Jesus co-atom to the only begotten Son of God. The Christ manifests the great miracles. This perfection in healing should be the goal of all Initiates. Jesus promised that we would heal as He healed.

Dwell upon the Spirit of God, the Eternal One. Unite with our Father, Conditioned God, who enables you, by His dwelling within you, to reach Absolute-God consciousness. "The Father that dwelleth in me, He doeth the works." (St. John 14:10)

Absolute God represents the Word to be made flesh. Conditioned God represents the works made flesh.

The Father is a caring God. God as Spirit enables all to care, to love, to live.

The total system of Cosmos, Cosmic and Soul is set upon equal measure for measure. *"With what measure ye mete, it shall be measured to you again." (St. Matthew 7:2)*

> *Whatsoever a man soweth, that shall he also reap.*
>
> —*Galatians 6:7*

In Sixth Light-Stream healing, which is Absolute Healing through grace, Spirit for Spirit is at work in all aspects of healing.

Restitution as Spirit for Spirit, forgiving as Spirit for Spirit, produce a lasting healing or Absolute Healing. Those who have reached initiation through the Sixth Light-Stream have done so through measure for measure. All units of energy obtained through grace use the Absolute-Life powers of healing as used by Jesus.

In the Spirit for Spirit or giving, one prospers. In the Spirit of obedience, one is healed of rigidity diseases. In the

Spirit of humility, one receives in Spirit for Spirit or equal measure the power to heal, to prosper, to be happy.

Spirit for Spirit balances, heals the impossible, the improbable. To accept Spirit-for-Spirit Principle is to be equal in instruction through obedience.

Spirit for Spirit supports the Life Fiat in Life; keeps one living in the vitalities of soul-vitality and supremacy. Spirit for Spirit is peace in Earth as it is in Heaven. To accept Spirit for Spirit is to live abundantly in grace within Spirit Eternal.

By what measure ye do these things, it is measured unto you as a right *Way,* as a right *Justice or Truth,* or as a right *Life.* In this Self-Genesis period, men will become more aware of this great law of equity through Spirit for Spirit; thus, a right way, right justice and a right life will manifest for God in this Earth.

"As ye sow, so shall ye reap." Retaliation, or hatred for hatred, is the most degraded use of Spirit for Spirit. Revenge is of God. True Spirit for Spirit, when expressed and experienced as reconciling love, is Absolute Healing within the Presence of God.

In the Sixth Light-Stream, Jesus is the door to Absolute Healing. "Do these things," said Jesus. So do we seek to live in the Sixth Light-Stream as a shining Light for God.

The Sixth Light-Stream values on the Sixth Light-Stream provide the Nisciene with direct and open knowledge of the inward healing powers. One by one, a Nisciene incorporates all values expanding his consciousness, extending his spiritual aptitudes. All is grace in God in Knowing or Niscience.

In the Sixth Light-Stream work, one encounters the Ishta gates—that is, the most close Omnipresent Beings to his Illuminati Grace. These flow into his soul-powers encased in an etheric circle or mandala with four gates. At each gate is seated a Maha Deva which God, Life and Fate have assigned to him over the many aeons and ages.

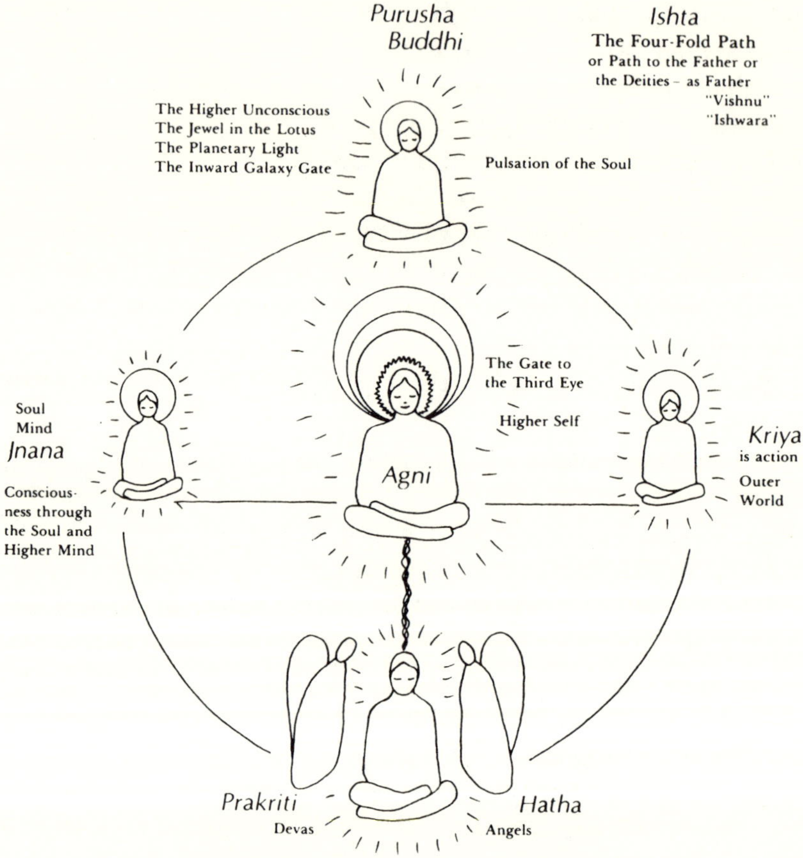

THE GATES OF EXISTENCE

The Ishta gates become the Omnipresent communicative points of contact within the higher vibrancies of Heaven. Through mediation and meditation upon the Ishta gates, the disciple learns of Heaven as related to Earth. Also, through his familiarity with these Ishta reinforcements of Omnipresence, he learns of holy synchronization between all worlds, gravity and etheric, and of coming worlds. He is in the constant company and companionship of the Angels, the Great Immortals and the Bodhisattvas.

A person using psychic-matter action has no access to the Ishta gates. He reaches only the gravity-controlled electricities of the lower devachan or astral communications.

Ishta means one's own personal Omnipresent Divine Companion in alignment with one's own life of the soul throughout the ages. One's own Ishta is an assured Eternal Companion containing the same soul-waves of the Eternals in his own natural Grace-Self or Higher Self.

There is a direct circuit connection between one's own Ishta and one's self. All healing, all spiritual action is multiplied thousands of times into healing and into the soul-extension powers of grace through direct circuit contact with one's Ishta gate.

To visualize and meditate on the Ishta Mandala and call upon Ishta presences, one should:

1. Begin with the Bindu point or *Agni gate* which starts at one's own heart center and moves up between the eyebrows and the crown of the head.

2. Then one descends to the soul or Jnana mental higher-mind gate: The Great Immortals. The attitude should be one of holy reverence for the mind as the vehicle for enlightenment.

3. At the Angelic, Deva Ishta gate, one dwells to think with gratitude for the presence of the guardian ones who enable the disciple to move over the darkness in the lower worlds or events and to keep the samskaras regulated in the subconscious.

4. He next moves to the Kriya Ishta gate, representing the physical world and all phenomenal action therein where the Ishta Light keeps one on the level of the Coinciding where Spirit for Spirit is represented as justice instantly.

5. The Most High Ishta sifts to the disciple the filtering powers of soul as Buddhi, where God-Realization is made possible.

SEVENTH LIGHT-STREAM

To extend our understanding of the Light-Streams, we visualize all seven Light-Streams as no longer enclosed in cyclic fixity, for it is in this time that Light-Stream action is in a master stage of opening all aspects simultaneously. Thus, men at large are asked to make synthesis with each value. In the advanced teachings, the Seventh Light-Stream now supports the synthesis and synchronization processes.

Never before has mankind of this Earth been subjected to such pressure; for all must move out of enclosure-enticements into oneness of will as souls with God. All of the Earth—the smallest of the knowing to the greatest—will go forward in God's Increase.

Love of brotherhood is expressed in the Seventh Light-Stream. Love of soul is sought. Strong mind-impulses of the past are surfacing into the composite mental body of the present. Man in Earth will claim the stars as brothers through this Seventh Light-Stream quickening.

For the Initiate, this means the carrying of the soul-burdens for the ignorance of the past. The collective body of the Most High Unconscious works to aid those who, through Intentional Suffering, take on these burdens. Instruction with ethic in right timing produces right and true ethic—ethic to return men to God.

The Seven Light-Streams re-emphasize the seven steps of initiation: Will, Devotion, Organization, Law, Science, Healing, Ritual.

The seven steps on the Seventh Light-Stream are under the tutelage of Master R, who was Joseph, the father of Jesus. Among his other lives before being Joseph, he was Noah. In the time of David, he was Hiram Abiff, called the great Master Phoenician.

The Master R spoken of as the mysterious Saint Germain and the Great Immortal Master R are not the same; there is no comparison. The so-called Saint Germain is an occult identity, while the true Master R is one of the Elect.

At the present time, Master R works to bring religiosity to religion. In healing, he works to produce Hierarchy-nature healing of mind over the body. In science, he works to bring science to a spiritual birth. In law, he works to produce justice and acceptance of law. In organization, he seeks to bring order on Cosmos and Cosmic scale. In devotion, he works to reveal the soul-nature of man and his ahimsa heart. In will, he will produce a higher genius use of the mind.

When you incorporate all the Light-Streams,
you become a ritualist of transcendental order.

13

PRINCIPLES OF PROSPERITY

Beloved, I wish above all things that thou mayest prosper and be in health, even as thy soul prospereth.

—1 John 2

Volition and Honorableness

Since thou wast precious in my sight, thou hast been honourable, and I have loved thee.

—Isaiah 43:4

A true Teacher never tells a student he *must* do something. The Teacher leaves all of the student's decisions to the *volition* of the student.

The Teacher's union with God is based upon the Teacher's honorableness in the sight of God. This honorableness has been tested over and over in the initiatory fires. The Teacher, having proved trustworthy and faithful to God, is honorable in all vows, covenants and dedications to the Creator of life.

A student, through the gift of volition, expresses his choices and decisions. If the student is honorable, he will observe his part in the Teacher-student relationship with integrity, faithfulness and conscientiousness.

If a student proves honorable in his association with his Teacher over the years, he will be a good candidate for the Divine-Marriage Anointing and the Greater Inheritances of Grace. Such students, through volition, will always remain true to their vows, covenants and dedications to God. In these rare students, volition and honorableness go hand in hand; they are inseparable.

Honorableness begins in a student's keeping of the Laws and Commandments of God. Volition is present in all decisions regarding each Holy Law and Commandment.

Honorableness increases through volition when a student fulfills his Teacher's suggestions, directions and guidance. Each time an aspirant observes with gratitude a creative assignment, a devotional practice or a spiritual dedication, it is an act of volition coupled with honorableness.

Honorableness is the key factor in all of one's relationships with God, his Teacher, in marriage and family association, in business dealings and in friendships. The quest for union with God begins the moment one uses the gift of volition inspired by the Virtue of Honorableness.

Attendance at meetings conducted by one's Teacher is an act of volition based upon a desire to learn and to serve. There are many other areas of volition for a student. If the student is honorable, he will use the gift of volition to come closer to God.

The decision of attendance at Classes, Pilgrimages, Special Events and Holy-Day Services is entirely up to the volition of the student. If a student has the Virtue of Honorableness regarding attendance, the Teacher can work more closely with the student. The Teacher recognizes that such students blessed with the Virtue of Honorableness are being singled out by God to become future Teachers of His Word and guardians of the Dharma.

> *The borrower is servant to the lender.*
>
> —*Proverbs 22:7*

The Teacher's task is to unite his students with the Omnipresent, Omniscient and Omnipotent Spirit of God. One aspect of union with the Spirit of God is union with His Providential Grace.

If a student feels he must loan or borrow from someone else, he has yet to unite with the Providential Grace of God. To loan or borrow from anyone is to become their servant. If large sums of money are involved, this servitude may extend for many years.

One of the Maya traps is to become a servant of someone other than God. To become a servant of God is to turn to God alone for all of one's needs. God's Wisdom determines how and when His servant receives the answers to all of his needs in perfect timing.

God works through honorableness. It is honorable when a devotee purchases only that which he can pay for through his own honest labors.

Earning is a spiritual Principle of great importance related to honorableness. It is an ethical philosophy, a way of life for the righteous. If a devotee of the higher life is not grounded in the Principle of Earning as a way of life, he will incur debts in order to purchase objects or things *before* he has earned them. This attitude is dangerous in the spiritual life because such a person will also expect Gifts and Powers of the Soul before he has *earned* them.

"The love of money is the root of all evil." (1 Timothy 6:10) Many would-be students of the higher life have a deep-rooted love for money. This love for money stands between them and union with God, for their love for money is stronger than their love for God.

One cannot borrow or loan spiritual gifts and soul-powers; these must be earned. They are earned after many rigorous trials and tests regarding one's integrity, character and honorableness.

Honorableness is a beauteous virtue that shines as a bright sun in a darkened sky. Students with the Virtue of Honorableness are as radiant lights in the darkness of the world.

Every historic spiritual event on the face of the planet Earth begins with the dedication of a Master Teacher under the Guidance of God, and with the Volition of students and devotees who are expressing the noble Virtue of Honorableness.

An honorable restitution made for present-life sins and past-lives transgressions holds the key to the receiving of Spiritual Gifts and Holy Inheritances from God. The Creator rewards those who are honorable in His sight with the Greater Anointings of Grace and Truth. These Anointings are the *true prosperity,* for they present one with spiritual riches that are infinite, eternal; thus, the wise seek to make an honorable restitution for their offenses against the Holy Law of Tithing, the Ten Commandments and the Commandments of Love.

Each prayer, offering, penance or pilgrimage made in the spirit of restitution takes one closer to the Inner Kingdom of God: the Godhead. Only the honorable may gain entrance into this Dimensional World of Knowledge and Truth that links the Solar System with all stars and galaxies in the Universe. Only the honorable may receive the Christ Mind, which is a Cosmos-Eternal Mind. Therefore, all who aspire toward union with God are diligent in their expression of the Virtue of Honorableness.

Be honorable in all things.

—*Ann Ree Colton*

DEDICATION AND STEWARDSHIP

> *As every man hath received the gift, even so minister the same one to another, as good stewards of the manifold grace of God.*
>
> *—1 Peter 4:10*

After a truth-seeker dedicates his life to God, he should realize that he has given all of his possessions and energies for God to use. He will no longer desire to own or possess anything for himself alone—for all that he once claimed has been given to God. Henceforth, he will have *stewardship* over whatever the Creator places in his hands. This includes monies, properties, persons, inspirational thoughts, and spiritual gifts.

As long as one knows in his heart and mind that God is providing him with his needs—and desires no more than is being provided—he will continue to receive the joys, rewards and inheritances that come to servants of God and stewards of His Grace.

As one proves the sincerity of his dedication, he unites with the *Increase* of God. In this, his stewardship increases in old and new areas of expression and service.

The Virtue of Holy Poverty protects one from feeling ownership of anything provided by God after words or vows of dedication are spoken to Him. The heart experiences frequent testings of its motives until one's dedication and stewardship sound pure and clear tones of Truth. These tones of Truth unite one with the Pure and Clear Tones of God's Truth. Thus, one's union with God as the Eternal and Omnipresent Truth prospers as he proves his heart's love for God through an unwavering dedication to Scriptural Laws and Stewardship Principles.

"But be ye doers of the word, and not hearers only, deceiving your own selves." (James 1:22) If a seeker after truth

retains any remnants of self-deception, the initiatory process centers around those areas. God focuses His Light of Pure Truth in each area of self-deception until one either turns away from the spiritual Path or determines to work with God to overcome all tracings of self-deception. An area of self-deception may relate to possessiveness of monies, properties or persons. A probationer's problems or troubles contain the clues to his discovering his self-deceptions. To become a wholehearted servant of God, one must release *all* to Him in the spirit of Holy Poverty and Sacramental Stewardship.

"The tenth shall be holy unto the Lord." (Leviticus 27:32) Through the Holy Law of Tithing, God's Word is preserved and prospered from generation to generation. Thus, tithing is an important expression of stewardship gratefully fulfilled by sincere servants of God.

The entire *Chakra** system is dependent upon one's attitude toward tithing. When a tither meditates and prays, the heart chakra is open to God through the fulfillment of this Holy Law. The love-currents of the heart shepherd the energy-flow of the other chakras Godward. In this, the energy-flow of the Chakras becomes part of the *Holy Flow* of Creation. Non-tithers, regardless of how much they meditate or pray, cannot open the Door to the Flow of God's increasing blessings because their heart-chakra energies are moving in the opposite direction to the Holy Flow of Creation.

When tithing is supported by a worshipper's love for all other Laws and Commandments of God, he becomes *centered* in the Holy Flow of Divine Love and Providential Grace. The Teacher's task is to teach his students the

**Chakra* is a Sanskrit word relating to the energy-portals of the soul within the human anatomy.

importance of each Holy Law so that they may *immediately* move their chakra energy-flow into harmonious union with the Holy Flow of Divine-Love, Providential Grace and Universal Creation.

Tithe as a citizen of the world,
and the world will bless you.
Tithe as a citizen of the Solar System,
and the Solar System will bless you.
Tithe as a citizen of the Universe,
and the Universe will bless you.
Tithe as a citizen of the Kingdom of God,
and the Kingdom of God will bless you.

THE TEACHER AND WEDDINGS: TO PROSPER IN MARRIAGE

> *But from the beginning of the creation God made them male and female. For this cause shall a man leave his father and mother, and cleave to his wife; And they twain shall be one flesh: so then they are no more twain, but one flesh. What therefore God hath joined together, let not man put asunder.*
>
> —*St. Mark 10:6–9*

A Teacher of the higher life is often requested to conduct weddings—and to *bless* the bride and bridegroom. This blessing is a very great responsibility for the Teacher, especially if the two to be wed are students of the Teacher. When students become householders, their physical marriage is part of their preparation for the Divine Marriage with God. If the souls' records of the bride and groom contain sin-shadows that will endanger their future marital harmony and happiness, the Teacher, through the Covenant of Intentional Suffering, will heal the sin-shadows as part of his *blessing* given at the time of the Wedding Ceremony and Sacrament.

If the souls' records of the couple to be married are heavy-laden with unresolved sin-debts of the present life and past lives, the Intentional Suffering by the Teacher can be intense. However, the Teacher endures with love this Apostolic service rendered in the Name of the Lord Jesus, for it will make straight the path for the married couple, who will thereafter serve God as "one flesh."

Students who are part of the Teacher's Mantle receive this priceless *Wedding Gift* as part of the Teacher's blessing and consecration of their marriage. Devotees who dedicate their marriage to God experience a *Sanctified Marriage* through the Wedding-Blessing by their Teacher, thereby assuring the perpetuation of the Dharma in the world. As stewards and guardians of the Dharma, the newlyweds will add to the world the joy of their love and the beauty of their pure creations.

All marriages consecrated *in Jesus' Name* come under the Mantle of His Love and Blessing. The Intentional Suffering of Jesus becomes a strength, a quickening, a supernatural Presence in the Wedding Ceremony and throughout the marriage. The Teacher, as an Apostle chosen and anointed by Jesus, is part of the Mantle of Jesus. The Intentional Suffering endured by the Teacher during the days or weeks before the Wedding is a gift of love, assuring the freedom from certain ancestral, parental, personal and other karmas that would otherwise intrude upon the joy and harmony of the marriage. Thus, the husband and wife, as devotees of the Lord, will remain free to accomplish the sacred purposes of God Who has joined them together in holy wedlock.

The degree of righteousness of a Teacher of Truth determines the power of the Spiritual Blessing bestowed upon the bride and groom during the Wedding Ceremony. This Blessing never ceases; it is a perpetual benediction. To be joined in marriage by a Master Teacher, a Living Apostle of the Lord Jesus, is a rare and great Blessing that will manifest increasingly the Presence and Glory of God in the marriage.

After the Wedding Ceremony, one or both marriage partners may *negate* or *nullify* the Marriage Blessing by the Teacher by failing to tithe to God, by failing to fulfill the Sabbath-Day Commandment of Worship, or by failing to keep the Morality Ethic within their Marriage Vows. To ignore, deny or offend the major Statutes of God is to fall from grace—whether one be single or married. The Wedding Blessing by one's Teacher becomes an expanding fountain of Love and Grace when husband and wife honor and fulfill God's Holy Laws with loyalty and love.

Every sincere and dedicated student of an Anointed Teacher is blessed by the Teacher's Covenant of Intentional Suffering. If the student is unmarried or married, he or she comes under the Grace of God through the Living Teacher's ministering in Jesus' Name.

If a student *requests* the Teacher's blessing in marriage with a mate or in marriage with God, the Teacher will use the spiritual powers with which he is endowed to seal into the student eternal blessings. These blessings given in Jesus' Name will be with the student for the remainder of the present life and for all future lives.

To be blessed by an Anointed Apostle of Jesus is to be blessed by one who has attained the Eternal-Life Consciousness, the Christ-Mind Consciousness, the Love-of-God Consciousness. Therefore, to be blessed by such an one in the Sacrament of Baptism or Christening, the Sacrament of Marriage, the Death-Ritual Sacrament, or in any other Sacrament ordained by God is to receive *eternal blessings throughout all lives to come.* Whether one is single or married in future lives, as long as he is mindful of the Commandments—worshipping, loving and serving God—

he will reap the everlasting rewards that come through the Blessing and Anointing by his Living Teacher under Christ.

> *Verily, verily, I say unto you, He that receiveth whomsoever I send receiveth me; and he that receiveth me receiveth him that sent me.*
>
> *—St. John 13:20*

LEVELS OF THE HOLY GHOST: TO PROSPER IN NEW IDEAS

> *Receive ye the Holy Ghost.*
>
> *—St. John 20:22*

There are different levels of the Holy Ghost. Those who have experienced *conversions* from lives of sin to become evangelists, priests, ministers or other dedicated servants of God on the level of fundamental religions and traditional religions have received the Holy Ghost *on that level.* The majority of such persons remain on that level; they do not realize that the Holy Ghost may be experienced on higher levels.

Teachers of God's Word on the fundamental and traditional level are vitally necessary to shepherd other converts from lives of sin to lives of worship and observance of the Commandments. However, one who is graced with a mighty increase of Holy-Ghost power will be lifted to a higher expression of spiritual-creative skills for God. Such persons will present *new ideas* through their stronger union with the Holy Ghost, and therefore will attract criticism or persecution.

These inspired individuals are either expelled or excommunicated from their former religions or church affiliations because of their new ideas and daring creations for God.

Many Holy-Ghost-filled evangelists, priests and ministers cannot comprehend individuals who are filled with the

Holy-Ghost on the level of *Cosmos Realizations* and *Solar-System Revelations* regarding the Sun, the Moon and the Planets. The future of the world depends upon servants of God being filled with the Holy Ghost on the level of the Stars and Galaxies. The Lord Christ came to open the Door to greater Holy-Ghost Illuminations through the Galaxy Consciousness.

Ann Ree Colton, a Cosmos-Genesis seer, on the Galaxy level of the Holy Ghost, tells of man's beginning to bring to birth an *Omniscient Cell* within the brain. When this new Cell appears in the brain, man will think through a greater, broader and deeper range of consciousness and conscience.

The Omniscient Cell will unite man with the Omniscience of God and the Mediation of the Christ in remarkable ways. When this occurs, Time and Space will be overcome. God is beginning to send certain souls who have begun to manifest the Omniscient Cell; therefore, their thinking goes beyond the thoughts of others in the present age. These Omniscient-Cell ones are the forerunners of a great new age. The *new* that will result in the new age is much greater in scope and daring than mankind can presently comprehend.

Each time a student receives from his Teacher a Cosmos Principle to contemplate or a spiritual symbol to meditate upon or to draw, he is being given the opportunity to stimulate the Omniscient Cell within his brain.

Omniscience, which means All-Knowing, is an attribute of God. Man, created in the Image of God, has Godlike powers within him that are yet to manifest. The Teacher comes as a Gift from God to awaken in his students these supernal skills and dimensional versatilities.

"Blessed are the pure in heart, for they shall see God." (St. Matthew 5:8) The pure in heart are the pure in mind. The pure in mind will see God through the Omniscient Cell within the brain. The Omniscient Cell will then prepare

man for greater hierarchy-nature powers and abilities. These also will manifest through purity in heart, chaste motives; and through purity in mind, selfless thoughts.

When men seek to emulate the Lord Jesus, they will be centered in the New Covenant as Galaxy-Knowers. Utilizing powerful Cosmic and Cosmos energies, they will glorify the God of the Universe through mighty and miraculous works. Over the coming centuries and ages, men will experience the Image-of-God Quickenings that will contribute toward an increasing number of persons becoming more like Jesus.

> *In the etheric brain there is developing an Omniscient Cell. The Omniscient Cell in the brain is the Jesus Cell. Men will be ultimately like Jesus.*
>
> —*Ann Ree Colton*

Many teachers, gurus, ministers, priests and others dedicated to religious and spiritual callings are brilliant in their understanding of Scripture and can teach beautifully and articulately. However, they never teach anything *new.* Such persons have yet to awaken certain gifts of the soul through which come new truths.

A truly enlightened Teacher is always presenting new truths because the Spirit of God is constantly anointing him with this priceless knowledge. New truths signify that one is close to God and the Christ on a high level of the Holy Ghost. It is only through this closeness with the Creator and His Son that a Teacher may qualify to be a revelator of new truths.

Teachers who teach old truths are rendering a great service. Teachers who teach old truths and introduce new truths are rendering a greater service. The former is working with the Preservation Principle. The latter is working with the Preservation Principle *and* the Revelation Principle. There is no higher calling than to be a Revelator for the Eternal God.

The Spirit of Truth . . . will shew you things to come.

—St. John 16:13

PRAISE

Praise ye the Lord from the mountain top.
Praise Him from the bottom of the sea.
Praise Him from the center of the Earth.
Praise Him from the core of the Galaxy.
Praise ye the Lord, O ye Earth and all who dwell therein.

Through the praise of God, one prospers. The continued praising of God—regardless of the adversities and vicissitudes of life—keeps one attuned to the Providential Grace of God.

The receiving of the Sacrament of Communion in the spirit of praising and thanking God for the Lord Jesus and His Miracles enables one to quickly overcome his tribulations and become more firmly centered in the Holy Flow of God's Grace.

When one begins to experience the Glory of God within his Spiritual-Birthright Inheritance, he will have increasing cause for praising the Omnipotent Creator.

To praise God for His Forgiveness, Mercy and Love is to draw closer to His Forgiveness, Mercy and Love. To praise God for His Universe of Stars and Galaxies is to draw closer to the Soul-Gifts through which come realizations regarding the Cosmos.

To praise God for His Image is to awaken new facets of the Divine Image within one's being. To praise God for one's Teacher is to be anointed by the Holy Light radiating from the Mantle of the Teacher.

Those who praise God are the hope-bringers, the prophets inspired by sacred knowledge. Praise comes from a soul quickened by love for God and one's fellow man. To praise the Host of Heaven is to become a praiseworthy one in the sight of the Lord of Hosts.

> *I will hope continually, and will yet praise Thee more and more.*
>
> —*Psalm 71:14*

THE JOY OF GIVING

> *For it is by giving that we receive.*
>
> —*St. Francis of Assisi*

He who gives receives—this is the law taught by Jesus, Saint Paul, Saint Francis, and the other Enlightened Ones.

Giving is a joy. To give to God is to receive from God. To give in Jesus' Name is to receive Gifts from Jesus. To give in the spirit of sacrifice and dedication is to receive blessings from the Saints and Angels.

He who gives continually receives continually. To commune with Heaven, one should follow the example of Jesus, the Great Giver.

When one gives selflessly, the Spirit of God anoints him with Miracle-Grace—which the giver immediately gives to others.

To become a Teacher under Christ is to be a giver under Christ. The Anointed Teacher is always in the state of giving: giving instruction, giving comfort, giving direction, giving cheer, giving hope, giving consolation, giving inspiration.

The joy of giving is a real joy, a positive joy, a continuous joy. To taste the sweet nectar of God's Love, is the daily delight of the giver. Therefore, O devotee, give; and thou shalt live in the Peace and Joy of God, prospering in His Wisdom and Truth.

> *Give, and it shall be given unto you; good measure, pressed down, and shaken together, and running over, shall men give unto your bosom.*
>
> *—St. Luke 6:38*

Part III
Personal Journals and Diaries

The recognition of the Cycles in one's life is connected with Self-Realization and Soul-Realization—and that is when one gets into Cyclic Law.

—*A. R. C.*

ANN REE COLTON

1898 August 17, born in Atlanta, Georgia.

1916 April 16, marriage to Alexander Taranko.

1917 April 7, gave birth to first daughter, Harriette.

1919 Heard her name called three times by a voice from the heavens. The voice was also heard by her father and husband.

1919 Moved to New York City.

1921 Contacts with the Master.

1922 September 1, birth of her second daughter, Ann Ree II.

1922 Union with the "Wind" and the Sound Current of the Holy Ghost. Also experienced the physical manifestation of the Master.

1925 Began a seventeen-year period of kabalistic paintings.

1926 January 1, left New York City to make her home in Florida.

1932 The beginning of her Ministry.

1941 Received the Holy Ghost and experienced the *Initiation of the Wilderness.* Made union with the Ancient of Days.

1946 January 6, concluded her Ministry in Florida.

1948 Visited California for the first time.

1948 In Florida, she was in the water one day when a voice from the heavens said: "You are loved."

1950 Moved to California.

1951 Experienced and received from the Holy-Ghost Archetones and Archetypes: the beginning of the System of Niscience.

1951 Guided to return to Florida for her meeting with Jonathan Murro.

1952 Eighty evening meditations produced the manuscript for the books *Islands of Light, Vision for the Future* and *The Lively Oracles.*

1952 September, new manuscript through daily meditations at *Shadelands* in North Carolina.

1952 November, New York City. Beautiful manuscript related to the Plan in Cosmos. The word *Niscience* made its first appearance during meditation.

1953 February, return to Florida. The System of Niscience begins to formulate through charts and revelations.

1953 June, under the Divine directives, Ann Ree and Jonathan receive guidance to go to California.

1953 Ann Ree has a moving experience with Jesus at *Wooded Place,* near Santa Barbara, California.

1953 September 4, marriage to Jonathan Murro.

1953 *Islands of Light* published. Ann Ree begins to teach in the Los Angeles area.

1953 November, moved to the Los Angeles area.

1953 November 25, the birth date of the Ann Ree Colton Foundation of Niscience, Inc., a nonprofit religious and educational foundation blending religion, philosophy, science and the creative arts.

1956 November 1, conducted the first Guild meeting in Glendale, California.

1958 January, purchased the first property for the Headquarters of Niscience.

1958 Wrote *Draughts of Remembrance* in Santa Barbara, California. Suffered her first heart attack.

1959 Published *Draughts of Remembrance* and *Precepts for the Young.*

1960 Published *Vision for the Future.* Wrote *Men in White Apparel* in Sausalito, California.

1961 Published *Men in White Apparel.* First Niscience Conclave in the Carmel area: *Cherubim House.*

1961 December, serious heart condition. Rapid recovery after requesting the prayers of her students.

1962 Published *The Lively Oracles.* Prepared *The Venerable One* for publication.

1963 Published *The Venerable One.* Worked with Jonathan on *Prophet for the Archangels.*

1964 Published *Prophet for the Archangels.* Wrote *The Soul and the Ethic.*

1965 Published *The Soul and the Ethic.* Experienced a major initiation after a heart attack. Wrote *The Human Spirit.*

1966 Published *The Human Spirit.* Dedication of the *Chapel of the Jesus Ethic* in Glendale, California.

1967 Prepared *The King* for publication.

1968 Published *The King.* Wrote *The Jesus Story.*

1969 Published *The Jesus Story.*

Ann Ree Colton, 1947

1970 Wrote *Ethical ESP.*

1971 Published *Ethical ESP.*

1972 Suffered a serious heart attack. Made another rapid recovery after requesting the prayers of her students. Wrote *Watch Your Dreams.*

1967

1973 August 12, levitated while conducting a Sunday Worship Service.

1973 Published *Watch Your Dreams.*

1974–1977 Wrote *Kundalini West.*

1977 First East Coast Conclave in State College, Pennsylvania.

1978 August 17, Eightieth Birthday.

1978 Published *Kundalini West.*

1978–1981 Worked on *The Third Music.*

1982 Published *The Third Music.*

1982–1983 Worked with Jonathan on *Galaxy Gate.*

1984 Published *Galaxy Gate I: The Holy Universe* and *Galaxy Gate II: The Angel Kingdom.*

1984 May 19, Suffered Stroke.

1984 June 28, passed away at 2:50 A.M. from pneumonia. 85 years of age.

1985 *The Pelican and the Chela* published.

JONATHAN MURRO

1927 October 31, birthplace . . . Brooklyn, New York.

1928–1937 Early years . . . New Jersey.

1937–1945 Education . . . Florida.

1945–1947 United States Army . . . South Carolina (Clemson College), Georgia, Kentucky, Japan.

1947 College . . . Saint Petersburg, Florida.

1948–1951 Realtor . . . Florida.
Professional Athlete . . . Georgia, Florida.

1951 Prayer to serve God.
Meeting of Teacher, Ann Ree Colton.

1952 Compiler of Teacher's manuscripts . . . Florida, North Carolina, New York, California.

1953 September 4, Marriage to Ann Ree Colton.

1953 Editor of book *Islands of Light* by Teacher . . . published in California.

Co-Founder and Administrator of the Ann Ree Colton Foundation of Niscience, Inc.

1964 Co-author . . . *Prophet for the Archangels.*

1967 February 6, Ordination . . . Glendale, California.

1972 January 23, Prayer to become more aware of God's Love.

1972 Union begins with different degrees of bliss, ecstasy and joy within God's Love.

1972 May 14, six new songs received during prayer-communion.

1973 Composed the song-cycle *Beloved Son.*

1973 August 12, present at levitation-miracle.

1973 November 3, Visitation of Jesus' Presence.

1975 Author . . . *God-Realization Journal.*

1980 Author . . . *The Path of Virtue.*

1984 Co-author . . . *Galaxy Gate I and II.*

1985 Co-author . . . *The Pelican and the Chela.*

Chapel of the Jesus Ethic, Headquarters Chapel of the Ann Ree Colton Foundation, Glendale, California.

. . . Jonathan Murro

14

THE SACRIFICIAL PATH

Greater love hath no man than this, that a man lay down his life for his friends.
—St. John 15:13

During the years that Ann Ree Colton and I served God together, there were books and lessons to write, classes to teach, people to counsel, chapels to establish and maintain, and individual students to assist in their spiritual progression. A beautiful Ministry has evolved—a Ministry dedicated to the powerful Commandments of God and the noble Ethics of Jesus. A lovely Headquarters Chapel sends forth rays of reverent love into the world during each worship service and sacred event. Many new songs by the members contribute to the joy and devotion of the Sanctuary activities and programs. Creative movement to sacred words has produced a unique form of dance called *Pleasance*. Conclave pilgrimages, monthly home-study lessons, chapels and research units in different areas of the country—all contribute to the overall effectiveness of a modern-day Ministry dedicated to God and to the Christ.

My work with my Teacher for over three decades has been to assist her in whatever ways possible. Almost every single day, I have recorded her beautiful thoughts and insights. From the moment I first heard my Teacher speak during a worship service, I *knew* that I must preserve her words so that others could benefit from their beauty and wisdom.

Over the years, I have not only preserved Ann Ree's words, but I have also assisted her in establishing the Ann Ree Colton Foundation of Niscience. As administrator of this nonprofit religious and educational foundation, I have witnessed the ways that God works through a Ministry dedicated to the high standards and moral principles of the Holy Bible.

Ann Ree and I shared an unusual life together in that she was my Wife as well as my Teacher. I thank God for this grace, and pray to be a good steward of the many blessings that have come through our Guru-Chela association and Wife-Husband relationship.

Ann Ree and I have served God as *householders.* The householder life is a wholesome and effective way of serving God when both husband and wife are wholeheartedly dedicated to God. More and more persons in the future will serve God as householders. When there is pure love between husband and wife, God is with them in their physical, emotional, mental and spiritual expressions—and their love, sanctified and anointed by His Spirit, contributes to the Creation of the Universe.

A Teacher of the higher life protects his students or chelas with great love and devotion, and provides for their needs, even at the expense of suffering. Therefore, in soul-symbology, the symbol of the Teacher is the *Pelican.* It is difficult being a Teacher of Truth in modern times; nevertheless, Ann Ree Colton accepted her soul's covenant to fulfill the role of Pelican in her students' lives.

God had asked difficult things of Ann Ree all of her life. As a child, she labored in the early morning hours in cold weather milking cows for her family; she also was required to do many other heavy chores not asked of her brother and sisters.

She was beaten by both her mother and her father; especially did her father beat her brutally on several occasions. Her mother punished her for speaking about her clairvoyant visions.

She was the sole provider for her two young daughters during the time of the Great Depression, working long hours in a department store for very little pay.

She was a woman minister in a time when most religious leaders frowned upon women ministers.

She was persecuted for her Gift of Prophecy.

She was asked by God to establish a new spiritual system of worship and instruction. In an age of increasing apathy and immorality, she established the System of Niscience, writing numerous words of wisdom and revelation.

While establishing Niscience, Ann Ree suffered serious physical-body afflictions. In 1961 and 1972, after severe heart attacks, doctors told her that she would not live. With God's help, she was healed in each instance. In her 80's, she suffered greatly from heart pain and arthritis.

On Saturday, May 19, 1984, Ann Ree suffered a major stroke that affected the right side of her body and also her ability to speak.

God always asked difficult things of His Prophet and Revelator, Ann Ree Colton.

Throughout all of her eighty-five years, Ann Ree did not complain, but continued to serve her Lord to the best of her ability, always fulfilling the Teacher's Ethic with dignity, constancy and love.

During my years as Ann Ree's student, I observed and admired her steadfastness, dedication and faith. She amazed me constantly with her brilliance of mind and beauty of soul. Her love for God and for her fellow man inspired her to live a life of selfless service to others.

I have come to look upon Ann Ree Colton as more than a Saint. History will weigh her worth on the scales of wisdom

Ann Ree Colton and Jonathan Murro, Easter Morning, 1982 in Mary's Garden, Glendale, California.

and greatness. She walked the Path of Self-Denial and Intentional Suffering with humility, honor and integrity. All her actions were motivated by pure love. All her works of soul-wisdom and spiritual beauty were living testimonies of her oneness with God in a very special and holy way.

When an evil or immoral person experiences suffering, people immediately know why. However, when a good and righteous person begins to suffer, it is not known why—except by the Angels and the Saints and others who understand the Covenant of Intentional Suffering.

When a Holy Prophet of God, such as Ann Ree Colton, suffers afflictions, she is following the Path of the Crucified Jesus. The suffering of a Great Soul is to free others from their sin-bondages in the present generation, future generations and coming ages—for these Enlightened Ones are serving the *Eternal* God. Therefore, that which they endure for His Name's sake seals Eternal Blessings into the Earth and into the souls of men.

In numerous cemeteries in the world are those who died in battle so that precious *freedoms* may be gained and preserved in their nations. Each freedom gracing a nation has been won through the blood of many brave souls. Millions of lives have been lost; bodies have been broken and maimed—all for the cause of freedom.

So it is in the *Holy War* between the Christ and the Antichrist. Those who follow the Christ are dying on the battlefield or are being wounded and maimed. The cause for which they are fighting is *freedom* for the human spirit, mankind as a whole, the children of God in the present and future generations.

The bloodiest and most savage war is the ongoing struggle between virtue and vice, good and evil, grace and sin. Those who serve God and His Son are walking the *Sacrificial Path.* To lay down their lives for the future good of all, or to be wounded and afflicted for the sake of righteousness, goodness and ethic is to walk the Sacrificial Path in service to God and one's fellow man.

The Sacrificial Path requires courage, a willingness to sacrifice properties, possessions, families and friends in order to *win* freedoms for coming generations.

Jesus traveled the Sacrificial Path with honor, dignity and great love. The sacrifice of His life was the beginning of many new freedoms for mankind for all time to come—freedoms of body, heart, mind and soul.

All who teach and minister in Jesus' Name are walking the Sacrificial Path. These dedicated ones are helping the Lord of Love to accomplish His work as Messiah and Saviour of the world. The cost of any freedom is very high. Freedom is purchased only at the expense of someone's efforts, someone's blood, someone's willingness to make sacrifices of all kinds. These sacrifices are motivated by love, compassion and a prophetic vision inspired by the Image of God.

Every age and time requires its sacrificial ones, for there are always old freedoms to protect and new freedoms to be won. The battle rages. The tide is gradually turning the human spirit Godward. Light will win, for the lighted ones, the sacrificial ones, are endowed with the virtues of courage, perseverance, constancy and love. These eternal attributes of the soul will eventually overcome every obstacle, every resistance to God and His Perfect Will.

Ann Ree Colton has walked the Sacrificial Path for many lifetimes. She works with the Saints and Great Ones who also travel the Sacrificial Path. Because of these Great Souls, the progress of the world is assured through the increase of freedoms. However, one should never forget that each precious freedom is being won at the cost of martyrdoms, persecutions and afflictions.

Blessed is he who follows the example of the Pure Ones who are treading the Sacrificial Path. The Light of God is in his forehead, anointing him with the grace of understanding. The Love of God is in his heart, blessing him with fortitude, faith, guidance and soul-gifts. Receive freedom and lose it not. Cherish freedom and preserve it forever.

*

Over the years, Ann Ree Colton dictated to me many pages of manuscript that have been placed in her beautiful books. She also made numerous personal comments regarding the years of her life before we met, as well as observations related to our Apostolic Ministry as Founders of Niscience. Often, Ann Ree would provide me with explanations and prophecies pertaining to my progress as her student and co-worker; at times, she would preface these inspiring comments with the words: "This is from the Master." Her personal comments placed in this section of *The Pelican and the Chela* contain priceless knowledge related to the initiatory process; they also reveal the extraordinary versatility, wisdom and dedication of a Master Teacher.

Dates from our personal journals and diaries are given so that the reader can gain insights into important *cycles.* One who realizes that God creates in and through cycles has a distinct advantage in comprehending the creation-dramas of galaxies, stars, souls and lives. To know that everything is cyclic in origin and purpose enables one to work *with* God and to move in harmonious accord with His Will and Design.

The Teacher's task is to unlock the greatness in your soul.

A Solar Archetype
Ann Ree Colton, 1954

. . . Ann Ree Colton

15

1962–1973

Thousands of lives make an initiate; millions of years, a Master. The Masters, living in the eternal aspect of time, never grow impatient with their proteges. Sometimes the Master appears in meditative vision; or in crisis times of initiation the eyes of the Master may be seen, speaking a tender message, giving a counsel of strength and love. For there is no greater love outside of Christ than the love of the Master for his disciple. Beyond even the love of a mother, the Master loves, understands, and guides.

A Solar Archetype

The painting *A Solar Archetype* was painted in the city of Pasadena, California in the year of 1954. This painting describes the spherical Archetypal-Light action. The projection of light in color portrays the raying spherical light-spectrum of the Christ. The blue form in the center portrays the Archetone or the Holy Ghost sounding His Vibrational action, setting free the great Archetypal Hum or Word of God.

To understand and to respond to the Archetypal system of instruction is to be free. We who walk the Path today are more than mystical novices in light. As scientists we must look to Jesus, the great Manifestor, who used the mighty Archetypal ideas and powers to manifest the Will and Mind of God to the world.

When we see Jesus and His miraculous powers within the frame of the Greater Archetypes, we can see that He truly did make the Word flesh in us through His mighty channeling of the Word of God. Since His coming, we are destined to increase our soul-expansion and our minds' light, becoming more aware in each age of the Word through Him. With a great age such as we are now experiencing, we are looking beyond the storm of chaos, determining to hear His voice above all others speaking for the Word of God.

All souls of the Earth, all creatures, and all sentient and non-sentient life are presently undergoing a synthesis receptivity from the great and mighty Archetypes or the Word. The Word is once again being made flesh or manifested into the soul, mind, forms, names and actions of man as never seen before in the Earth.

Through epochal and cyclical action, the Word during great intervals is sent into the world to receptive minds. Receptive souls respond; men rise to greater heights to create with their Creator—God. It is the destiny of all that one must produce from what he is (spirit). The Word or Spirit of God during a greater synthesis Archetypal Time literally turns over the souls of men to compel them to do mighty and new creative things.

During a synthesis Archetypal Time, the Solar or Sun Archetypes flow into the souls of men, uniting them with the Time-Spirit or the *Ancient of Days.* All who have followed the Light respond to this Solar Archetypal Light. The Christ, the Son of God, makes Himself known to those who are vessels for the Light.

The age now before us is literally a "time and times." In this great new age, lasting 2500 years, men will learn of and use the energies of the soul, mind and planets, thus becoming masters of Time and Space. From this will come forth another Golden Age to the Earth and to man.

In these times, all resisting the Light will suffer; all resisting the Tone will come under the purging aspect of the Sound or the Great Vibration of the Holy Ghost. So does God reinforce His creation through and by His Word. All have the opportunity to rise and to be cleansed in preparation for the New Day.

When the Solar Archetype is quickened, this brings about the radical upsetting of decadent fixations. The Solar Archetype produces certain daring and creative inventive incentives until now dormant in the minds of men.

The Archetone within the Archetype sounds when the Archetype is ready for manifestation. The Spirit of Truth and the Holy Ghost stir and flood the upper planes of the Astral World or the First Heaven with ideas and pictures which fall into the minds of prophets, seers and advanced disciples; and this in turn produces the transcending changes in the outer life of the world.

I was first initiated into the Supreme or Greater Archetypes in December 1952 to January 1953 in the city of New York. The Archetypes unveiled their meaning to me, producing the System of Niscience.

1962

December 12, 1962. Ann Ree heard these words from the Master and saw light by Jonathan: "You are called as an Apostle, my son."

1968

August 3, 1968. Ann Ree from the Master: Faith is the jewel by which you can purchase the things of the spirit and not the things of the world. By faith, the spiritual molecules are mastered. Things or possessions are energies projected through spiritual faith, and are only retained if they are consecrated to and used for things of the spirit.

August 21, 1968. White Brother to Ann Ree for Jonathan: You are in need of a more philosophical attitude, which will give you acceptance of things as they are—and more flexibility. Inasmuch as you are going to open wider portals concerning religion, you must open the vein of philosophy, that you may have an overlook into the human affairs of men.

It is necessary to suffer for a time in every life to light the lamp of illumination, but to suffer all of the time produces a martyr. Your labors do not require martyrdom. They require sacrifice, endurance and survival; a whole perspective rather than a singular must be incorporated into the will and into the mind.

It is no longer a question of sorting out what was bad or what was good in your life. The question and the answer are both contained in your asking yourself: "What is asked of me? How may I best use and be used? What has been given to me?"

August 22, 1968. Carmel, California. Master to Ann Ree for Jonathan: Fear destroys the volatile juices of the body. You must deliberately cultivate a hopeful and optimistic spirit. You can take oceans of carrot juice and it will go only so far—you have to be cheerful and hopeful. One must eat and drink with a happy spirit, with a sacred spirit.

Man is never absent from taking food of some nature. Joy keeps this food alive as a vital energy which overcomes fatigue and poisons of the body. If you would use your mind to the uttermost and be in a state of mental and spiritual health, you should act the part of hopefulness, identifying yourself with joy.

You are not clinging to vanishing stones when you remain calm, joyful, hopefully expectant of the good of God in you and through you.

It is urgent that you know joy. It is urgent that you think on joyful things. It is also urgent that you feel joyful within your thinking.

The body is obedient to a joyful spirit. The body lies down as a tired horse when it has for a rider a depressed spirit. Take care that you do not in moments of depression attract a wrong rider for your horse or body.

Prepare to mount your horse or to live in your body as one who rises to the ramparts of the overlook. Having a chastened will, thou art mounted upon thy steed or living in thy body as the master of thy going.

*

August 23, 1968. Master to Ann Ree for Jonathan: Keep in mind your soul as a sun lighting the darkness of your sickness. This sun, as a serene blazing light, cleanses the effect and reveals the cause. From this is rectification for the tomorrow.

August 25, 1968. A. R. C to J. M.: You are now working to come under the *Divine Mother.* This will bring a new facet of the mind, a better memory.

August 27, 1968. Carmel. From the Master to Ann Ree for Jonathan: Keep the vision of the Word for the All-Seeing Eye or the Tone of God vibrating between the brows and acting as a searchlight searching out your affairs and beaming its light into the right path for your feet and your works. Never lose sight of this vibratory Eternal Hum, for this is God's tongue speaking to you—and also His searchlight in you.

It is superior to your vision—all men's vision being immature through the two eyes. One must depend upon the Eye and Word of God centered and sounding between his eyebrows. When this occurs, you tip the brain-mesh forward and light up the reasoning faculty with a higher reasoning. Not only in meditation must it be practiced intensely but all of the time—the feeling of seeing intensely and truly through this centered Eye and Word of God.

Your muscles are friends of the nerves. When they are placed on the shelf through inertia or misdirection, they are unsuitable supports for the nervous system. The emphasis of the psychic energy is thrown more heavily upon the nerve system—and finally the nerve system as an overcharged electrical wire blows a fuse; the result is debilitation of the body. If the muscular system is taken in hand through the practice of walking in Nature's environment, one slowly walks towards balance in health and in mind. As long as man can be on his feet, he should walk on the ground in Nature's environment.

Man is a running creature only to escape danger. It is his destiny to walk toward his goal rather than run toward his goal. To be in a constant state of running, mentally or physically, is to violate the ego-arteries or the glandular system.

Running towards one's goal injures the adrenal akasic will-center of the body. Walking is a rhythmic practice and should be accompanied by philosophical thoughts. This occurs when one makes a convenant to walk.

*

A mounted divine son is given food and is set forward on his journey, but he is never absent from Divine Mother.

August 30, 1968. Ann Ree to Jonathan, a talisman from Divine Mother to visualize before meditation: Before meditation, the Divine Mother will slip a jewelled ring on Jonathan's right forefinger. This is a talisman between you and Divine Mother. This will keep your thoughts steady during meditation and will keep the union steady with Divine

Mother. The jewels will change their shade from time to time in meditation. Seven jewels. Jonathan has now opened six starry portals of Divine-Mother power and initiation.

*

Ann Ree: The Divine Mother held Jonathan with her legs crossed, with Jonathan on her blue-sky life-ether lap. She had nestled him, and now he was being seven years old and weaving his first manhood garment of white fine linen. She had placed him on a young elephant. Jonathan had first insisted on riding the elephant with his back to the elephant's head. And she had picked him up and turned him around with his face looking toward the elephant. The elephant would henceforth beat a path through the fearful jungle of the world and of his senses. Jonathan has no need to fear the jungle, as the elephant is charged with Divine-Mother intelligence. Under her command, he will take Jonathan where Divine Mother bids.

Under the right arm of Jonathan are cakes of honey or morsels of life to feed him and to keep him strong.

Divine Mother sends her sons into manhood with strength. Her strength is in the life of her own. Jonathan is a son of Divine Mother. He will not stray, having henceforth six feet rather than two. The elephant, appearing two-three years old, will grow as Jonathan grows, into divine manhood.

Mantram to think or feel whenever Jonathan feels a rising tide of spiritual lifting. May be during meditation or during any other time of the day:

O Angels of the Star Portals
to Divine Mother,
Protect the Gates of my Illumination.

Divine Mother to Jonathan: Your soul-cry has been heard. You are breaking through now to a personal meditation, or to your Divine Ornanta nature—personal between you and Divine Mother. There will be an unending stream of guidance. This will be spiritual experience directly through your own Divine Ornanta nature. You have all of the other skills finished.

Ann Ree: You are entering into a divine-guru ministry. You are a divine son in the eyes of Divine Mother.

Divine Mother: Before this you have been trying to walk through the jungle of your senses—and he who tries to go through the jungle of the senses unmounted will be devoured by wild beasts. She who teaches you (Ann Ree) has always been mounted.

August 31, 1968. Carmel. Master M to Ann Ree for Jonathan: The ego has been partially off its axis. Now these actions are like pulling a switch; the ego will take command, absent from certain vanities. As the Divine Mother has a talisman ring, its main insignia being a circle, the Master places around your neck a talisman of protection—prayer beads—an *etheric protection necklace* of insulation.

Mars produces many energizing actions when on the ascendant. Mars now being active, it is no accident that martial music is being used to re-channel the will and to transcend it to spiritual will rather than physical force. It was physical force destroying your body. So many aggressive thrusts from the lower subconscious were destroying you. This pressure caused the ego to be tipped from its axis.

In the night and the day, the Mars stimulus is working to transcend. Only your prayers, devotions and meditations can make this possible.

An ego-caused sickness must be healed by the ego. Some of these aggressive tendencies came from the subterranean worlds, playing upon your sympathetic Plutoan temperament. This has been withdrawn now. The transcending has begun. On the day that you say, *"I am alive,"* with joy, your ego will have reassumed its theme.

August 31, 1968. Carmel. For Jonathan to use during Morning and Dusk Meditation. Meditate for a few mintues.

It can gradually be increased, but be careful as to tension or zeal.

1. Praise Chanting Mantrams—approximately five minutes; longer if desired, depending upon one's feeling making union.
2. Roll eyes upward toward top of skull, keeping lids closed.
3. Let the vision screen of the Divine Eye open the pineal gland. Remain so poised for a reasonably brief period, being careful to not lose consciousness. Be aware of everything seen. If so desirous, speak soft mantramic words, entreating the Divine Eye (God) to reveal Himself to you.
4. End transcendental exercise with deep inhalation of breath. Hold for a few seconds and exhale firmly. Be careful of tension in breathing.

   When you look up, you are looking right into God's Temple, into the Holy City. Each meditation will give off something that is Intelligible and of God.

To Jonathan: You are going to reawaken the horns of Moses.

With every vision you have in the City of God, there will be an equal phenomenon on the physical planes; there will be a counterpart manifestation on the physical planes. What you see in the City of God, you will see in the flesh in the world of man.

September 1–3, 1968. Carmel. From the Master to Ann Ree for Jonathan: You have now put on a belly-band (beautiful silk sash about ten inches wide) of insulation to protect you from the soiled, psychic probing and psychic ignorant thrusts.

The whirling pain in your body is psychic fire. When your pain or frustration has reached its total crisis peak, you will experience the Pentecostal flames of the Holy Ghost. This fire Ann Ree knew in 1951. You must now know it that you may teach.

You will practice each day before Ann Ree a portion of free logos. Your first subject under the Master is *God.* It will come freely with no intellect. This is the freeing fire. You will stand before her as if she is thousands of persons, and without mental self-consciousness you will speak to her of God. When you have completed speaking, kneel and pray, and your knee will be healed.

The only things standing between you now are mental reservations. These will be dissolved through God-Realization.

The Master says that Ann Ree's dispassionate attitude towards persons and towards her work will help you and her for the rest of the way. It will be the opener to the great floodgates in the work.

Your hands are being bathed in intense white spiritual fire. This fire is inside of your hands as well. This is going to be slowed down now so that it will be healing love. This white fire has been cauterizing you so as to consume the converging karma of many lives.

You will have *your* kind of illumination, which is your own divine-ego right as an identity under God. Also, you have speeded up your spiritual powers for ages. You are working to clear away karmic processes of future lives; as an illumined one, a divine son, you must be free of this karma. You are doing this with the assistance of Divine Mother.

This does not mean you cannot err. You will dissolve the erring processes in light as you go.

You have also been making a ring-pass-not to prevent the karma of others to weaken you, or even to distract you, so that you will be out of the range of being drawn into their karma. This is the most powerfully important issue of all in the present initiation.

You are working to have the dispassionate releasing so as to attain a level of healing beyond the level of healing consummated in the past. This does not mean indifference. It means that your Light will have greater power in its revealing and protecting aspect.

You are working with the composite medallion of the Masters. And it can be a different Master dependent upon what degree of karma you are working upon.

Your own dear Master initiates you in the morning, at dusk, and in the night. He wishes you to call him "Dear Master."

The interflow of ideas and pictures you will receive throughout the day and even throughout the night can come from any of the Masters, for each Master has a specific karmic remedy, that the initiate may dissolve the various facets of karma in converging-karma initiation.

You do not realize it now, but the time will come when you will be grateful for this experience and call it blessed.

Your mind is working towards acceleration and there must be care taken that there be not over-acceleration and become psychic and not spiritual. The regretful thoughts you have been having have in a way been putting a brake upon mental acceleration so that you will not become psychical rather than spiritual. When regrets have been drained off through the white-fire alchemy action, acceleration will be maintained without danger. From this will come deep wellsprings of inspiration and illumination.

Every hour beginning with arising, flex your right knee slowly ten times. Do this every hour for nine hours. Also, the hands must be shaken thoroughly ten times so as to change the contraclockwise fire into clockwise fire, that the etheric stigmata may be opened in the hands. Do this every hour for nine hours.

The condition of Jonathan's hands is caused by a lack of coordination between mind and hand. When your shoulders gave out, you ceased being a burden-bearer. You now work to be a burden-lifter through the Light; you cannot do it through your singular will.

In heaven there is one who weeps for joy for you, for she is being shown around the bend your true destiny. Henceforth, telepathies received from her will be less and less colored with astral electricity. Unconsciously, she damaged the nerve force of your body, playing upon your conscience and sympathetic nerve system. Now, a golden padlock locks away that side of her nature from you. In her Chinese memory of a former life, when you were her little son, she returned to the reverence for the masculine judgment, which she had lost in this life. She sees the masculine judgment in you as mature now. She will help you to trust yourself and to trust in your judgment. This is part of her healing mission for you.

You are now working to develop *audience magnetism*—whether to the hearer or to the reader. Your emotions previously being covered with restraints, karmic and emotional, are now moving out of the self-sensitive antenna range into the mass antenna range. To acquire this aptitude and to use all of its accompanying gift aspects, one must raise the total nerve system and muscular system of the body into higher frequencies.

The transitory period you now experience is initiatory, designed to perfect three vital Gifts, that you may serve with authority, with poise: Healing, Speaking, Teaching. Your teaching will have contributory aspects—Writing, Painting. All are interrelated.

An initiate who is not honest with himself weights down the magnetism in the lower part of his body. It can neither feed him nor feed others for any lasting period of time. Magnetism working with the adhering nature of ether must be used by one who is removed from certain self-centered interests.

The weight of magnetism went into your feet due to a desire to excel through the muscles rather than the mind. An initiate learns that all parts of one's nature are sacred and uses them in a balanced moderation. You have not gone too far out that you cannot be retrieved.

Your ego is now centered in its highest aspect. You have acquired the first virtue on a higher level—humility, teachableness.

All you have suffered is of the personal ego. The inner self wishes to keep you polarized to the Higher Self. The inner self is your higher ego. Your Higher Self is your Eternal Self.

September 5, 1968. From the Dear Master to Ann Ree for Jonathan: When the true Master has drawn the disciple to his heart, there can be no severance. I have drawn you. Resisting the Master's heart is painful. The Master's heart must reveal itself to the disciple, for the Master, too, has walked in the same path of pain, suffering. Having mastered these things, it is my work to teach you how to master them. Return to the dance of your spirit. Return to the joy of your living. Return to the eagerness of new discovering. The self that would cast you in gloom is not the real in you.

Close the fingers of your hand if you would catch some of the rainfall of wisdom from the Master, that you might drink of it, bathe in it, and be healed by it.

It is not an offense when you ask me to heal you. It is merely your weakness reaching for my strength, that you may recover your strength.

To keep in your mind a steadfast thought that you may be healed through psychic intervention of being healed out of timing would be of error. To keep in your mind the thought that from my knowledge I may give you certain knowledge you have yet to attain concerning your weakness, this is of good. In a kindling blast, these right-proportion thoughts come to the one who suffers. You will receive them. Such healing does not patch up the condition. It is a firm remedial action between subconscious reflexes which are the direct cause of your sickness.

Divine Mother in command of the unconscious has through your prayers made your unconscious as a cleansing oil, that the fires of your spirit may use the subconscious and give to you an instantaneous ignition guidance.

Do not expect your powers to be the same as the one who walks with you. Your powers will be a unique harvest gathered from the spirit of service over the ages.

The spirit of service in you will not be denied. It is your vocation and avocation to serve God.

Dwell upon your own unique fitness in the sense of being willing to serve God. In this manner you will melt away the block of your sense of being foolish or unprepared or inadequate.

Trust in divine selection which has chosen you to keep strong the ramparts supporting the household of the spirit. The white stone is once again being glossed and polished in the inner planes that it may speak in your forehead and mind of the Real.

*

When you have the feeling that you have not gone far enough to make union, this is the sign that you should prolong the act of meditation. Meditation is an intuitive spiritual action. The one meditating should remove the tension in his thoughts while longing to make union with the Divine through a tender devotion and inoffensive contemplation.

The very thirst for a prolonged meditation should be an intuitive function between the disciple and the Master. He should not expect each meditation to be the same. No two phases of meditation are ever alike. One will find that each meditation offers something different.

During meditation, keep firmly in the mind a soft willing, avoiding forcefulness. The soft devotional approach to meditation is as a shrine bed of roses laid upon the altar of inspiration and illumination.

God desires to speak in your mind. Prepare yourself to hear Him by stilling the will clamors of your little fears and doubts. With mind-stilledness, subdue all intellectual questionings or queries or curiosity during the state of meditation.

One cannot remember at first what he experiences in devotional meditation; in time, with the Divine Mother's assistance, he will remember deeply what has been given in meditation. From such memory will come the parabolic or symbolic chain technique.

True vision in meditation contains many molecular energized thoughts of Divinity; so is one instructed in the moments and hours after each meditation.

September 29, 1968. Ann Ree to Jonathan: The Ikhnaton life has changed its clutches on you now. It has changed to *I WILL LIVE.*

Your emotions have affected your circulation. You must have no regrets or self-reproaches or blame anyone or anything.

The Ikhnaton life has left its sediment of seeing a God-centered faith as necessary of the one God.

In your meditation, you must make union with God. You must find self-realization of your own creation, pushing aside the belief of inadequacy, which is also a form of egotism.

You must identify yourself with your own creation. And you must claim to defend the right to create through your own identity. You had to choose either to give up or to get up. You have chosen to get up.

October 6, 1968. Carmel. Ann Ree to Jonathan: You are presently working for Divine Intuition. This Divine Intuition will be enlarged more and more.

You are preparing to inherit Ann Ree's Mantle in the next twelve years. What you are going through now is a small price to pay for the Gift to be given you. You are a fish caught by the Christ. Men will eat of you (means your Divine Intuition).

October 8, 1968. Master to Ann Ree for Jonathan: You will be a "pole vaulter of the spirit."

November 7, 1968. Ann Ree saw the Disciple paintings by Jonathan become an electrical vibration in all of their mixed powers. This electrical power moved toward Jonathan's feet, and she was told that Jesus was washing his feet—preparing him for the Holy Ghost.

November 8, 1968. Meditation vision: Jonathan is now under the disciple John and is being given "tarrying" longevity; he is going to write under the Christ.

Jonathan's Recording Angel to Ann Ree: Jonathan must keep his Bible always in his hands that he might incorporate the disciple powers and be in direct contact with the Holy Ghost.

November 16, 1968. The Master to Ann Ree for Jonathan: It is the ethic of the Master to show two choices to the disciple through which he may evolve. He showed to Jonathan the choice of suffering of the body or of harmfulness to the soul. Jonathan chose suffering of the body rather than harmfulness to the soul, as did all great sages, martyrs and the apostles choose suffering of the body rather than a blemish upon the soul.

Suffering is sweet when it leads to the door of spiritual liberation. All saints know this, brother.

Be aware of the saintly holy comforts in this time; yield not thyself up to self-condemnation, for thou didst choose this way rather than the way of soul torment coming from miseries self-inflicted by lust and sensuality.

November 1968. Vision by Ann Ree: Jonathan is now working with an emotional atom—to enlarge and expand the emotional atom so that he can expand his emotions to the whole embodiment of the work.

December 17, 1968. The Holy Ghost to Ann Ree for Jonathan: Thy sins are forgiven thee. The Father will use your contrite heart on the Altar. The flowering of the Ministry begins with your taking up your true Ministry on the Altar.

Prophecy from the Holy Ghost for Jonathan's work: This is the house of Israel raised up unto Christ—a new religion for a new generation. He who enters into my holy place has been given the sign of the covenant. And he will keep the covenant with a light perpetual within his heart and within his loins. Thou hast been working to keep the light of thy loins equal to the covenant of thy heart.

When the sands of thy undoing have fallen from the glass, which is now toward its ending, thy doing shall encompass the very Earth in this ministry. Thou art a workman for God. Until thy chaste mantle is complete, the Lord Jesus Himself and the Angel of Light shall cover you with the mantle of chastity.

By holy absorption you shall become free. And even as a virgin of chastity, thou shalt serve the Lord.

The wood is cut down ready for the fire and the flame, to be made into ash. From ashes man makes a new beginning, and rises up as the phoenix bird.

Behold, the cloak of prophecy has come upon you. Only one thin veil of your own fears obscures the cloak of prophecy.

The heat in thy nostrils and the heat in thy private parts are the hand of the Holy Ghost cleansing thee in the fiery furnace to transmit the energies of thought and draw upon the sacral fire as a blower's torch. The cavity portals of outgoing light are being blown open.

Your only sin now is despair and self-denigration. Now the Angels wash your body in the lavas of a fresh spring, singing and cleansing.

(Next refers to Jonathan's dream of small indefinable print.) The inscription last night in dream will increase

until thou hast received the total scroll of thy pleureferent destiny.

Thou couldst not have served the Lord's Altar save thou didst experience the past months: thy fall was a fall in part. But thou didst have a string to keep thee over the precipice so that thou wilt not go into the chasm. Thou art now on the trembling edge of return.

Behold the crucible fire which maketh thee into a transcendent man and the insensible irritants which seem to be real shall fall away into nothingness—and thou shalt be erect as a whole man for God.

The Ark of the Covenant has returned to the Earth. It now is resting on the Niscience Altar. The Cherubim watch over this Ark; and thou art the Aaron high priest: To reinstate it to the people that the Messiah did come and dwelleth as Light in the world.

When dark thoughts come, speak the words of Michael: "May the Lord rebuke thee."

No matter what, the fire in your private parts, in your forehead and in the feet is being used to initiate you—for the working of the selfsame Spirit.

1969

August 22, 1969. Saratoga, California. Jesus appeared to Ann Ree for Jonathan: To you, J. M., He is the simple Jesus. He appeared to me as your paintings show Him. You are to be in your life under Jesus a combination of Schweitzer and Saint Francis.

In this moment of rebirth, He touched your spleen; rays of His light went all around your spleen. And He gave you His life into your body. You became co-atom to Jesus. Your etheric body was healed and set into a new course. Jesus' face transfigured over your face—and then followed a blessing from Mary, from the Great Angel. The Saints put a crown on you. From your Mentor Master, you received a blue indigo jewel out of your mouth and it was also part of your mind. In the background the Angels kept singing: "Holy. Holy. Holy."

August 22nd is to be commemorated all of your life as the time you had your new birth. Your mantle has been fused in. You have disconnected the old umbilical cord with Jehovah. A radiant life of bread substance—spiritual substance—rather than a stone.

Jesus changed the blood pictures in your spleen. He changed them over from the ancestral-blood-pictures responses into the great Apostolic pictures and the higher responses.

1972

Ann Ree to Jonathan: The Master's Light has supervised our lives for twenty years. We have built a future for hundreds of persons. To our best ability we have fulfilled. We have not regretted these years in the Master's Light. He has opened worlds to us never considered in our mortal minds. He has made the invisible visible. And through His encouragement we have made the impossible possible.

*

In the year of 1922 in New York City, I was in the living room in the evening. My two children were seated at the table with me; the younger was in her high-chair. I was working on a painting under the direction of the Master. When the Shabd or Holy Sound of the Holy Ghost occurred, the curtains draped back between the dining room and the living room were lifted up by great gusts of the Holy Wind, and the sound of the Holy Ghost or Audible Current was heard by my children and myself. The sound articulated itself as an "OOoooooM." It filled the room and moved around the room. This sound terrified my children and filled me with tremendous light.

The Holy Spirit works through the body of the Holy Ghost.

Another time I was at the Rosicrucian Fellowship in Oceanside, California, and the Great Sound Current penetrated my eyebrow center, charging me with a thunderous roar. I was blessed and charged in all of the currents of my body. My vision was clarified.

May 14, 1972. Six sacred songs were received inspirationally by Jonathan during a 3:00 A.M. prayer in the Chapel in Glendale, California. Ann Ree made the following comments regarding the spiritual significance of each new song:

These six songs are the steps of Initiation into God-Realization. To listen to and follow this sequential flow of music by Jonathan Murro is to share his God-Realization Illumination experience. The soul opening with the six phases of music provides the steps of union with God.

1. JESUS, O JESUS . . . *Jonathan's agony-cry and petition to Jesus is a prayer spoken out of the soul hunger to unite with God.*

2. ALMIGHTY GOD . . . *In phase two, God is realized as Almighty, as the Power in all. The soul in Jonathan Murro becomes as a mighty cathedral resounding the Omnipresence as Reality within Infinity.*

3. MY HEART HAS SUNG A SAD SONG . . . *Phase three: the cleansing of the past and the reminder of the suffering on the ladder of initiation are experienced as a necessity, for the death-pangs of the undersoul must be, that the fire for the Light of the soul be made perfect. When the fire of the undersoul reaches the ulti-*

mate Light, the troubled heart comes to peace; the mind becomes as steel clear of the clouds of passion and fear.

4. MY PEACE . . . *Initiation into God-Realization demands supernatural struggle involving the subliminal powers in consciousness. Peace comes to Jonathan through Jesus, the Lord of Peace. In this phase, Jonathan has surrendered; peace through Jesus falls upon the fevered past—cooling, healing.*

5. THE LORD IS IN HIS HOLY TEMPLE . . . *Omnipresence is realized through the Holy Spirit. The joy-cry of a soul housed as a worshipper of God gives the knowledge of the Omnipotence of God and the need to adore Him.*

6. GOD BE WITH YOU . . . *The blessing of God flows through Jonathan. He is now God-Realized. Henceforth, all who come into his proximity will receive this unending blessing.*

> *To hear, to heed, is to experience, and enter into the Eternal. By music, God speaks His Creation. By the sound made holy in the temple of the soul, His Word is made flesh. Amen.* *

1973

On Sunday, August 12, 1973, while conducting a worship service in the Chapel of the Jesus Ethic in Glendale, California, Ann Ree experienced a Levitation Miracle. As her

*The six songs received inspirationally by Jonathan Murro are on the long-playing phonograph record *"On This Star-Filled Night."* Ann Ree Colton Foundation, Post Office Box 2057, Glendale, California, 91209.

physical body arose in the air, her legs and feet moved over her head in a total arc; then she landed on her back in the aisle of the Chapel several feet away from her original position. Ann Ree gave the following description of her experience:

> First, I saw Jesus coming up through the floor in front of the marble altar. The floor looked like a drawbridge being lifted up. The open side of it was facing the East. The radiating Christ Light was so powerful in my body that it overpowered me and took me out of consciousness. As I arose over the prie dieu, I totally blacked out.
>
> Then I saw inwardly a great golden circle in front of me—and the force pulled me into the golden circle. The golden circle was filled with little wheatlike grains of light with shimmering light around each one. The outer rim of the circle was colored with a beautiful indigo blue. The circle of light was of the Christ, and I was protected in my fall. This was both a physical and spiritual phenomenon.
>
> I was not aware of falling or how I fell. It was said by those who saw me that I was lifted up in an arc over the prie dieu. My feet did not touch the prie dieu.
>
> When I awakened, I was on the floor of the aisle. Then I was moved to one of the benches where I rested and listened to Jonathan's sermon. I felt that I wanted to get up at the end of his speaking and give the benediction mantram. Then I went into a regular faint at the lectern.
>
> The Christ on this day took command of all our souls. He used my body to demonstrate His power physically and spiritually. This occurred on August 12, three days before the birth date of Mary, the Mother of our Lord.
>
> When I came to and was lifted up, I looked into the faces of all who were looking at me. Everyone appeared to be dressed in pink clothing.

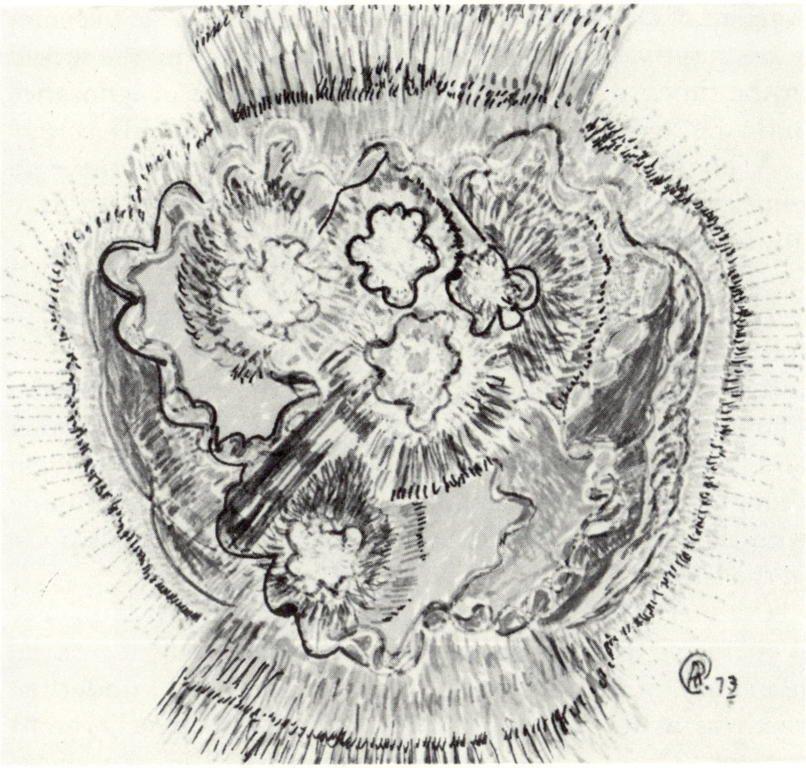

Step Beyond Gravity
Ann Ree Colton, 1973
Painted after Levitation Miracle

August 19, 1973. In 1946 the Ancient of Days appeared to my upward gaze. He floated as on a cloud of clear, white light. His face was radiant with a jewel-like shining. His features were benevolent, relaxed, yet smiling. He was bearded with a white, snowlike beard. His eyes were blue as the sky.

I was initiated into vows, promises and timing, and the telling of truth, that I might become a witness of holy things. When one is graduated from the school of the

Ancient of Days, he becomes more that witness, he becomes a bodhisattva-presence fated to reincarnate in the world in the times of stress. He becomes a deliverer of ignorance and an instrument to shorten the time in karmic suffering.

A bodhisattva takes the vow that he will continue to reincarnate into the world until all men of the earth have attained salvation.

*

In 1946, I had an out-of-the-body experience while in full consciousness, and went to the North Pole and there received the great Northern lights and their universal tone-sounds into my body. After this, I went to Pennsylvania and began my assembling of the Niscience Archetypal thoughts. I walked the hills of Pennsylvania communing with the grandeur of the Cosmos, categorizing man's place in the Universe as a universal being.

October 17, 1973. The Master shows me that Niscience is operating to a Universal scale rather than to the terrestrial planetary, Sun and Moon scale. It has been kept under the earth as a universal seed responding to many Hierarchy systems. Thus, it has remained under earth in its roots to come forth to flower and to give fruits instantly to the need of a cosmic era and generation.

Niscience is cosmically regulated by Hierarchy, as are all true systems of teachings that come to release Archetypal flows of knowledge and spiritual power.

Hierarchy in other eternity systems work in combined light-sending to stimulate and give birth to new phases of Archetypal power in a new eternity system. Thus, Earth is a younger eternity system.

The coordinating Hierarchs or Overlords working with this eternity system work with Jesus, its selected World-Saviour, the Christ Spirit and the Father to bring to man a mental and spiritual identity only to be obtained in this Earth system. The time is now ripe for the cosmic era. In this, old governings and institutions are to be eliminated. Every man's light must become a part of the Universal light.

Niscience is the blueprint for the coming cosmic man. The Niscience educational, philosophical techniques will be used as a blueprint for systems of instruction. The blueprint for worship and devotion is now being inscribed into the receptive souls through the Niscience method.

The ethic upholding this system based upon the Ethic of Jesus will keep the roots of Niscience steady and firm, assuring their birth and their resulting fruits of a good, harmonious, natural and healthy spirit. Only in the spirit of Agape or holy concern for one's fellow man can there be a true religion and education.

16

1974–1979

August 16, 1974, the day before Ann Ree's 76th birthday: Niscience is a gift of the 20th Century. My work has been to bring the Light, to clarify Scripture, and to unite souls.

In every century there must be a link added to the knowledge of reincarnation. Madame Blavatsky gave the knowledge of reincarnation related to the 19th Century. Until each person of the Earth knows he is a reincarnating soul, he is a floating unit of gravity sensuousness and materiality.

The universal whole is speaking unto us through Niscience, Knowing. The scars of estrangement are to be healed.

Niscience comes to provide the 20th Century with the impetus for the new era, that the souls coming forth to birth may probe the Eternals within themselves and within all worlds.

I have been in this world 75 years. Tomorrow I will be 76. I have lived three-quarters of a century. Tomorrow I will be moving toward the goal of 100 years.

I have walked with the Masters. I have sat at their feet. I have made union with the greatest Master of all—Jesus.

It has been my grace to see the East and the West as blended through the Christ.

Bodies of worship failing to recognize the true powers of Mediation are empty shells serving only ecclesiastical ambition.

As I move toward the ending of a century as a person, I see that these old decaying forms are ending. The true charisma and glossolalia shall return. The original vertebra of worship established in Ephesus by Saint John the Beloved, where miracles were consummated through faith and transcendental powers, is once again coming forth. The Angels over the churches through Jesus once more have placed the church on trial, for in this new era, ". . . unto me every knee shall bow . . ." (Isaiah 45:23) through Christ, our Lord.

November 17, 1974. While in the hospital in Glendale, California.

MY PRAYER

O Lord, forgive me, for I am a sinner.
My greatest sin is spiritual ignorance.
Let me enter into Thy Paradise of grace
And good and purity.

My sins in Thy sight are forgiven.
I am not condemned or judged by any save Thee.
Thy Love looks into my heart and shines its
Wisdom for my beginning and my ending.

Let Him who is the Shepherd King bear me up,
that I may endure through love and strength.

May I forever keep a forgiving heart,
That I may walk with joy in this life and
In all lives to come.

November 19, 1974. There is no mind in this earth able to interpret God totally except Jesus. Any one who claims that he can is filled with ego-pride. THIS IS A SPIRITUAL SIN. I remind myself so I will not be tempted to have it. To me, a sin is unknowing.

When I find myself in any way not using the total of what God has given, I can be tempted. You have to empty your ego before God can come in. There can be no guidance or direction or willing of God until you have emptied yourself entirely of the ego.

I have not reached the state of perfection where I am absent from error. Every person must learn—and he only learns from making mistakes.

If I were to say I was a perfect being, I would be the greatest of sinners. I always prepare my prayers and consecrations for Sacrament with: "Father, have mercy on me, for I am a sinner." But I do not feel myself unworthy or in a state of guilt, nor do I dwell on my errors. I look upon my errors as concealed blessings, for through them I have been taught to forgive others and also how to know that God is my Solution and True Teacher.

The word *sin* means moon or illusion. When a person is in the moon state of the ego, he thinks that he does everything himself. He is in a state of sin.

Jesus was *sent* down. We *come* down. This is the difference between incarnating souls. When a person is one who comes down, he involves himself in the world as a sinner. This is the state of *Maya.*

Man who has shaded aspects to his soul-record sins and is sinned against in the world of Maya.

There is a grace state before death where one, by acknowledgement of error and unknowing, can clean his record of sin of the past.

It is not only necessary through meditation to prevent one's sinning in future lives, it is also necessary before entering the last phases of life to ask simply and humbly as a little child—while in a state of pure soul-knowing—for forgiveness for unknowing and knowing transgressions, and thus acknowledge the wrongdoing in former lives as well as the wrongdoing in this one. The heavy weight of imperfection falls away in this time, and one steps forth free of bondage to sin of Maya-relativity.

All Great Souls must clear their record in the ending of each life. It is this portion of greatness in each soul which enables the one dying and the one reaching forth to new birth to bring the pure white Light, as did Jesus.

When persons are weighted down by the shadow of past lives, it is inevitable that they return to commit the same sins over and over in each life. Jesus came to free us from Maya. It is not enough that Jesus knows this; we also must know it.

Mastery over the law of relativity moves us out into a degree of light beyond Maya. This is the Omnisphere of the Christ, where the Omnitron Light gives a perspective into dimensions beyond the hypnotic compulsions of returning and of repetition.

We are here in this world of Maya to master its relativity processes. We can only do this when we give good for evil, love for hate, light for spiritual darkness.

December, 1974. While in hospital. I was shown the two egos I had been in the two previous lives. They were consumed in total light, and issuing forth from them was a golden, radiant light. These lives were transformed into total radiance.

Because I have reincarnated so quickly between the last three lives, discarnate shells of the past two lives remained with me, hissing discordant impulses upon my consciousness during periods between initiations. When the sound became so intensely painful, the present body was affected; and each time when I was initiated, I dissolved something of these shells. Now, with this present initiation in which I have discovered the great Omnitron Light and its spiritual calm and joy, the experience of transenergization over these two past lives gives me the freedom for my future labors.

The grace extraction has been made. My Sattva Guru, Radiant Master, and all of those in the chain of Gurus whom I represent are free to touch all of those who seek liberation in the Omnitron Light.

*

Through one of the proteges of Saint Rose who bore her name, I was used as a healing channel to heal an impossible disease of the blood. A woman by the name of Rose from Peru was brought to my attention in a request for healing. She was healed of a critical blood sickness. In her gratitude, she invoked Saint Rose. On her return to Peru, she made a novena on the Catholic altar—and sent me a silver medal of Saint Rose she had worn since birth.

During this period of time, I also received an actual manifestation of a physical gold medal, miniature in size; finding it at my feet, I saw it to be a medal of Mary and Jesus. From this, I made union with Saint Rose, and was told that she was my Patron Saint.

Saint Rose has appeared to me in many manifestations of healing since this time.

1976

April 16, 1976. Ann Ree to Jonathan. You have twelve very strong years which are the root-shower. You will be 62 when there is real culmination of all the gifts that you have worked out and established.

May 4, 1976. On the 10-year and 20-year cycles in her life, and the Holy Ghost: In my 23rd year, I united with the *wind* of the Holy Ghost and with the Sound Current of the Holy Ghost.

In my 33rd year, I united with the directive from the Holy Ghost that I was to be the instrument for the white magic to overcome the black magic within ceremonial magic and superstition.

In my 43rd year, I received the Holy Ghost and experienced the *Initiation of the Wilderness.* In my 43rd year, I united with the Ancient of Days. I experienced soul-illumination and moved out of Time and Space, and began to be instructed by the Great Archetypes supported by the Christ.

In my 53rd year, I experienced and received from the Holy Ghost Archetones and Archetypes the beginning of the System of Niscience.

In my 63rd year, I had a major initiation in a heart attack. This began the first stages of the distribution of powers and gifts through the work of the Holy Spirit upon the Ministry. The composite body of devotees and initiates began their initiations for the use of their gifts and for the support of the Archetypal instruction whereby the religious impulses of the world would be purified.

In my 73rd year, a second heart attack produced more direct manifestation of gifts, spiritual powers, dedication and manifestation within the Ministry. The accumulative creativity, talents and application of the rhythms and practices, the research into the vortice-pools—or myths, symbols and rituals within all religions and religious impulses—began to produce its productivity.

The general public began its response to the fermenting action within the united soul-powers and gifts of those dedicated to the System of Niscience, its methods, practices and presentation. Tested stewards stood firm; perseverance and devotion attracted to the axis-center of Niscience more and more souls having recognition of the quality, versatility and confirming-truths within the System.

My 73rd year was followed by a levitation experience near the Altar in the presence of approximately 100 people who witnessed this miraculous event. I proved that we are not gravity-bound creatures while living in the body. When I had the levitation, the Christ literally raised the Niscienes from the dead. I saw our Chapel taken up from its foundation and shaken—and it re-settled again with more porous openings to support the Power of God.

July 13, 1976. Commenting on her ministry in Florida during her 30's and 40's: There was not a person who left my office that I did not give a spiritual interpretation of his karma. The more spiritual I became, the less they could stand what I had to say.

Fear and hate are companions. And their fear of the truth about themselves attracted to me enemies who persecuted me. Among these were persons who were karmic pawns in my initiatory dissolution process.

December 25, 1976. Christmas. I have three vices, which are virtues in disguise:

I love to serve God.
My love for my husband.
I love to read.

1977

April 9, 1977. It took me 55 years before people were kind to me with my gifts. Until that time, I went through a cruel inquisition regarding my spiritual gifts. I certainly paid back the Blavatsky-karma in full, full measure.

July 17, 1977. Ann Ree for Jonathan from the Master: He who goeth into the pit in the spirit of sacrifice shall rise up sanctified.

October, 1977. Regarding the time A.R.C. left Florida in 1946 and went to Santa Barbara, California: The world as a cannibal was eating me up alive for my prophetic powers, and I was finished. I was absolutely walking out on everything and everybody. I burned my files and everything connected with the past.

Commenting on her hearing the words "You are loved," while in the water in the Gulf of Mexico in 1946: When I was told "You are loved," that was the *Bhakti Anointing.*

*

From 1926 to 1946 I went through a 20-year Kali Cycle of paying off karmic debts.

December 30, 1977. Ann Ree to Jonathan. It was *soul* recognition that brought us to marriage.

1978

January 2. Santa Barbara. Ann Ree to Jonathan on his writings on Virtue: The last thing people think on now is virtue, but later they will need it as they need air.

January 12. The *amazings* are beginning to happen.

February 22. While in Florida visiting her daughter and some of her grandchildren and great grandchildren. I am intoxicated with happiness.

March 10. After visiting Washington, D.C. Washington is like a hen sitting on a glass egg, thinking it is going to hatch chickens.

June 24. I left New York City on January 1, 1926. I finished my ministry in Florida on January 6, 1946. Then I established the Chapel in Glendale, California in 1966.

Ann Ree Colton, East Coast Conclave, State College, Pennsylvania.

July 3. Carmel. Ann Ree to Jonathan: Your whole initiation was the mastery of Voltage, to gain the Transcendental.

July 5. New Moon: The Master appeared to me in the upper Northeast portion of the United States—and he showed me the Niscience instruction in all the States.

July 13. As the scientist understands the genetic-chain, I understand the Galaxy-chain. I teach through the Galaxy Universals. I have the Galaxy Consciousness.

July 14. I feel young. I feel the joy of youngness. I feel the enthusiasm of the Esse.

July 20. Ann Ree to Jonathan: What we have accomplished has been out of pure guts and God.

July 24. It has been a very interesting life.

September 1978. Ann Ree to Jonathan: You are a cosmos evangelist.

September 10. In my past life, I let everybody talk for me. In this life, I talk for everybody else.

*

I was 25 years old when the Master said to me: "You are chosen." But it took me until my 56th year to be totally centered in the Voltage. This is when the System of Niscience formulated. Since my 56th year, I have been working to expand more and more this Centering, and to be completely immersed in the dynamics of the Superconsciousness.

Each moment of my life, since union with the Niscience Archetype, has been one of constant revelation. I am always in the midst of the miraculous. From this Centering, I teach and heal.

It is my work now to take hold firmly of the Archetypal Light, to make myself each day a better vehicle or conduit for the Archetypal Light. In my darkest times of this life, and in the memory-processes of former lives, I have never been absent from faith in God.

In this birth of the present life, I knew my Saviour, Jesus. I talked with Him often. I saw Him. In major and minor things in my life, He visited me. I saw Him in vision. I experienced His voice.

Lower-Devachan impressionability—so strong upon my stubborn self-will nature—I did not always obey Him, but He never forsook me. In one grand accumulation of grace, it was the Will of God for me to break through into freedom of the Knowing or Niscience.

He who reads my books with a heart open to spiritual experience will walk with me on the Path and experience God after his own native soul-potential. My books were given to me as a gift for the many who seek to rise beyond the delusive states of sin and sorrow.

Every book written by me supporting the Niscience System, which is an initiatory school, was given from the Realm of Light where dwells the Lord Jesus, the Archangels, the Christed Light, the Archetypes.

My first book I wrote in the Akashic Light beyond the reaches of the lower Devachanic suggestibles.

In my last life, I wrote through the reflected light of the Archetypes in the fourth plane of the astral world. These writings were true writings, as they were given to me in the Tibetan polarity of the Great-Immortal Masters. While visiting and being apprenticed through Initiation by these Masters, the true secret doctrine as passed on by Tibetan Masters was indented into the banked recordings within my etheric brain.

The reflected Archetypal Light, as expressed through me in books for the world, was experienced by me not as my own personal living initiatory experience in that previous life. Every day as I wrote these books, the banked recording of the secret doctrine was opened in a form of clairaudient, clairsentient and clairvoyant dictation. That which I wrote was spoken to me while I experienced in the great Himalayas the induction.

As a stream of revelation, this knowledge flowed into the reservoir-retentions of the banked recording. Thus, I became a vehicle to give to the Western world the true knowledge of the initiatory processes in this world where each soul may be led to the ultimate of direct revelation through his experience and union with God, the One.

In this life, through the process of overcoming my past-life inherited Devachanic inclinations, I have mastered the Devachan planes both low and high. There are no words to describe the bliss-joys I receive from the higher Devachan beings or Shining Spirits. These Great Devas are peace-beings of joy to the one who has reached their shores of shining purity and spirituality.

The Bodhisattva Light dwells in the higher Deva Planes of the astral. Buddha functions in the inner worlds at this time through the Great Shining-Spirit Deva Light. In the Christian theology, the higher Deva Planes are called *Heaven.* In true terminology, the Deva Planes are, in reality, the First Heaven.

September 24, 1978. Sometimes you have pseudo-bliss in meditation; and sometimes you have genuine bliss. The Teachers tell you that if you are having pseudo-bliss, enjoy it.

September 25, 1978. Post-sleep or A.M. arising visions and assurances from Omnipresence: Gave my day to God. Saw visions of happy Saints on right side in front of me. I felt strength that they were supporting my feeble trying. I am especially aware that I must accept the ones who are sent regardless of their soil and ignorance as to morality. Somehow, I must gather up the strength to teach these in their kind of weakness which is *moral weakness* rather than physical.

September 25, 1978. Afternoon post-nap vision: I saw J. M. and myself dressed in gray wool cloaks, knee-length, gray color. We were walking south on a narrow path. We were very close together, melted into one another as one body. Our bodies suffused in blood; we were walking as pilgrims in blended martyred blood. I knew this later to be a recollection of many former lives together when we had given all to God and were martyred. It was an old story—no accident that we are together now. The pilgrim's blood

1978 Christmas letter handwritten by Ann Ree:

Christmas!

Christ Jesus Our Lord.

We long for thee Jesus
and seek thee on this day of thy coming
to birth in earth.

Renew us.
Receive us.
Bless us.

Thy crib and thy bassinette in the manger
is our Temple-refuge.

Be with us
Anoint us.
Reassure us.

On thy sacred day

Free us
Reveal to us
Thy Star.

That we may chart our course
toward thy love....

Merry Christmas Beloved [illegible]

Ann Ree . Jonathan
and by our fellow disciples

is now grace. As one identity we are walking; as one blood we give.

September 26, 1978. Awakened refreshed with *will-resolutions* toward service to God. Was reminded in Bindu Chakra flow or banked recording of the former dragonfly absorption experience while in "Esse state" last spring. I *became* in that time the dragonfly, etc.

This morning I experienced the meaning of the power and energy released in me through "being" the dragonfly. I became a dragonfly again. The sound of the Hum of the dragonfly became the Hum in me. I united with the Audible Hum and experienced the movement ecstasy of the Esse as vibrational sound of God in all life forms, sentient and conscient.

October 5, 1978. 2:30 A.M. Sitting on side of bed for two hours. Said Jesus Prayer repeatedly with Pilgrim Posture: chin on chest looking down on my heart, saying, "Lord Christ Jesus, Son of God, have mercy on us," sometimes using "on me." Experienced a crown of gold with emeralds—large stones—placed on my head over the crown. While I spoke the Mantra, a scene appeared painted by El Greco of Jesus, Mary, Saints, Angels, except they were not static, they were moving. I experienced a great, a holy joy. Felt it connected with Pope John Paul, who recently died and was rising into higher dimensions of Light through victory over death. Over my head extremely high was a scene of glorious color.

Noon Meditation: Experienced Archangel energy going before me preparing the way for my teaching in Monterey. The energy was like trillions of bees humming, synchronized molecules providing a body for me to work in. Praise, Praise God.

October 21, 1978. 8:30 A.M. San Francisco, California. Ann Ree said to Jonathan: "This is my little nugget for you." Then she spoke the following words on Virtue-Beauty:

The most wholesome beauty is virtue-beauty. Virtue-beauty is the beauty of the soul emergence into the whole of life, producing a whole person.

Virtue-beauty is centered in mortal and immortal goodness shining forth upon the countenance, the movements of the body and the expression of the person.

The lamp of grace keeps alive virtue-beauty. It spreads as a hope and a blessing upon everyone and everything.

Anyone containing any form of conceit or inflation of ego is devoid of virtue-beauty.

The deep, sweet memories of a beloved face, of a beloved deed, passed on from a pure soul leaves the undying mark of good which all crave, desire and hope for.

Ten minutes later, Ann Ree gave a blessing to Jonathan for his forthcoming 51st birthday. She titled the words of the blessing "Initiate's Poem," and said "To my Scorpion, a mighty prophecy":

Rise up, O eagle.
You have vaulted the exalted places.
You have seen into the crevices of men's hearts.
Your beak has plucked the seed from the fertile earth
    that the soul of man may come to birth.
With your eye fixed upon the illustrious Sun,
    you have seen the beginning and ending
    of things to come.

No season or cycle shall stay your flight.
No blight or twisting shall delay your right
    to rise, to climb, to overlook.

Behold, O Scorpio, the mystic scroll
    in thy eagle claws to be unrolled.

Before the gaze of all—
from East to West, from North to South—
the words of birth, of life and death
shall be read on the screen of the sky,
where the eye of man shall see and try.

November, 1978. A.R.C. to J.M.: O, Jonathan, you have been in the real ballgame on the Big Diamond.

You are a Marking-and-Tracing Initiate.

Saturday, November 25, 1978. Sacramental Fast for the 25th Birthday of Niscience:

A.R.C. pouring oil: This oil is of the Life of God. This oil is filled with the Igniting spirit of God, the Holy Spirit. I pour this oil in the Name of Omnipresence manifesting everywhere as God. I pour this oil that I may shine forth His Holy Countenance in God-likeness everywhere and to everyone.

During the anointing of the head: I accept this oil as an Anointing vehicle through which the Spirit of God increases my virtue, that I may manifest the Great and Holy Virtue—Faith in God. O God of all, Absolute God, in the Name of Thy Son, may I have in me the Holy Increasement of the Holy Powers, that I may bear witness to Thy Word through the manifestation of holy works in this Earth and in Heaven. Thank Thee, Father.

1979. Ann Ree to Jonathan: Our life together is one of the most wonderful love stories ever written. It has been a love story for God. God took the difference of our ages and blended them. He extracted your naivete and my wisdom and made a vehicle for *His* love. It is a miracle—and so many have benefited.

1979. Ann Ree's Dedication of Day. Each morning upon awakening: My Day belongs to You, God. Lead me and guide me. *(Put feet on floor and say:)* Thank God I am free.

*

It has been my grace to retain the basic virtues I had gained in former lives. It is my grace in the present life to be in a constant state of enabling others to move beyond the rajasic chimeras within their Undersouls.

I had to go through a 20-year cycle of exposure to rajasic roughness to develop the character I have in the present life. In this time, I paid off the debts of two just-previous-life karmas, resulting in final sattvic peace-revelations through states of Samadhi.

January, 1979. A title for a new book about the Angels: "Dynamic Dimensions of the Angels." What the Angels do. Where the Angels are. The transportation with the Angels. The Angel is Law.

The Angel Law functions in the most inner artery of God-Law which is Love. The Angels, having love-atoms which know no hate nor can conceive of any, are on the wave-lengths of God's unceasing Cosmos Love.

The Angels live in the Love-Body of God.

The Angels accompanying men who live as Souls in Earth and Heaven are free in the atmospheres of man seeking love and to be loved.

Angels arrange a quiet moment in time so that their very smallest energy or thought may be transported to the suggestible side of the ear of man. How the Angel knows—how angelically ever-present he is—to the need. All grace, all pure.

January 3, 1979: As usual it is always difficult for me to keep a day-by-day diary. Had a severe hemorrhage following a heart failure attack yesterday. Am weak today. I am full of the necessity to clarify the Esse with Ethic before I leave.

The inner-life practices must be accompanied by sacred movement—movement with awareness of Esse as Omnipresent Grace and Blessing of God.

I feel the winds of death today very close. I am thankful to God for all—J. M. first; all, second; life. J. M. is a Saint in action. God help him.

May I return with the shining souls God has given me. Amen.

*

Thank you, Jonathan.
Thank you, Father.
Thank you, Jesus.
Thank you, Angels.
Thank you, beloved friends in Christ.
Thank you, Harriette and Bunny.*
We will all meet again and again.
We will not perish.

January 9, 1979. Ann Ree on arising asked the Father: Why must I suffer so? *The answer came:* You made the choice between health and knowledge.

January 9, 1979. Ann Ree to Jonathan: I want you to take the Night Ministry Mantrams and keep them in their sequence, and put them in a book on Dreams. You can use my interpretation of people's dreams as well as your own.

*

After I pass from this world, you, J. M., will find your equilibrium on the sixth day after my death. The Holy Ghost will fill you on that day, and the post-passing euphoria of the Holy Spirit will guide you from then on.

With calmness, integrity and dignity, you will meet the world as a Cosmos Disciple united with the Cosmos-Disciple

*Ann Ree's two daughters.

initiated ones. The Archetypal Flow will keep you steadied within the Ethic of the Lord Jesus.

God will send you a Telepathic Disciple to take over your Mantle when you leave this world.

January 19, 1979. Ann Ree to Jonathan: You are one of the most heroic men in the world.

To find a disciplined man in the world is like finding a pearl in a hen's egg. And that's you; that's you, husband.

January 22. Ann Ree to Jonathan: You are teaching the markings and tracings through the Bhakti-energies so that one may observe the Bhakti or love-energies in his own morality.

Love without morality is disenchantment.

To be not loved is to be useless.

To be eccentric or insensitive in love is to be an outcast estranged from the Bhakti-flow assuring life-survival.

Love is angelic steel.

February 4. For 20 years I was in a Yang rajasic-cycle (from 23rd year to 43rd year). Then I went back into the Yin Cycle for 20 years. Now, I am Yin and Yang balanced in this time within a Yang Cycle, and am strong enough to take the exposure from the blows against my gifts. Whatever has been of the past has been mastered. And whatever is of the present and the future is of grace, for I am centered and polarized.

February 13. Ann Ree to Jonathan: When I am out of this world, you will be the recipient of greater powers than you could realize through personal comparisons.

February 19. During illness. The Father is my Employer—that is why, when I do not work, I feel terrible.

March 1979, Ann Ree saw Jonathan's hand turn into a tiger's head: Your right hand is a tiger pen. It is the pen that is on the hunt for new knowledge.

March 22. Ann Ree to Jonathan while she was reading the chapter on Saints in his book The Path of Virtue: Savonarola used a flail of fire; you use a flail of light.

May 20. Season past—beautiful response from all, and added Members. Colorado section now shows promise under supervision of John Goldhammer.

Every day the Voices prepare me to go home; to be ready. So I live constantly preparing for the drop-off of the residue collected. As I look back on 80 years, I have never lived for me, just me, always for others. Perhaps I can observe that me more closely soon. Lord, Thy Will, not mine.

On Thursday of this week, I received a transfusion of the White Grace from Gustave and from the Master. Gustave Doré, my Illuminati mentor since 23rd year. Master of the H.P.B. days, always near!

Thank you, O White Grace.

My body in the Esse of yesterday felt free, light, young.

The Brhaspati series going well, good attention; and at last *The Venerable One* is being utilized—a master book for those open to the Master of Masters.

The *Galaxy Gate* will be worked on—I hope by J. M. and me as a co-authored book.

June 13. The world of the Illuminati is a golden city of light. That is where I think I am going to be after death. Any person who has any contributing knowledge to leave to the world is in the golden city of the Illuminati.

July 5. Carmel. Ann Ree to Jonathan: The Master calls you a "self-remembered man." That is up the road—it is coming.

July 5, 1979. Carmel. Moon in Scorpio. Ann Ree saw a vision of Jonathan, an abyss and the Christ. She drew a sketch of the vision and titled it "Walking the Abyss under the Christ: The Self-Denial and Virtue Path." J. M. on the Path—and abyss ones try to pull him down to their level. J. M. will not be pulled into the inferno with them. That is called the *sucking abyss.* The Christ is over Jonathan.

July 7, 1979. Carmel. Moon in Scorpio. Ann Ree to Jonathan: You are under Gabriel and I am under Michael. I am under the West Gate and you are under the South Gate.

Drawing by A. R. C., July 5, 1979. (See page 309)

It is good for you to look into the Bible and to see the part that Gabriel played in the life of the human race. He was a transmitter for the Holy Spirit, the Holy Ghost, in the Annunciation of Mary. He was with Muhammad when he received the Koran. He was with Daniel after Daniel confessed his sins and the sins of his people.

From Gabriel to A.R.C. for J.M.: He who is under Gabriel need not apologize to any man for his faith. He who has been tried in the Gabrielistic fires has emerged clean and pure, and therefore a holy vessel for God.

He who has been tried in the Gabrielistic fire has met the tempter face to face. He carries with him the cleansing flame, that all may come to be pure and to live as the pure.

He who is in the Gabrielistic light is the manifestor of miracles.

July 14. Re: Ann Ree's birth: I was delivered by Doctor Grace. I was born on Young Street.

July 14. Ann Ree for Jonathan from the Master: You are now entering into the shaggy professor period. You are going to be so caught up into this syndrome of revelation that you will need the help of strong angels to assist you in attracting supporters supporting your revelatory tasks.

You are to become a Galaxy-surveyor, a knowledgeable entriant of Space, passing on to those who will observe and apply your instruction a freedom in the use of the energized voltages within the macrocosmic light.

Space is your *illiate* or element. Illiate means atmosphere. Much has been required to open to you the Gate of Space or the mathematics beyond relativity. Mankind of the future is to think through illiate or Galaxy-spacelessness.

July 16. In answer to Jonathan's question, "When did you become aware of Initiation?" From 1935 to 1939 I went through the Satanic trials. From 1939 to 1945 I went through World-Dweller Initiations. Then I entered into the Bodhisattva Light in 1945 and 1946, and I began initiation into the Deva and Angelic Kingdoms. 1949 to 1952 I moved from the wavelengths of the Hall of Learning into the Second and Third Heaven Initiations, and I made union with the Great Archetypes in the new year of 1953.

July 19. Ann Ree and Master to Jonathan: Never make a friend of a student, or you lose your Teacher's position.

July 21. Carmel: Never felt freer with so much space in house and in air and water. Walking some, thinking much. J. M. simply a God-grace gift for my life in this time. Thank You, Father.

August 1, 1979.: Now that I am 81, I feel ready to teach.

August 8. After worst earthquake in 68 years in Northern California: An Earthquake is an Esse of the earth.

August 8. A.R.C. to J.M.: You are loved; you are blessed! You are giving birth to the ear-chelas—those who hear and heed and do these things in the Name of Jesus.

August 10.: I am less than nothing. I am a channel for God.

August 30. Ann Ree to Jonathan five days before their 26th Wedding Anniversary: I love everything about you.

October 30, 1979. A.R.C. to J.M.: "My Birthday Gift to you from the Masters": The Master has shown me that you, Jonathan, starting on your 52nd birthday on October 31st, 1979 into the year of 1999, will have 20 pure, white years of spirituality, of ethic presentation, of revelation, and of returning the Saints to neglectful men. In this, you will be sustained in health, in body, in mind, in presence, in logos, and in affiliation with true and sincere friends who share in anointing you with the gifts that pour down upon you from Heaven.

You have been found by the Masters an earnest and true pray-er, a true servant of God and worker. In His green pastures, you will be found on a Throne of Truth.

The venom of the false teachings polluting the world of men will be pierced by the Word through you and in you.

Because you are not asking for an exalted place, you will find yourself in exalted places.

Because you have not denied your lineage, you will be looked upon in Heaven as a son of righteousness supported by right works.

The gullible inclination in you of the past will be changed into insight.

Your precision habits will be fortified by machineries (computers) which extend your proclivities and aptitudes.

Your stewardship of conversations, confidences, of monies, of lands, shall be in equilibrium supported by the Karmic Lords of Materiality who support with diligence the energy-processes in form.

You have passed your third trial in initiation. The next 20 years will be the fourth, which will round you out as a whole servant for God.

November 29, 1979: Marriage inside equals marriage outside. Marriage outside equals marriage inside.

*

If only those who say before a talk, "I give praise to my Teacher," would say, "I honor my Teacher and walk the Path of my Teacher."

December 1, 1979. Ann Ree to Jonathan: You are now working for the Mantle of a Cosmos Disciple.

Masters to Jonathan: Holy son, we have prayed for you in the Holy Cloisters. These Cloisters are the Master-Bodhisattva Cloisters. Be prepared for the thunder to follow the lightning of your prayers.

December 13. A.R.C. to J.M.: You have to have the love-flow to oil the mind-flow you are receiving. The love is the oil and the mind is the light which comes from igniting the oil of love.

Love, to ignite this light, must be of a very special heat which comes from the Fire of the Love of God in the life of all men.

December 1979. Ann Ree to a new student critical of Jonathan: When you scourge Jonathan, you scourge me.

December 1979. A.R.C. to J.M. regarding his teaching of the Law: You are the other side of me and I am the other side of you.

December 16, 1979. The moment I am dying I hope that I will be talking for God. I hope I am saying: "God *Is.* God is Great!"

December 17. Ann Ree to Jonathan: Our goal is to provide the Teachers of the inward life with a new Ethic and to make firm the moral principle governing right conduct or action in the physical world.

December 21. All my life has been restitution—from my first breath.

1979. Words heard inwardly while offering the Sacrament during a worship service in Glendale, California. Ann Ree knew the words to be from Saint Polycarp, the Patron Saint of the Chapel of the Jesus Ethic: This experience with Polycarp is equal to my levitation experience witnessed by approximately one hundred persons on August 12, 1973.

WHERE IS MY BREAD?

Thus saith God:

Thou shalt build My Altar and My House of Prayer with thy holy tithes. From this thou shalt preserve thine own house, and thou shalt prosper thy soul and the souls of thy brother, thy wife, thy child.

And thou shalt live in this world as a steward of thy God; and thou shalt know Him as thy Lord over thy life. And thou shalt render unto Him that which a son has reaped from the providences which abide in His Kingdoms, domains, realms, regions, planes.

Thou shalt assure thy purity and the Presence of God in thee through the taking of the Holy Sacrament. Thou shalt take into thy body through the Bread and the Wine the life-atoms of thy Lord who shall resurrect the truth and power of the Holy Spirit in thee.

Thou shalt not live in a craven sense of guilt and in self-unworth. Thou shalt remember the Lord has made thee, when thou prayest to thy Lord. Thou shalt keep open the ear of thy heart to His Holy Law which abideth in you. Thy guilts shall be made white by thy holy confession of thy faith in God; and His forgiving love shall bless thee with His revealing Law. His Word shall tear aside the veils of ignorance in thee. He will reveal His countenance to thee.

Thou shalt make thy covenant in His house of worship and keep thy vows made in His Holy Name.

Thou shalt hear His Voice. With the ear of remembrance, thou shalt recollect what He has sealed into thee from the beginning. And thou shalt live in the world as a creator with God.

17

1980-1981

January 5, 1980. Ann Ree to Jonathan: You received the *Internship* from the Archetypal Guardian Angel of the Niscience System. You received your first book, *God-Realization Journal,* in the Gabrielistic light of the Archangel Gabriel. You received your second book, *The Path of Virtue,* in the Bodhisattva Light of the Greater Saints, drawing upon the Sacramental Halls of Worship in the Second Heaven.

January 22, 1980. Ann Ree to Jonathan from the Master: You are going to have whole Brhaspati revelation.

You are known on the inner planes as *Jo*-Nathan. You are the protege of the prophet Nathan. You are supported by all of the prophets whose names begin with Jo. Your Holy-Scripture polarities are Joel, Jonah, Job, Joshua, John the Baptist, John the Beloved.

Jo-Nathan is your call-name. It is the name that gives you the vibrational telepathic-interplay between you and all the prophets with names beginning with Jo.

January 24, 1980. I went to Florida in the year of 1926—in my 28th year. I became Yang. I took hold of my life and supported myself and sought to support my children. In this period, I developed strong traits of character, stability and earning capacities. Before reaching 35, I began my public work, teaching and counseling. In my 35th year, I turned Yin, and invoked my Kali karma from the past life.

From the 35th year to the 42nd year, I went through crucial challenges. Emotions in my own nature, little understood by me, caused me to make several wrong decisions regarding my personal life. This attracted and drew to me gossip, slander and opposition. During this time, however, I was slowly developing another sort of emotional body, which was to be the vehicle or matrix for the future System of Niscience.

I was always in contact with the Masters.

In my 49th year when I came to the State of California under the direction of the Master, I fixed myself to the polarity point of the supra-psychic flow in the State of California, where I was to meet the golden horde, or advanced students, some as yet unborn who were to be the students of the new and regenerating system under the Niscience Archetype.

In my 56th year, the ground-work was cemented for lands and properties which were to be the future home of Niscience.

My past having been dissolved through a major consuming of initiation during a Wesak period while in retreat in the city of Los Angeles, California, I was polarized to be as a new being so that the flow of the Dharma for the West could come without the default-karmas of the past lives and of this present life.

Since my 49th year, I have been a vehicle for the Niscience Archetype. Under the Christ, none other have I served.

My karmas of the past having been absolved, I took on the karmas of those affiliated with me through initiation under the Niscience Archetype.

In my 63rd year, I had my first massive heart attack, enabling me to loosen my silver cord that I might give more and more first-hand recorded experience as to my knowledge received from the Spiritual Worlds.

January 31, 1980. Full Moon in Leo, Sun in Aquarius. Ann Ree to Jonathan, who has Leo rising: It is a very significant time of initiation when the Sun is in the opposite to your rising sign—and both are yang—as in today, Sun in Aquarius, Moon in Leo. Then one makes a thrust into greater expansion of knowledge.

February 9, 1980. Re: the sale of her books. I made a dedication when I left Florida that I would not profit on anything as a channel for God.

February 9. A.R. C to J.M.: You have to give them the rough side of morality, which is *the Law.* This Law is absolutely fixed in the Universe. There can be no deviation from the Law, if one would find happiness, harmony, peace and contentment.

February 16. New Moon. Ann Ree after Noon Contemplation: To beat a path to the door—that is Jonathan.

February 19. A.R.C. to J.M. regarding his being born in the Year of the Hare: You're chewing on work all the time; you never stop chewing. *(Then she moved her mouth like a rabbit eating.)*

February 27. One must make union with the Holy Ghost before he can know anything about the Holy Ghost.

I have had the Holy Ghost since I was 23 years old.

Every time one "stones" a person who is anointed, he is sinning against the Holy Ghost.

That which works through a prophet is the Holy Ghost.

To give false witness or lie about a prophet; to stand in his way of preaching, healing, teaching, or of serving God—are in the modern times the act of stoning.

Every anointed person is an anointer. To persecute the Holy Ghost in him is to stop the flow of his anointing. Persons born to the world without peace are those who have cut the arteries of the spiritual flow of the Holy Spirit.

March 3, 1980. St. Petersburg, Florida. Jonathan asked Ann Ree's blessing before he left for Sarasota, Florida to conduct a meeting. While blessing Jonathan, Ann Ree had an experience with Ramakrishna and said: Ramakrishna was transmitting the Vivekananda powers to you. He touched you on the shoulder, and the blessing went down your arm like an electric current.

May 8, 1980. In my 32nd year, I heard the voice of Lucifer; it was a mocking voice—and it was terrible.

May 21. A.R.C. to J.M.: It would be good for you to write a book called *The Anointed.* You would put Christ as your central theme as the Anointed—and all Anointed Teachers too. You will experience the great religiosity that I experienced in *The Jesus Story.*

July 30. I am a realized witness for God.

October 2. The Master says I am in my *Tower* years the next five years. I am not going anywhere physically, but I am over-looking everything spiritually while writing.

October 3. I am a Science-of-Ethic Teacher. I have a Grand Intuition.

October 8. New Moon. Ann Ree to Jonathan regarding their one-year stay in Carmel: This year is necessary. My association with you is to *seal* into you the last portion of the Mantle so that you carry the Mantle and be a Teacher in your own right.

October 10. Moon in Scorpio. A.R.C. to J.M.: I stayed in the body to give the Passing to you. I have been giving you the Passing all these years.

October 24, 1980. Written by Ann Ree to be read at her Memorial Service at the time of her death:

MY GIFT

My Gift given to me through *Mother Grace* is sacred. And to my dying breath, I must watch over it, knowing it to be my lodestone, my guiding star.

In the midst of my heart, I must watch over my Gift.

My Gift has been my sense of direction under God.

My Gift has been the means of my healing thousands of people.

Through the gift of my Gift, my tongue has been loosened for God.

Through my Gift, my body has been made strong to do all of the tasks given for me to do.

My Gift has made me friends and strong enemies.

My Gift has been my honor, my shield, my light, my candle.

My Gift has been a baggage light with gold, to be distributed as I go.

My Gift has kept the door open between my heart and the hearts of suffering.

My Gift has made people to walk, to stand, to work, to believe, to hope.

My Gift has given me the way to span a continent with my works.

My Gift has given me many gifts, that I might reach the minds of men in every part of the earth.

My Gift has crossed rivers, moved on starry highways.

My Gift has fed bread, given comforts, built buildings, children and men.

My Gift given to me through the Mother Grace has given me the comfort of being of worth in the sight of God.

My Gift has kept me in tune with the third musics of the soul.

My Gift has opened to me vistas and dimensions beyond the senses, whereby I cross over the thunders of Maya into the lightnings of Heaven.

My Gift put upon me the yoke of discipline, of hardship, of tears mixed with blood.

My Gift put upon my ankles a checkrein.

My Gift loaded me with the burdens of the many.

My Gift gave me insight into terrors, struggles, sufferings, sorrows, death.

My Gift gave me friends who bore with me my afflictions, whose forebearance of me gave wings to the use of my Gift.

My Gift gave me hovels to live in, very little bread to eat, and few baubles of indulgement.

Of all of my Gifts, these were the most important, for they were the guardians over my Gift, that I sell it not for a mess of pottage, or trade it for a pearlless pearl.

Now that I am waxed old, my Gift has been burnished with the acids of my learning. It is shining.

Already my Gift is mirroring the face of the one who will receive it so that it may be spent in the world and lived in the living side of things.

For the Gift has been deathless in me, and through the Gift I have lived as few live in the world.

And that one whose face is mirrored upon the burnished shield of my Gift comes from the Mother Grace which is now Passing to the one that it may be worn with honor, with love.

I go now to take on the Gift prepared for me, which this Gift given to me by Mother Grace I have earned.

That Gift waiting for me shall find its niche, to be worn, to be used.

I can see plainly my Gift to come. It is filled with the countless treasures I earned in the Gift I have borne.

I will return with Gifts in another day earned from this day through the Gift given to me in the Mother Grace.

October 25, 1980. I am the mother of prophets.

November 7. New Moon and Sun in Scorpio. Ann Ree to Jonathan: This is the year of your real apprenticeship.

I am doing to you what the woman who came in from the river did to initiate Ramakrishna.

November 11, 1980. Ann Ree received her first inspiration and guidance related to the Continuum Sacrament. Over the following days, she dictated a manuscript describing this beautiful and powerful dedication to be observed each morning. *

From a continuum of the Bread and the Wine comes the perpetual Epiphany.

The Continuum Sacrament keeps one in touch with his hierarchy nature and with the Supreme Spirit which has created all.

To awaken to the Continuum Sacrament is to enlarge the circumference or sphere of Eternality. To be aware of the Jesus-atoms in the Bread (body) and the Wine (blood) within the Sacrament is to remain in Jesus as the Way, the Truth and the Life.

November 17, 1980. A.R.C. to J.M.: Your Saturn in Sagittarius and Mercury in Scorpio are your regeneration power through the emotions. The water principle (Scorpio) to regenerate and purify the emotions; to master the sexual powers which seek to live in one's body as a master.

December 15, 1980. Referring to herself: One long life of work.

1981

January 17, 1981. Carmel. A.R.C. to J.M.: You are a wonderful person.

Ann Ree was looking at me intently and suddenly said the above. This was a heartwarming moment shared with

*The complete description of the Continuum Sacrament is in the book *The Third Music,* ARC Publishing Company, Post Office Box 1138, Glendale, California 91209.

my beloved Teacher and Wife of almost 30 years. It is the Father Who is wonderful to let me be with such a brilliant Teacher and beautiful Wife.

January 18. In my next life, I hope to be closer to the Stars in knowing. I hope to be a mathematician of a high order. I hope to be born to a Cosmos-conscious family.

January 21. Thirty years of agony to get a System. That is what I've had. It was no accident.

January 24. I'll give my last drop of blood if anyone in this world will be better or happier.

January 26. Carmel, California. A.R.C. to J.M.: We have reached the equi-poled creativity between us—and that is when the Dharma can really flow.

February 12, 1981. The Teacher takes on the soil of the ignorance of his students. This is what crucified my heart.

The unshakable Absolute: That is what I have been feeding on!

February 19. Carmel. A.R.C. to J.M.: You are in the Master R's aura and he is in your aura. Master R is closer to Jesus than any Master because he was His father—Joseph. Joseph is the Master Carpenter and Jesus is the Lord of Prospering. Joseph is also the watchman over the Archetypal Blueprints supporting the New Covenant or Dharma. The 7 is his number. He initiates his proteges through the formulas of 7.

March 2, 1981. The biography of the processes of my Illuminations is written in my books. In the sequential order of my books, I move in gradated stages beyond the Devachan impressionable and suggestible reflections into the Archetypal Light.

Each book is a record of my victory over my past lives and the past in this life. All of my books beginning in the direct Archetypal Light are Archetypal statements received and transmitted through the Archetypal Light. All of my earlier books are books I received in preparation to be initiated into the Archetypal Light.

This life has been a struggle to overcome the Devachan impressionability which I experienced in two former lives in the earth. In this life, it has been my grace to master the lower Devachan karmas, to be blessed by the higher Devachan, that I might receive the Archetypal Revelations.

Ten years of this present life were spent in Kali-trials influenced by the mirage deluding-processes of the lower Devachan impressionability. In this ten years, through the Kali side of my nature, I worked free from massive karmas and paid a debt to my own unrealities. I still bear the scars of the agonies of these years.

On the human plane of judgment, I do not seek to justify myself. The fetters which hindered my soul-self and God-Realization came free through accumulative initiations opening me to the Archetypal Light.

In the terms of religion, I have been a sinner. I am not a saint. I have known salvation. Every day of my life in the present is a day of restitution. Every person I counsel, every effort I make in an unwilling and protesting body, is a restitution for the years which have been dissolved in the waters of spirituality.

March 2, 1981. Hierarchy-Nature Covenants for the next life: In the Hierarchy Nature, you make a Covenant. In the earth nature, you make a desire. These work together when placed equally in the Will of God.

In my next life, if it is the Will of God, I make a Covenant in my Hierarchy Nature to be versatile in astronomy of the Space and of the Cosmos. I make a Covenant to be versatile in astronomy, atomicology, botany, chemistry, cosmology, dynamics in forces, etymology, fatherology (yang), genetics, geology, harmonics, harmony, kinetics, motherology (yin), music, physiology, radiation, reincarnation. In all of these sciences I desire to be versatile in one cognizing realization. This is my Hierarchy-Nature Covenant: to be whole, to be one with God, with a full consciousness of Knowing or Niscience.

I long for this versatility in the state of precognition, knowing that only God knows everything. Therefore, I make no demands on when or where I receive or obtain this knowledge, knowing that the initiatory processes through which I gain this knowledge will come in God's Will and Timing.

I give thanks that I am in this Earth as an initiate being initiated through the learning processes of myself and will. I use my will as free choice under the blessing of God: to make free choice to be ever closer to the Will of God for me. By this I will be that which is ultimately for me: a Nisciene glorifying everything and every aspect of the Omnipresence of God.

One must be a Christ to be a full-knower. By accepting the learning aspect of knowing, one removes himself from childhood and grows into a mature being or son of God.

March 7, 1981. Carmel. A.R.C. to J.M. regarding Francois Rabelais (1490?–1553), French physician and humorist: He has reincarnated in this world and will become your Telepathic Disciple when I leave the world.

March 13. I went through an exactly three and one-half year cleansing period from Florida to Niscience.

March 20 and 21, 1981. During a Conclave Pilgrimage to Washington, D.C. during the sacred days of Lent, Ann Ree experienced the Dolorosa Initiation. Friday, March 20, 1981 was a unique day of timing: the day of the Full Moon in the second ten-day cycle of Lent; the day of the Vernal Equinox; the day of the Sun entering Aries. The Full Moon was in Libra, Ann Ree's ascending sign. On Friday evening, Ann Ree gave a beautiful talk on the subject: Inseparable Co-Atom Souls. At 12:00 midnight, she began to suffer heart pains which were to last twelve hours. From 10:00 A.M. to 12:00 Noon on Saturday, March 21st, Ministers and Elders of Niscience were serving the Sacrament of Communion to members in attendance at the Conclave. The spiritual power of the Sacrament was increased due to the pilgrims observing a day-long sacramental Group Fast. The following words by Ann Ree describe her Dolorosa Initiation:

The Dolorosa Initiation started at 12:00 Friday midnight and continued for twelve hours of pain (angina attack).

On Saturday, during the Mary Hour of 12 Noon, Natiti Stanigar and Tiliti Lane were with me observing prayer and meditation. Natiti and Tiliti were kneeling at the Continuum Sacrament table. I was lying on the bed.

In my heart was a thick golden cloud. It was moving like a vortex in a galaxy. Out of the core of the vortex and void came the Voice of Jesus, resonant, deep. He said: "*I am bearing the sins and the sufferings of the world. You are bearing the sins and sufferings of the world. The nail holes are rusty. These must be cleansed with the pain of suffering. You must bleed them free for the sins of the world. It is so sorrowful.*"

When Jesus' Voice came through my heart—"I am bearing the sins of the world"—I knew my heart condition was caused by the sins of the world.

I burst into terrible crying and sobbing—and I was relieved in my heart.

I experienced a Holy Crying, a Holy Phenomenon.

All the words of Jesus were spoken in the language of Senza,* but my understanding was in English. With each thing said in Senza, visions and illuminations came.

I spoke aloud in Senza the words of Jesus coming out of my heart. At the end, I no longer spoke Senza but Latin. The only word I remember was *Dolorosa*—so sorrowful.

Jesus stated: "*We are one in suffering.*" Then I started speaking in Senza again. My heart was relieved of its pain. I knew I was not healed of future suffering.

**Senza* is the Initiates' language.

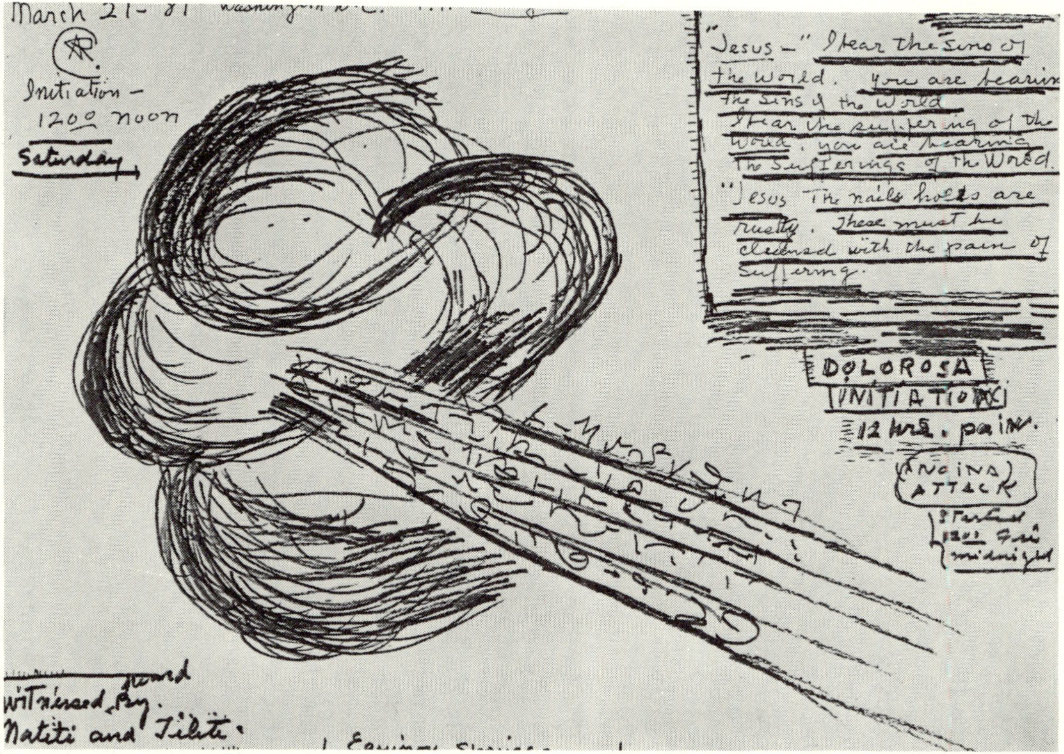

Drawing and Journal Entry by Ann Ree Colton describing her Dolorosa Initiation.

I had received the *Passing* from Jesus. I received the Passing from the *Passion* of Jesus.

My strength in God increases. I experienced what is called the "Holy Crying"—A Holy Phenomenon.

The Holy Wind of the Esse in golden color formed in the core of my heart in three or four circles. Jesus' Voice spoke in the core. Tender, true and pure, He spoke to me. His Voice came speaking out of my heart in this smokey gold. I experienced the English interpretation as I always do in Senza, heard the words of Jesus, and He continued to speak in my heart core. This continued for many moments. My great sobs blended with the tender, grave and pure words of Jesus.

Natiti and Tiliti heard my words of Senza.

My heart pain ended after twelve hours of suffering: 12:00 midnight Friday to 12:00 noon Saturday.

The Golden Light that is formed in my heart I can use endlessly to bless others. Through the Golden Light, I am Passing the Passion, cleansing the sins of omission. Henceforth, the Golden Light is limitless.

In post-observing of the Dolorosa Initiation experience, I realize that I was out of the body approximately two feet above the bed in a suspended state of holy movement within the Senza.

In the Levitation experience in 1973, I was physically lifted upright vertically and moved over the prie dieu. In the Dolorosa experience, I was etherically suspended *laterally*.

March 23, 1981. In Washington D.C., two days after Ann Ree's Dolorosa Initiation experience with Jesus, she made this comment to Jonathan regarding the Niscience group-body: I am carrying the sins and you are carrying the conscience.

March 28. I was so hungry for knowledge all my life. I was so hungry to learn, to know.

Ann Ree Colton

March. My total life has been mortification. It has been one humiliation after the other. My total life has been mortification to keep me down so that I would have no prideful arrogance whatever. A scapegoat person must bear the sadisms, the humiliations and the scourgings. I have had all of those.

April 18. On Good Friday, I experienced transfiguration. Looking in the mirror, Jesus' face as an opal-like foam had formed. His eyes looked through my eyes. I experienced again, inwardly and outwardly, something of the Dolorosa tears.

I said to Tiliti: "How can men do these terrible things to each other?"

April 27. A.R.C. to J.M.: Your tests fall on Friday, Saturday and end on Sunday because you are being tested by genetic memory.

Saturday, May 2. Saturday is my day of the Angels.

May 4. A.R.C. to J.M. after he prepared the evening meal: You are mastering the Dharma of cooking.

May 5, 1981. Until the last breath I will be working for God—if it is His Will.

*

I am a scapegoat for the healing of others. I make restitution for their sins which also include my own sins in this life and other lives. Jesus in the core of my heart gives me the freedom to make restitution for my sins and the sins of others. To call on His Name is to be instantly in His Presence, which resides in the core of my heart. Placing my weakness in Him and the weakness of those I would heal receives the instant twinkling-of-an-eye healing for the cause or the sins which caused the sickness.

May 19. Day after Wesak Full Moon. Carmel. I am taking on the group suffering. I am making it possible for them to enter into their practices and to simplify and glorify their lives.

May 24. Anyone who enters the Path with the intention of healing others and teaching others enters into Intentional Suffering.

June 6. Ann Ree to Jonathan: The love we have is so rare. It is the love creators have together.

June 8. My motive and my conscience: These are what God weighs in me.

June 14. A.R.C. to J.M.: You have opened yourself beyond Yantra now into the Coordinating Worlds.

June 23, 1981. In my meditation of the night, my Divine Companions monitored to me that Jonathan has received the healing powers of Omnipresence and of the hierarchy-nature healing. The Omnipresence of God possesses Jonathan's soul and mind as the breath in his body possesses his lungs, his heart and his body. There will flow from him henceforth the healing power, giving unto him the seven stages of Mediation and the twelve prototypal healing powers, which by visitation he will in the night and in the day be present in the spirit and the soul with those who come into his ministering and counseling.

June 26, 1981. Every time I take on suffering, I am releasing people from their Undersouls so that they can come into Enlightenment. When this occurs between me and one or a cluster of students, it is not what they are doing to me; it is that I am as their accepted Teacher undergoing Intentional Suffering.

In the heart pain I suffer, each time I am close to death; that those for whom I suffer must die to their sins. In this Intentional Suffering which I take upon myself, I undergo labor pains through my heart, that those who turn to me with the weight of their suffering may be healed.

Jesus, in taking on the suffering of the world, labors unceasingly. Through Intentional Suffering on the Cross, He mediated for all in the world.

I have taken on Intentional Suffering to discover *new* and expanded gifts of healing.

June 26, 1981. Carmel, California. A.R.C. to J.M.: This year I have been Passing to you. Before the end of our year here, you will receive your Sacred Name.

June 28. Around 3 A.M., Ann Ree received Jonathan's Sacred Name: Ahbey.

AHBEY means joy in enlightenment; anchored in truth through obedience.

Pronounced AH-*BAY*.

AH—reverence.

BEY—the appointed one of God; a first servant of God.

It is a first name out of the Eternals, like my name *Ti-Seila* is a first name out of the Eternals.

It does not come out of a race or a country—it comes out of the Constant.

You have moved out of the Rudra into the Most High Chakras and, consequently, you are within the Archetypes.

Jonathan Murro

Your first soul-cry stemming from your Sacred-Name Crowning:

> O God, bring all my unknowing
> before the court of Pure Reason
> where Thy Truth exists undefiled.

Jonathan is your Soul-Grace Name and Ahbey is your Sacred Name. This is the birthday of your Sacred Name.

The Sacred Name does not come out of a race history or a nation history or a blood history. A Sacred Name comes directly from the God-Sent sound retained from one's own direct star or former eternity system from whence he comes.

The Sacred Name dwells in the Constant, retaining its direct-star supremacy as a sojourner for God.

The Sacred Name sounds what its bearer is. If one is Truth as a Constant, it is sounding "Truth, Truth, Truth." If one is in the Constant resurrection and exorcism, it is sounding: "Resurrect. Resurrect. Resurrect."

The ego resounds: "Me. Me. Me." The soul resounds: "I am. I am. I am."

The name the Constant resounds—and the virtue it represents—is one's own mantra.

Ann Ree to Jonathan: Yours is "Truth. Truth. Truth." Also, "Obey. Obey. Obey."

Mine: "Resurrect. Resurrect. Resurrect. Exorcise. Exorcise. Exorcise."

Note: Ann Ree was 23 when she met the Master.
Jonathan was 24 when he met Ann Ree.
Ann Ree was 52 when she received her Sacred Name: *TiSeila.*
Jonathan was 53 when he received his Sacred Name: *Ahbey*

June 28, 1981. A.R.C. to J.M. regarding his disinheritance by his physical father: To be obligated to him would be a curse.

July 12. We must have joy and enthusiasm to our last breath.

July 19. You are not ready for Intentional Suffering until you are ready to take the Cross.

July 21. A.R.C. to J.M.: You are working with the true Esse Essence which comes from the Constant.

Eleven years ago, Ann Ree told Jonathan: "You are becoming a Marking-and-Tracing Initiate. It is beginning now." On July 26, 1981, she said: You came officially designated by the Higher Worlds as a Marking-and-Tracing Initiate. You were the first Marking-and-Tracing Initiate. Right after that, you opened the Rudra Center and began your Yantra mastery, leading you to the Greater Archetypal Flow.

July 30, 1981. Solar Eclipse. The Initiation I am having today is a *Thorn Initiation.*

As householders in His Household, we walk with Him the Path of Intentional Suffering.

Every person who is agnostic and cynical concerning Jesus contributes to the thrust of the thorns on the Crown of Jesus.

To clear the rust from the nail holes invites the crowning of the thorns, where mental pain as a fire frees the buds of knowing in the Crown of Knowing.

The agnostic is superciliously insensitive to compassion, mercy. His ego-environment is limited to self-supremacy. He sees the one who wears the Crown of Thorns as an idiot. He sees the one who must transubstantiate the rust in the nail holes into glory as stupid.

The agnostic cannot live in the Household of Jesus. He cannot know the code-key to the Passion containing the Passing, nor can he know the transenergizing of the bitter poison, of the taking of the Cup.

He who wears the Crown of Thorns as a householder in the Household of Jesus has made the bitter, sweet; has made the rust into living waters; has made the Crown of Thorns into Illumination.

Agnosticism is an agony path.

The disciple on the Path of Intentional Suffering must contend with the World Undersoul.

He who is Jesus is fixed and impaled upon this Cross in the first matrix-energy.

He who walks the Path of Intentional Suffering must open the stigmata points of the nail holes through his own suffering.

July 30, 1981. Sun Eclipse, Sun and Moon in Leo. Ann Ree's Sun and Moon are in midheaven. I count every eclipse a birthday.

July, 1981. Everything in Niscience is free and green with new growth. The Lord has led us unto the Green Pastures of Niscience-Knowing. The master-enzyme energies of the green in our learning give unceasing spontaneity of new ideas and creation; ideas to lead us, to restore our souls and to vitalize the Name of God, to take us away from death, evil and temptation.

We are fed in the Green Pastures of the Units, of the Chapels, of the love co-atom relationships. In Niscience we are fed in the Green Pastures of the undying spirit of Regeneration-Grace.

I pray that all students bring forth from themselves their souls' treasures accompanied by the true selfless humanitarian Agape for the total and whole Earth—a holy concern. I desire for them healing hearts and work-service hands. I pray for them to become first servants for God, as Jonathan has become a first servant for God.

It is not too much to ask in this world—so sick, so insane—that there should be one nucleus of souls who maintain the vortex of a perfect God-Realized life and lives. This is my holy anxiety for you: that you *truly,* not ephemerally, serve God and realize Him by daily God-Realization, demonstrable ways in your life.

I stretch my whole capacity and all of its energies into all of the stressful needs in the world. My intensity, I pray, shall become a will in you, a dedication in you, to serve God, to be slave to none, and to never in any particle of your nature surrender yourself to the wills of those who would seek to erase you from the Path your soul has chosen. This God-Realized Path is the Archetypal Path.

Prepare your hearts. Strengthen your determinations to cast out the demons in your own nature, that you may exorcise the world-demonic seeking to possess all souls in the Earth.

Prepare your hearts. Arrange your hearts—and receive the blessings which come from a rearranged life, a centered life. Unite with your Constant, which is in control of your true nature.

Glorify God with your practices. Esteem yourself as a child of God. Change your day-by-day foresight to insight.

Never forget that the first artistry of your soul-expression must root itself in your householder-stewardship nature. Each day weigh your stewardship with your morality and ethic. Balance them on the scales of the Lord of Love—Jesus.

God has given you an army to fight your battles. This army consists of millions of mind-faculty assets you will never encounter through your ego. United with your Constant, you are in command of this army of potence, this army of valor.

Remember, our Lord said: *"All power is given unto me in heaven and in earth." (St. Matthew 28:18)* You are His steward. He is your Commander over the treasures of your soul. Through Him, you are armed to share your treasures and also to protect them and enlarge them.

You may think that your life, framed in what is called *the commonplace,* is not of value or concern save to yourself. Your fumbling, your frustration, your unknowing are not yours alone to resolve. The Lord cannot get on with His whole and complete business until you lay your burdens at His feet. Remove your little ego from your burdens. Even though you set them into motion, in motion itself is the resurrection through and by His Love.

There is the call now from the Calling Place in Heaven—calling you and me. Its name is Niscience. Your name is inside of the Niscience Vibration sound. It is moving you out of your burdens. Move with it. Dance with it. Love within it. The Archetypal Tone is sounding. *"Be with the brethren."* Seek to make pilgrimage in the mountain, by the ocean, in the city, by the river.

Behold, the Lord said: *"I will make all things new."* Be willing to die each day to the lower side of your ego. Bury this nature in the cemetery grounds of your Undersoul. Exorcise the ghost of the dry bones you have buried. Live on the high side of your ego.

Niscience has come. Through the Vibrational Archetone-sound of Niscience, electrify your burdens. Serve God. Unite yourself with Omnipresence. Live in the state at all times of the only true morality as stated in the Sermon on the Mount.

August 29, 1981. The Intentional Suffering by Bibi* and A.R.C. is bringing down upon the Mediative body of all Niscienes a Holy Remission which provides a neutralizing of our outstanding karmas. Bibi's experience and continuing victories over and beyond a death sentence is our victory that we may move into freedom to use our spiritual anastasis gifts. The anastasis gifts are the gifts all early Christians used.

Inasmuch as in these times greater sin and evil abound than in the time of early Christianity, greater gifts are therefore needed to meet and gain victory with the utilization of soul-gifts and soul-powers. In every soul-crisis time, man as a whole is required to move forward with greater energies, with greater assumption of responsibility. Through this, he moves the human race with him, that they may do "greater works" as promised by Jesus.

I put religiosity into the Gifts. This is the essential spirit the early Christians had.

Even though we have had profound Mediative Miracles in Niscience, they have been submerged by those who experienced and witnessed them. Henceforth, this nonrecognition of the miracles in Niscience no longer exists. The Angels who are the chief disbursers of the good tidings related to healing through the Miracles of Jesus are now active so that mediative healing as experienced in Niscience will be openly witnessed by the many. It was necessary that

*Bibi Madden, Minister of Niscience, passed away on November 15, 1981.

there be this repression of witnessing so that it would become deglamorized of any form of magics as related to psychic phenomena.

The nail holes of Jesus are now flowing forth to bring new stigmata healing-powers devoid of rust.

Holy transfusions accompanied by the Archetypal Statements have now begun to come under the "single eye" of recognition and acceptance by those who seek as physicians to heal themselves and as mediators to heal those who appear upon the screen-consciousness in mediation.

We are entering into Vast Healing through Pilgrimage. We bring healing to communities. We polarize and heal communities. We have Denver because it represents the crossing of the East and the West or the polarization of the Nation. We have Washington, D.C. because it represents the Archetype of the United States, where a new human race is pressing forward into religiosity rather than religion.

September 1, 1981. A.R.C. to J.M.: You made your first leap into the Fiery Trial. You made your next leap into the Rudra. Now, you are experiencing the third aspect of the Mantle, which is the leap into the Archetypal Light.

September 5, 1981. (Age 83) I am more alive now than I have ever been, because I am alive in consciousness.

September 5. A.R.C. to J.M.: You are the angel carrying the virtue-bucket.

September 8. This is the most beautiful year I have ever spent.

September 13. Full Moon in Pisces. A.R.C. to J.M.: You are my Guardian Angel. You are the Guardian Angel of Niscience. You are the Guardian Angel of millions of people not yet born.

September 14. It took me from 1945 to 1955 to go through my dissolution process—10 years. And I came out a chaste person.

September 14. On her Levitation Experience: You have to be in a weightless state in your consciousness to have Levitation—and in that moment I was in a weightless state. In the Vibration of the Christ, I became vibrationless—and He lifted me up over the prie dieu. I was sucked into the Great Wheel of Light, which was like a great filigreed mandala. Approximately 100 people witnessed my levitation in front of the Altar on August 12, 1973.

September 21. Carmel, California. This (the 21st West Coast Conclave) is the accomplishment that God wanted—on the Archetypal level.

October 14. Ann Ree to Jonathan: You are God's talent scout.

October 16. If I had twelve tongues in my next life, I would never stop speaking of God.

November 8. Re: the tree in front of her home planted by her about seventeen years ago. It has given me so much pleasure.

On her work: . . . to take the ugly, the neglected, and to make it beautiful.

October 29. Carmel. To J.M.: You are God's gold mine—and you need to be protected.

November 2, 1981. Carmel. To J.M. regarding Barjona II: The Mind of God as Spirit built this building—and you and I are the channels.

November 14. Carmel. A.R.C. to J.M.: God has chosen us because of character.

December 9. I moved out of the Family-Genesis in 1926. On January 1, 1926, I left New York City and sailed for Jacksonville, Florida. That was the end of my life in New York—five years after the Master made himself known to me.

December 14. Glendale. After Saturday night Post-Pleasance Party: I have never given a party that I enjoyed more than the other night. It was a most important day for Niscience.

December. Patience and love built this Ministry. A ministry built through pressure builds neurosis, irritation, upon which cliques and separateness thrive.

December 16. Master to Ann Ree regarding Jonathan's observation about a student: "You can't expect a chicken just out of the shell to lay an egg."

December 17. Jonathan commented on the Teacher's Blessing for the student. Ann Ree replied: And the student's blessing for the Teacher: his faith and love and devotion.

December 19. If a student receives a gift from someone whose heart is against tithing, and requests that he does not tithe from the gift, he should not give a tithe from this gift. Niscience cannot prosper from dictates limiting giving. However, the student can use such gifts for other Agape-purposes rather than supporting the Altar.

December 25, 1981. Christmas Day. A.R.C. to J.M.: We have worked so hard to make others happy.

1981. I have been working with the Moon ever since I began my inner sciences. Throughout the years of my life, I have grown to discern the interplay of the Moon forces upon human nature, human behavior and spiritual potentials.

All men are Moon-cradled in an Earth which is living within the Soul of the Sun. One must master first the Moon forces in his own nature to become a Sun Initiate.

I have Sun and Moon in the midheaven. I am a Sun and Moon Initiate.

Clisome, my Moon *Grace Name;* Tiseila, my Sun *Sacred Name*—are seated as my true identity in the tenth house of my chart. It is my destiny to give inner knowledge. This has been my whole existence as vocation and as work.

Spiritual Archetypal ideas have showered me with truths related to man's future and destiny, but more than this, have rained upon me the meteorites of great truths related to man as to what he truly is in the now.

It is so sad for me to contemplate the waste of mind, of intelligence, of reasonable cognizant knowing. It is so terrible that men refuse to rise beyond subhuman exploration.

The Earth itself is the backdrop or scene for man's spiritual destiny in Earth, yet men continue blindly on, destroying, bruising, forcing.

Every form of life in this Earth has meaning. And every form of life in this Earth is dependent upon all other forms of life.

Man, in his ego-estimation of his own capacity, is moving in a revolving door of existence, or a merry-go-round of static confusion. The most profound dunce—if a dunce can be profound—is man.

This beautiful Earth. It is longing to give us birth. This beautiful Nature is longing to see man feeding each hungry creature. This blessed Earth spurns not any man. This blessed Earth. This Earth.

Only when man can realize this Earth is a starry field of Intelligible energies—every thing speaking to something else that it may live and grow—can he realize the wholeness of his soul in its meaning.

He who seeks to suffocate this Earth dies.

There is not anything that is not precious and priceless when it is seeking to reveal the Face of God.

December 31, 1981. In the 1950's, my prophecies began to change from the personal into the Cosmos Revelations. Everything I see now in the Dimensional Light relates to the Universal as well as to the individual.

This planet Earth is moving toward Illumination. Through the Christ, all men are to be *seers* under Jesus, foreseeing and fulfilling their destinies as directed by God.

The psychic impulses today, stimulating the unknowing, are but froth on the waves of reality.

A true prophet is one who lives in timing to the Cosmos Revelatory Scale of Time and Space.

The Gift of Prophecy is a *Soul* Gift which lifts not only the prophet but all who hear what the prophet saith through the Spirit of God.

*

1982 is an *11* year. Strong souls will come forward in command of forces; though often unknown to themselves, they will re-write the script for men in high places. In this year, death of unusual men will occur, and birth of unusual souls will come to the world.

He who has been laggard must prepare himself to run a new race.

Dictators in the larger countries will pass from this world through suffocation, strangulation, and conditions of heart and chest. Small-water territories' rights will create an unstabilized condition for the larger countries.

The year of 1982 into 1985 are crucial in finances. The money changes seen for 1985 bring ominous relatings to gambling on a world scale.

The individual who would follow a spiritual life should simplify and glorify his life, and sincerely re-appraise his relationship and his responsibility to his fellow man in the world.

I greet you with a holy kiss, with gratitude for the years I have spent for you.

I give thanks for the challenges of the coming year of 1982.

I prophesy that your well-being is certain through faith in God. Put your cares in Him totally. Trust Him. Lean on Him for guidance.

18

1982

I am going to live a long time because I am interested in the Universe.

*

We are looking for reverent persons and for persons willing to walk another mile in service to God.

January, 1982. If you live in the tithe-budget you can make it. I put Divine Mother and Father and Joseph in charge of my budget.

While watching a fire in fireplace. Man was made to look at a fire—and dream; that is where he gets his wisdom.

*

For the last 20 years I have had severe Intentional Suffering.

February 5, 1982. What is restitution but giving? Giving exceeds paying debts. If you make restitution without giving, you are still in debt—and thinking of your debts all of the time rather than how you can give.

The Mercy of God takes your nothing and makes it into something. Mercy is the Face of God's Love.

Love is never unintelligent. Love directs, guides, shapes, molds. And the Love of God which surpasses human love is the creator within the shaping.

February 27, 1982. If it takes a whole lifetime to make restitution, it is worth it. All make restitution. All are engaged in Intentional Suffering. Few are aware they are making restitution or are undergoing Intentional Suffering.

When one becomes *aware* that he is undergoing these two things, he enters the Path of Intentional Suffering, bearing with Jesus the burdens of the world and its creation.

March, 1982. A.R.C. to J.M.: You are having the real Melchizedek powers now.

You are under the selective side of Hierarchy which gives the Gift of putting everything in its right place, preparing for the right time.

You had this Hierarchy selectivity in knowing me. When one has this, he does not have to undergo the rivalry initiations separating him from his Teacher. He knows what his Teacher is and why he is with him. He accepts this without question. Through this, he serves God. He is like a perfected physician who puts his finger upon the true pulse of a sickness—and heals. He has the power of calling souls, and of placing them in their rightful soul-power environments where they may best serve God and create with God.

To J.M. regarding his visit to the Tomb of the Unknown Soldier in Arlington Cemetery: You received the Passing from the National Archetype to work with the grace of the dead. These soul-powers have never been tapped. Thus, the average American has very little patriotic sense and statesmanship ambition.

The conscience of the United States of America is to be stirred so that appreciation of the past as history and historical value must surface.

In the United States, the spiritual is preparing to be born.

March 27, 1982. Ann Ree to Jonathan: Your experience in the Kundalini Fiery Trial was the most astounding ever experienced by a Western Initiate. It is the only one of its kind to be experienced in the Western World. There are many Kundalini experiences in the Western World of a lesser degree which are short as to timing.

The prolonged intensity of fire burning away the sheaths restraining Kundalini was rare and exceptional in the case of Jonathan. That is why nobody can change you. That is why you have no compromise.

March 28, 1982. A.R.C. to J.M.: I came with the Yantra Door open. You came through the Yantra Door.

Your commission when you met me has now become a mission.

March 29, 1982. Re: the past year; the babies being born to students; the Washington D.C. Conclave. I think it is the most outstanding year we have had in our Ministry.

April 4. A.R.C. to J.M. regarding the domed meditation room in their home, Barjona II: High spiritual things are to be experienced in this room, and high spiritual revelation is to be given.

April 14. Concerning the visit by Jonathan and students to Arlington Cemetery where thousands of American soldiers are buried: In the Far East, a guru has to undergo Initiation in a cemetery where the dead are buried so that he may be initiated into the plane of the dead. By this he receives the power to overcome obnoxious spirits and to assist in preventing the earthbound stage after death. Jonathan's inspiration to go to visit the Tomb of the Unknown Soldier opened to him the power to extend his guru or teaching light. Those who went with him received the blessings from the Angels of Dissolution who work with the Destroying Archetypes. These Angels assist in the cremation of the lower etheric body so that souls confined to grave enclosure can arise.

June 7. Saturn rules the conscience. The Capricorn under the rulership of Saturn influences the conscience of others.

Jesus, as a Capricorn, used Saturn to reinforce the conscience of the earth peoples. Man reaches Jesus through contrition, confession and admission of wrongdoing, and thus frees his conscience. A stabilized conscience under Jesus is a Saturn blessing.

Jonathan, having Moon in Capricorn, received great resistance to his teachings in the beginning from those who refused to face their conscience. Stones were thrown against his ministry by those being devoid of conscience or ignoring their conscience who sought to have a religious life without conscience.

June, 1982. A.R.C. to J.M.: When you came into my life, we both came under the care of the Caring Father. He has cared for us ever since. We came into our Initiation of Kali. Until you had your Initiation trial by fire, we were under the Kali side of Divine Mother. We came under the Divine-Mother Grace and Coinciding Principle as soon as your Fiery Trial was concluded. From that time, we have increased the core-body of Niscience.

You are under the *Chinese* influence of Lao Tsu (Master R). You are going to have some sweet paradoxes and parables. His gift to you as a dutiful scribe is that you will think through these paradoxes and parables.

You are going to reach your finest hour when you reach your 56th year. You have gone through your Compression.

A woman who would not die; a man who would not give up—that is you and I. *(Ann Ree will be 84 in August.)*

July, 1982. A.R.C. to J.M.: Your life is the most amazing life! There is not one man in the United States who has the grace to be married to his Teacher.

Your full crown will be on you when you are 56.

To have retained the elasticities in relationship to the eccentricities of the human spirit in the 56th year, you are assured of God's Wisdom-blessings for the remainder of your years.

1982. Ann Ree is elated on reaching her 12th seven-year Cycle of Life: her 84th year. This is a pinnacle year!

When a person of spiritual character and inclination reaches the 12th cycle, which is 84 years of age, he has graduated with honor as to four-dimensional consciousness. And he has prepared for his next reincarnation cyclic-choice as to location in birth, placement in emotions, mind and soul.

The years following the 84th year—if one survives the year of 84—relate to automation-grace, which is memory-aptitudes of grace in the body as related to longevity.

If one is approaching spirituality and earns years beyond the 12 etheric cycles or the 84th year, and if he uses them only for his own vegetation, he is in dis-grace as to choice of place and time in coming lives.

To misuse wisdom in the latter years is an offense against the Light.

Numbers bring you abstract spacelessness when one moves beyond the relativity of Einstein into the transcendental.

There is a new kaballa entering the Earth through the technologies of men. This kaballa is directly from the Living God, whereby life as existence comes equal with the knowledge of being.

When one has become greater in Spirit than the body, he is Soul-realized. Men face this state of existence in this time.

All things are bought at a cost in this eternity system. In the Self-Genesis Age, all must make the effort to rise from the dry bones of mortality and take on the immortal flesh which houses the Spirit.

August 30, 1982. A. R. C. to J. M.: You write through the Christ-to-come. I write through the Christ-who-has-come. You write through the Holy Annunciation or the quickening of the womb by the Holy Spirit. I write by the Archetypal Destined Will of the Established Kingdom.

September 9. To J. M.: You are the only person I have

ever known who has no conceit.

September 14. My chief guilt in life is if I do not work.

September. Following the 22nd West Coast Conclave: It has been for me the most rewarding day of my life. This Conclave is the most vital one we have ever had.

The Post-Meditative period after a Conclave is very powerful.

We are carrying the Epistle of modern times.

It was a great love-experience—and very awesome.

This is my work in this life: to blend the East and the West and relate oneself receptively to this Flow; and to return the Ethic within the Holy Spirit to the Church.

The most rewarding and exciting life in the world is to teach the Dharma.

October 4, 1982. Ann Ree to Jonathan: You wrote your first book, *God-Realization Journal,* under the Gabrielistic Light; also the second book, *The Path of Virtue.* This book, *Galaxy Gate,* is being written under Sirius energies. This was especially active in the Archangel Uriel Gate (time) and then came into its own in the midsummer of August with the August Full Moon. It became extremely clear in the last of its function, leaving a lucid coolness of rationality to fall as peaceful Realization-snow upon the receptive.

Master to Ann Ree: In this period every year it will be a higher spiral. There is no reaching of the Interterrestrial Knowledge until the inside and the interior of the origins are experienced. By this, Knowledge is a golden retriever, whereby one recalls his beginnings and the plan of each ending.

October 14, 1982

It is a Dance,
a Maya Dance,
Until it becomes the Cosmic Whole.

It is a Dance,
a Maya Dance,
Until it becomes the Cosmic Soul.

It is a song singing to the Tone of the Cosmic One.
It is the being within the meaning of the Cosmic, Cosmic
One.
It is the Word without the verb.
It is the Word of the Sound Unheard.

It is the Union attracting the Real.
It is the life through which the Cosmic would heal.
It is the Cosmic Fleece woven into the Robe of Peace.
It is the Garment White,
the Seership right.

It is the Dance.
It is the Dance of the Cosmic Soul.

It is the Light, the Cosmic Light,
brighter than the light of the eye.
It is the Worm and the Man
within the Master Plan.
It is the Hand of God, of God.

It is the hailing and the nailing.
It is the failing and the gaining.
It is the hope and the wish.
It is the lapping of the waters in the Cosmic Dish.

It is the brine gone sweet.
It is the rough made neat.
It is the Cosmic Whole face to face with the chord and
the fame.
It is the Name of the Name beyond the claim.

It is the water dowsing all.
It is the fire.

It is the steam and the dream.
It is the walk and the talk.
It is the Cosmic, the Cosmic, the Dance, the Dance.

It is the Game without a name.
It is a Dance not of the foot.
It is a Dance of the Root.
It is the Dance of the plain and the mountain far.
It is the Dance of the gathering from the Evening Star.

It is the Whirlpool and the Energy Grace.
It is the awakening beyond the race to the Face, to the Face,
of the Cosmic, of the Cosmic.

*

J.M. to A.R.C.: You have a lot of music in you these days.

A.R.C.: It is the Music of the Eternals.

October 23, 1982. I am nestled in the Naga-Coverlet. That is what keeps me protected, and it keeps me in the constant state of receiving the Flow of the Archetypes.

November 8. A.R.C. to J.M.: I live in constant wonder of the Infinite Grace we are in.

November 11. I am going through a very intense Seraphim Initiation.

November 13, 1982

"The God Sent"

Jonathan is a teacher beloved of God. He is chosen.
He brings your mission of the heart into rightness through healing in the Law.
Jonathan's soul future is drawing you toward your soul's future.
Jonathan is authorized of God ~~to~~ carry the scripture to make it live in your [illegible]

November 14. The Seven Light-Streams and their values opened for me in 1946. I united with the Venerable One, and he in turn united me with all of the Immortals or Great Inward Masters. And finally, on writing the book *The Jesus Story,* I became co-atom to Jesus—and a Cosmos Disciple.

I began to understand why my life had been one of Intentional Suffering, for one who enters the Archetypal

Path cuts the cord of the Pleasure-Principle expectations and takes on the golden cable of oneness with God. Layer after layer, I stripped aside the creed and dogmatic scales on my heart. The divine virtue of the Heavenly Kingdom placed me at a distance from doctrinal prejudice and limitation.

Every step of illumination was gathered from phase after phase of Intentional Suffering. The rigors of pride were melted into humility through mortification. To many, my own life showing contradictions, brought upon me mortification and eradication of the sin of separateness.

In Intentional Suffering, one joins a world-company in which there is no separation, for in suffering all are alike, all suffer, all bear pain.

Suffering is the birth-lady elect of the soul. Suffering produces the wanderer, the alienated. Suffering demands barrenness that one may be *full* of the grace. Freedom from suffering provides the glory of the Light gained from the lesson in suffering.

Making synthesis in the Light-Streams brought me the wholeness, the flexibility, the union with suffering, producing an Enlightenment beyond the physical.

The more I suffer, the more I adore God, for in my suffering I know a law of rectification and revelation is being worked. And when the pain has finally agreed to bow down to the law, to right, then comes the Illumination, the Revelation.

The Second Light-Stream under the Venerable One taught me what true synthesis means. All presently in the Archetypal Path must become devotees true and whole in devotion to live as an Archetypal statement and representative in the world.

All in the Earth are Intentional-Sufferers. We entered this eternity system with the agreement that we would suffer, that we might gain a certain kind of consciousness, that we might build this eternity system. There is a consciousness beyond Maya consciousness; it is a consciousness seated in God, inwardly directed by the Image of God which in its constancy varies not as to the intent of all men for this Earth.

In every phase of suffering there is concealed a revelation relating to God and His Will for us.

The unity in suffering is ever alive. From this, men sculpt and mold a Galaxy mind. Their Galaxy tools are: will, life, light and love. These are the building necessities, producing mind-chastity and purity.

There is no family or person in Earth who has not known or who is without suffering in this time or in any other time allotted to men of the Earth.

He who hung on the Cross and agonized for the soul-birth of the human race holds the key to freedom from suffering.

What men call a life-span of a few years is but a trial of duration and of cyclic mastering. How one lives the life in the physical world determines the buoyancy of his own constancy within Divinity. His victories over suffering contain the suffering to gain reverence, to gain devotion, humility; the suffering gained to know obedience; the suffering gained to live in peace and in order; the suffering to prove the Law with the works of the Spirit; the suffering to become a healer; the suffering to become a most-high priest of Melchizedek or the Teacher-Adept in the world.

December 4, 1982. New Moon. O Omnipresence in me, You are so wonderful. The Omnipresence in Jonathan is a safe pilot to follow.

1982. A.R.C. to J.M.: You are a blissful one. You had the guts to stay and to get the job done.

19

1983–1984

January 11, 1983. A.R.C. to J.M. regarding their being together over thirty years: Every moment with you has been my heart's answer.

On Sunday, March 6, 1983, during her Lenten Conclave talk in Washington, D.C., Ann Ree spoke various phrases in Senza, *the language of initiates. As in a past Lenten Conclave in the nation's capital, she experienced "Holy Crying for the mass conscience." On March 14th, 1983, Ann Ree observed a New Moon Fast in Glendale, California. The next day she received for the first time the* Rapture of the Holy Fragrance.

March 15, 1983. Holy Divination is in everything when the Eye is open. Holy Divination has a language; it is in the Holy Writ of the Archetype and in the Holy Witness of the Archetone. Holy Divination as speech is the Hearing of the Word and the Healer Vehicle for the Soul.

I had the real Rapture. It was an astounding experience. It was awe-inspiring. That is why I burst into tears.

It was a total ecstatic Fragrance. I was aware I was experiencing a Saint's Rapture.

It was a Holy Fragrance, ecstatic, almost unbearable Fragrance, yet ecstatic happiness.

This I know to have been the holy polarity companion to the Holy Crying—and hereafter will accompany the Holy Crying when it has had its total effect.

This followed a day of Fasting (New Moon) and casting out of the karmas connected with Intentional Suffering.

It was a total Ecstasy. It was totally consuming.

You open the Holy Gifts when you fast; you encounter them.

March 17, 1983. I will never be the same after the Rapture. I knew my Eternal Self with a certainty. And I also knew my value as a God-projection.

It was just bliss, bliss. I had no sense of guilt or remorse or regrets. It was a total rightness. I made union with God.

It is not permitted too often to have the Samadhi Rapture. I have had moments or seconds, but never such an extended positiveness in God and rightness in everything. I was one in the One with no bars or restrictions or limitations. This was my Rapture at 8:00 A.M. on March 15, 1983.

The Senza was one side of the Polarity, and the Rapture was the other side. These come together in the Samadhi.

I pray for the extension of healing powers in the whole and total Ministry.

These Holy Phenomena are of the Nature Grace of the Cosmos. The Master calls them God-related incidents superior to Time.

March 20 and 21. It put me into the Divine Euphoria.

From the Rapture, I have gained the Divine Euphoria, which is beyond Revelation. Revelation relates to the relativity world and to the mastery of Maya. Divinity-seeing relates to the spiritual processes of the Divine World and Kingdom, where the Buddhi is at home within the Informing Principle.

I will be doing a lot of Buddhi transcendental work in the future, relating to the Transcendental states of consciousness. I will be writing on this.

The Rapture is the promise of what to expect in the Inner and the Transcendental life.

March 25. Since I had the Rapture, my whole world has changed and my place in it. I know Mediation to be a reality. Mediation is a consistent God-Increase Power.

One who uses Mediation as an aware vehicle for God is Power, representing the Omnipresence of God. The soul-faculties when at one with Omnipresence become Omnipresent, Omnipotent, Omniscient.

April 17. Sunday, in Mary's Garden. Mary to Ann Ree: If thou shalt pray through mediative and modified prayers through Me,* thy prayers shall not go astray. They shall go into the heart of My Son. Our Father and My Son are one.

June 8. To J.M.: The Law is using you.

June 16. My teaching is Cosmos Religion. It is religiosity in the soul. It is innately man's true way of worshipping and approaching God.

June 18. To J.M.: Your manhood is shining forth, your true Christed Self.

June 28. I am under the Tutelary Guardians of the Dharma. Through Buddhi, I am in contact with the Informing Principle which is under the guardianship of the Tutelary Deities or the Omniscient Guardians of the Word through writing and speaking.

July 7. When you step out from your Teacher, your karma comes in on you.

July 14. Written to be read at Ann Ree's Memorial Service after she leaves the world: When death is a creation and not a desolation; when death is an extension and not an extinction; when consciousness with soaring wings flies into the soul's Bhakti Home—there the me becomes the I Am, the Whole in God.

July 15. A.R.C. to J.M.: Our marriage has been a celebration.

*Begin prayers with petition to Mary.

You were born an athlete. You are God's athlete now.

July 18. To J.M.: We are fighting the battle together as of Time in Karma and winning the battle of Grace in Space. I am, with your help as a co-atom server for God, sustaining my units of measure for life, living and healing.

The field of energy filled with pain in my karmic state is simply a field of energy to which I must relate with Reciprocal Maintenance. Rather than live in this garden field of pain seeking to possess the whole of my consciousness, I build with you and through you another field of energy in consciousness where there is no pain, no resentment, no resistance, no separation.

August 5, 1983. Everytime I get down weak, I get stronger for God.

I ask myself, "Does the Soul cry? Can the Soul shed tears? Does the Soul agonize?"

I say to myself every day, "Why have men lost touch with Soul-knowing and Soul-understanding? Why have men lost Soul-union and Soul-guidance? What is wrong with a person or people or society when they maintain not the Soul or their Altars or their Beloved?"

Where is the music and where is the singing when the Soul has not heard?

I am seeing everywhere the clamors of ignorance and the languish of complacencies.

What is happening?

What is the Soul saying?

How can the Soul be made free to shine and to give of its golden self to safekeeping in God?

When a man dies, they say, "He has gone to his Soul." Where is this mysterious place? *Who* is waiting for him? What of the Soul-Home? Is it such an alien place that man cannot live in it while in Earth?

What is the Soul-journey? By what route do we travel to find the Soul? Must we await death to live in it, or is there space enough to know this Soul-Home?

Where is the desert? Where is the dry place that must be filled with a Soul-Home, where God can reside? How, find it?

God and His Angels await their coming into the Soul-Home of the many, for Christ is now hungry and starving for His board of Bread and Wine, that He may come in and sup in the Home of the Soul.

*

There are three God-sents. There is the God-sent of a beloved who is co-atom to you. There is the God-sent of the one who comes to initiate through the vajra for you. And there is the God-sent who walks with you on the Path as one of the 70 chosen 2x2 by the Lord.

August 12, 1983. Ann Ree telling a group of students about a vision experienced a few days earlier: Jonathan was kneeling in prayer by the bed three or four nights ago. He was very tired. He had been working very hard all day and he gets up early in the morning and doesn't go to bed until midnight; he is working on manuscripts all day long and on all other things that he has to do, and he only has one walk, which is the only privacy he has. So he was kneeling by the bed and I wasn't particularly feeling sorry for him; I was just sympathetic to the fact that he was tired and needed to rest. Suddenly, this vision of the most beautiful ocean appeared while he was kneeling, and I didn't say anything to him until he was finished. In back of this beautiful foam was a great white Sun. Jesus stepped out of this and held his hands out and Jonathan went forward to meet Him in his old checkered bathrobe. But it became the monk's robe of the same checkered bathrobe of the material of Savonarola. Jonathan reached out his hands to the Christ and the Christ had His hands out to Jonathan—and they met their hands. I told Jonathan of this, and I knew that he had really received a true union with the Christ. The wide ocean for miles had nothing to interfere with its great stretch of light—it was beautiful.

It is really interesting how spiritual holy phenomena always have something connected with physical appearance and apparition as well as spiritual. But I thought it was such a wonderful vision that I told Jonathan about it and, of course, he related to it with gratitude.

These are things around us ready for us. We do not always see them, but we always feel them. We have intuition of the Angels. We have points in our atoms related to the Angels that the Angels touch with their light. That is why when we have had an experience with the Angel there is always a feeling of a flow, of light, the response. We all pray for that.

August 24. To J. M.: You are His living testimony.

September 2. To friends: We will be married thirty years—the greatest years that have ever graced two people.

Wedding Anniversary on September 4: Thirty years of beautiful struggles and victories.

September 7. New Moon in Virgo. Ann Ree's words following Jonathan's comment on the Grace-Inheritance that comes after the 30th year of Marriage: The crest of the wave of a Cycle produces all of the bitter and the sweet together as one into a Samadhi-Realization of God, His Perfect Law, His Perfect Life, His Perfect Light and His Perfect Love. It is an ecstatic weightlessness free of the burdens and intoxications of gross suffering. You realize the burdens you carry have been adjusted. The soul-load has shifted into weightlessness. The mind is unburdened, reasonable, rational with a holy logic.

When a person reaches the end of his Cycle of Repentance—and comes free of his sins—he totally drops the old mind, and the true Mind in Christ begins its functioning. This is the Samadhi Mind. The cruel endurance one has suffered to cleanse away the different laps of sin finds him in the elevated position of true Ahimsa and selflessness.

September 7, 1983. A.R.C. to J.M.: My Mantle is almost entirely covering you. The threads of the Mantle which we are carrying together have now become totally absorbed as consciousness. The Androgynous Light of Enlightenment is being shared between us. When I leave this world, you will take totally this Mantle.

I am in the position of Elijah passing to you the Mantle. This is added now to your virtue. You are in the blueprint of Elisha who inherited the Mantle of Elijah.

Elijah became Jesus. Elisha became John the Baptist. The misinterpretation of the name of Elisha in St. Matthew was due to the translator's confusion as to this statement concerning reincarnation. The translators of the Bible were uninformed as to reincarnation, and also not understanding the true relationship between Elijah and Elisha as reincarnating saviours in the world. Many errors in the New Testament exist because of uninitiated knowing in the translators. In the reading of the akasic records of the saviours, one must have known them in the physical world and have sat at their feet as disciples or chelas.

September 7, 1983. Carmel, California. Ann Ree spoke this "Morning Letter" to Jonathan:

The morning Sun looks brighter because you are here.
Everything is lighter because you are near.
The pelicans are flying in the blue light of the water's
Sun,
The pages are turning—and because of you, our work
will be done.
I am seeing the dogs on the beach,
and the men running,
their legs bare with sweat.
I am seeing the seals and hearing their bark.

The pelicans are flying and striking for their mark.
Some people walking are clothed in dark, city clothes,
and some in casual dress, dressed in only what, God
knows.
If I were a child of two or three,
I would be digging in the sand with you close to my knee.
But now in my lofty top, cathedral room,
I must open the mystery of God.
Very soon, I must unroll the Scroll
of why I came and where I go.
A few notes remain, almost an octave,
but now scattered in stretched-out rhapsody.
I am hearing,
I am seeing,
I am knowing.
When I first met your hand in friendship warm,
I stood at the gate no longer forlorn;
The letter from your mind to mine was postmarked,
"Infinite, for all time."
Two strangers wandering in this Earth
found mirth and birth and joy.
Every stroke of the pen,
Every dot on the page,
Every line structured to heal the rage
of the unseen dark.
Two souls, co-atom yoke-fellows of Light,
this is the page on which we write.
This Revelation is that we can see only what is in sight—
This music, this love, this creation.

LIFE IS

Life is not a saddle to ride upon for comfort.

Life is not an eggshell to be cracked for consumption.

Life is not a pill to be taken with a grunt and a groan.

Life is not an assumption that your face will be known
on billboards heavenly, on neon-lighted shores.

Life is not for just pleasure or just pain or just laughter.

Life is a giving, a birthing, a dying, a sharing, a crying.

Life is a victory over unknowing.

Life is a climax of God-expectation.

Life is a misery making history immortal.

Life is a coil become a spiral.

Life is existence, discovering the Eternal.

What better way to live than to live? What better way to love than to love? What better way to know than to blow with the winds of experience, that the tree may bear its fruit of instruction, and that the life in the living, and the love in the loving, and the Niscience in the knowing may be seasoned in the timing of the having and the giving and the sharing.

*

God is Music and Poetry.

But we cannot sound this Music unless we praise.

To praise Him continually is to be found,

To be caught up into the round
of life as creation.

Life as creation is more than fate and insinuation;
it is riding the waves and rising with the Sun.

It is flowing with the leaves and the wind.

It is swimming with each small fish near the beach.

It is reaching and being within everything which seems
out of reach.

There is one climate for the dunce and one for the angel.

There is one for the knower, who knows, who reaches.

There is one for the teller and one for the see-er.

There is one for the necklace reaching from you to here.

There are Nature things and lacy things, making a
necklace true, reaching from the end of the world
and back to you.

There are dances of jubilance;

There are patient, hard-bitten smiles,
deceiving the self, and painting in the wiles.

He who has a broken heart and cannot see the mending
is suffering the death of a little ending.

There is no boat at the anchor longing for the sea,
tossed by the waves of being not free.

The heart which has pledged itself to Eternity
must affix its sails by night for the Sea of Infinity.

*

The monkey days are funny, filled with juicy
understandings of mind-restlessness, of wasted
moments, of vows unkept.
The greedy days are tormenting;

A tongue oversaturated with desires misspent, the
debts unpaid without remorse or repent.
The sattvic days are the happy days if a mind has
been swept clean, and every pasture and every field
is glowing with green, the green of healing
and growth and plenty.
The moistures are sweet with dewy pearls as small
balloons blown in rainbow swirls.

The musics are clearer, pure, sounding with the
Word of God.

Each day is a scramble between Maya and the Light.

Each day is a war against warriors unseen.

Each day is a target, honing and shaping.

Each day is a drum beating, and hands clapping.

Where is the soul in this time-district of learning?

Where is the mind in this fantasy-churning?

Where is the deathless work, the most chiseled mark?
Where is it writing its name, its right for Space,
its stand for place? Where is this day, and what is
the way in this time-allotment of Guna-shaping?

What is it saying?

What are my prayers on this day of Guna-light?

What is my praise at this day of enlightenment?

THE POET

When you have become a poet, you have weeded out all unnecessary things to say.

When one becomes a poet, he has moved beyond the traffic of the commercial lanes. He has united with the Angels and is standing back of the wings, looking on the stage of life, describing the fanes.

If in times one thinks himself a poet, he must weigh himself again, what he wrote and what he brought. He must timidly approach the pulse-beat in time to reach the heart of saying things which rhyme.

Celestial-primed to speak in verse what men have not the courage to converse.

Each poet writing in the invisible Sun must give birth to his death of lives many undone. He must tear away the flesh concealing the thrum of the soul.

He must unite himself with the sinews in the gold, in the elixir, in the Eucharist of the One.

He must see God as the Awesome, God as the Real, God as the Wonder, and God as the Spirit.

Within the field, the plain and the mountain, he must know and see and feel the emotion in each pulsing thing giving life.

He must be a surgeon with a godly knife.

He must be an architect looking for a house to build for a wife.

He must be as a bulldozer scraping out the unclaimed road.

He must be a towering building awaiting its erosion by earthquake and time.

He must teeter on the edge of life,

He must sink deep in the Earth, breathing its life.

He must find the passion to be passionless.

He must become the way-breaker for men yet to be born.

He must be a seer, a dancer, a teacher, a preacher.

He must be a healer.

He must outrage him who sleepeth.

He must not lose touch with his Angel who keeps open the chest of his treasure, that men may read him with leisure.

He must unite with the units of measure. With a telescope, a microscope, he must aim toward the Galaxy, beholding the Intelligible.

In every man, a poet is concealed. The poet who awakens him must find him when he has finished drinking the bitter of the cup.

He must provide him with a clean vessel from which he must sup.

He must give to him a new vessel lined with the gold collected from the soul-dust of his becoming.

In the Earth, he was a bumbler and a mumbler. In the learning, he was a tutor and a sender.

In his own legislature, he was a parliament made up of building blocks of error and failure.

As an educator he was waiting always for the tomorrow, as he was addicted to the belief that the scientist would bring him the answers beneath the furrow of his brain.

His brain which was bored and jaded from waiting for its insighting message gave off in repetition events which had long been outdated.

The poet is a seer living in houses not made with hands.

The poet is a magician, making something out of what men call nothing.

The poet is a sage turned inside out, exposed to the acids and winds of self-doubt.

A poet as a mantra in the cocoon stage explodes his territory and bruises his wings.

A poet, when explicit, loses his touch; when too vague, he incarnates with the Dutch, where in Holland, poets must inventors be and begin as tradesmen to set themselves free.

When in China, poets must abdicate their rights to the dynasty flow of oppression to light.

When in Russia, poets must use as their pen the iron bars of imprisonment on the Siberia plain.

When in Spain, poets write their arcane stale fragments on inquisitor parchments. They still reflect the Inquisition's diminished enlargements.

When in Mexico, poets write with Cortez in their veins.

When in all South America, the poet seeks to rise, he must hide himself behind the Andes pyramidal files.

Wherever poetry comes to birth, men are ready for a leap over the graves and dry bones of man's crying, striving and trying.

Every poem conceals a burial, a grave, a resurrection.

All poets have been stripped of Maya-sense. Caught between Heaven, the limbo and Earth, they must dare to give life to things long dead.

They must soar with the spirit of the Angels, which sees life and more life. They play upon unknown instruments hidden in the breast of men.

They must drink of liquids which are more than wine.

They must have discounted gurus of the mouth, who by speaking overmuch have lost touch with the sacredness of Light.

They must often come with clothing besmirched by the ears of careless listeners who give to give them birth.

Poets are lonely, thinking through energized hearts to tell something to the autistic closed minds, who work in the world to be settled but never set.

Poets are not thinkers completely free in thought.

Poets speak through a feeling tongue straight to the sensitive heart which has known pain and futility and uselessness.

But poets are alive with the nature of things.

Poets are non-glamorized by masses and things.

Poets are not funny or comic or clownish; they are not exhibitionists about things which rhyme.

The hammers of their balance are mallets or anvils pounding in the Divine, the beautiful.

The wonder of the poet is that he lives at all or that he speaks where there is no call.

The wonder of the poet is that he is not often read or quoted as something said.

The wonder of the poet is that in every age and clime, he rises again, that men may hear within the Universal Rhythm of the Rhyme within the Word.

September 27, 1983. Ann Ree to Jonathan, Archangel pointing to Jonathan: That Fire in you is going to light many altars and enlighten countless people. That light will not go out in you because it has been born of the Fire of the Holy Spirit. And that Fire in you—the evangelistical spirit—has now become the Light of the Christ endowed with Eternal Spirit, which no man taketh from you or putteth out.

September 27. Samadhi Marriage.

October 5 and 6. Carmel. A.R.C. to J.M.: You certainly belong to the Father. Preserve, preserve, preserve is your keynote.

You are now a Teacher. You are now working within the Archetypes. You have the organized Logos.

The rajasic heats which have overwhelmed the mystic body in the church and in the teachings must now return to a most pure, holy bliss consciousness within the Logic rationality with the Archetypal Omnipresence.

The bliss stillness of the Holy Spirit pouring forth into the rabid heats of dissension seeks to become Christ-Knowing within the religious body and religiosity hearts of men who seek to become servants of God as ministers, as priests, as Teachers.

Your teaching now will contain the Archetypal formats for worship, whereby the new ritual promise by the Masters in the red books will be expressed on the Altars.

The present church authorities of this day deny they are dying. Yet deep within, those who work in ecclesiastical presentation are deeply aware that their teaching and communicating faculties are inhibited by cross-currents out of their control. They have lost their sense of direction, failing to have concurred with the True Passion and Passing as given in the Lord's Supper or the First Communion. Churches which do not understand the true Eucharist as passed down to man through Christ Jesus have inhibited their Archetypal sustaining sound within the Word of God.

October 10. I am going to leave this world as a holy woman, and I am going to return to this world as a holy Teacher.

I have had dissolution and absolution. The threads of holy gold have become the threads of steel in the physical world. My life as grace is manifested among my students, chelas, disciples. The Word has been made flesh; the gifts quickened and the Power of the Holy Writ have ignited and set fire to the unuseful and obstructing.

Initiation is fire; it is Kundalini in action. The Holy Worm or serpent is setting many eagle nestlings to fly and to find their prey. These are the Teachers in the Christed Avatar Light. They are the God-sent who have committed their souls and soul-grace to Christ. Christ Jesus, the Lord of Love and the Light of Love, is the Teacher.

October 17. On being resurrected in her health many times: I have proved over and over that I have resurrection powers, and I have them for other people.

October 24. A. R. C. to J. M.: The Cosmos is your trestle through which your train goes.

October 28. The negatives have taught me great things and have schooled me in a sharp-school. The Maya system provides the negatives. Man provides the struggle. Soul provides the light.

November 11 and 12. To J. M.: I am at the feet of your illumination, and you are at the feet of my instruction.

I have made my Covenant, and you have made yours, and we have made our Covenant together.

November 15. My prophecy is now in its crown, and it especially affects the world's religions and the family-atom.

November 25. On Niscience's 30th Birthday. It is a building of love and hard work.

December 7, 1983. A. R. C. to J. M.: Our whole experience was *work* from the beginning.

December 10. They have tried to make me a little prophet to dig them out of their mortgage holes.

December 24. There are students who come and offer service to assist me. As time goes by, they begin to feel they should be paid for the service and press me for money. This is done on the subconscious level. In some cases, it erupts into separation and estrangement—having forgotten their original virtue-offer of service to God.

December 26. We have never had such a Christmas Day as yesterday.

1984

January 5, 1984. If one does not understand reincarnation, he cannot understand the Laws of the Cosmos that support our life.

January 13. Since I confessed for the group body, they have taken on more responsibility themselves.

January 14. Thank Thee, Father, for Cyclic Wisdom.

*

We have been carrying the incubus* of guilt from generation to generation.

Exorcising powers in a priest or minister is the power of annulment.

If one is plagued by incubus-persecution, the priest or minister should know: Has the person investigated or played with any form of psychical art? Has he taken drugs? Is he taking any form of drugs at present? Is he connected with alcohol or alcoholism? Does anyone close to him take alcohol or drugs? On what level does he pray? What is his childhood training in religion?

January 16. I gave everything up for the Dear Work. It has been my soul-venture.

*

A person without education in the future might as well have leprosy.

January 20. The Masters want those who can carry the real Dharma, which is Reincarnation and Cosmos Unity.

January 24. Saint Petersburg, Florida. You shed a matrix like a snake sheds its skin—that is according to Cyclic Law. A matrix is a literal encasement, a cellular system. It is a psychic-nature framework.

It is similar to the grid around the Earth and the grid system around the World-Soul Atom. This grid system makes it possible for the World-Soul Atom to polarize the planetary action. When the grid system of the World-Soul Atom and the grid system of the Earth coincide in timing to each other, the Galaxy Gate opens; one is initiated through the Cosmos. Man as a consciousness being at one with the Galaxy-Gate revealing is an adept of the Cosmos. He is a seer beyond prophecy. He is a world-builder of the mind.

*Incubus: a spirit or demon.

The soul-nature is at home within the open Galaxy Gate. Man as man in consciousness undergoes a mutation. His atoms are extended to comprehend rather than to question.

*

Be honorable in all things.

January 28. To be a Teacher of the spiritual life is the greatest calling in the world.

January 29. Raleigh, North Carolina. During Holy Crying, Ann Ree heard Jesus speaking to the churches the following words. She knew that His use of the word "water" related to the Immersion Powers of the Water or the Holy Spirit as in the Jordan experience:

"I have given you My water, and you have turned it into lead.

"To intercede is a duty, so that the Intercession of the Saints may come."

*

Your incarnations rule your destiny. It is destiny under God that one must have many lives, that he may produce the ultimate of perfection as an Earth creator.

January 30. A teacher who does not draw out his students is not a teacher.

February 4–11, 1984. Christ Samadhi is levitation into the Cosmos Consciousness.

What is a sin? A sin is anything against God and His Increase. It can be a sin against a person whose soul belongs to God.

It can be a sin against stewardship, against God's order in the care of possessions or responsibilities. Anything that is done with malice and defiance of God and for the sake of lust and self-survival for self alone is a sin against God.

*

When you come in the Teacher's environment, you show up your faults—it is inevitable.

*

Thank You, Father, for all Grace.

*

The intuitive and the scientific will definitely conjoin—this is inevitable.

*

People must return to the Archetypal Morality. In all nations, those who sit in authority must be at one with the authority of the people.

February 18. To. J.M.: You have really earned your crown of Living Teacher.

February 19–22. Our work comes out of the pure Dharma.

The Tutelary Deities or Guardians of the Word and the Law exact heavy penalties upon those who would exploit the Dharma.

*

My favorite exercise is talking.

*

Living Teachers are doing the living works with living results.

The Teacher lives within the Law and imposes the Law. And those who follow him will respect and fulfill the Law.

The Teacher must first entreat, that the student may lean in the direction of his better nature. The Teacher must next adjure, that his student act upon the Word, that he may *pass* the Word and thus live as an everlasting witness of Truth.

February 22. To J.M.: Your being the successor in the Elijah Grace, as Elisha you have the grace to give to the widow the jar of meal and to teach her to have the Prophet's Room for the Prophet.

February, 1984. The only way to make Restitution is to build Virtue. Virtue pushes out all sin. Sin flees when one has obtained Virtue.

*

The church does not give you the Inner Realization. When the Inner Realization comes forth, there must be a Teacher or a Teaching.

March 1. In our Teaching, the children come first in everything.

*

In Niscience, we have the Ethic of Owing No Man.

March 1. During Noon Contemplation in the Prayer Room in Barjona II: The invisible musics in the prayer room are sounding and soaring in our prayers:

> The holy currents of the mixtures in all faiths pouring the oil of blessing and grace upon the wounds of separateness:
> The uniting of the holiness in holy places;
> The domesticity of the Angels in the houses of God;
> The unison of all doctrines stabilizing Truth, Ethic, Morality;
> The house built without hands, structured within the Guiding Principle;
> Blessed in the Bosom of the Father,
> Exalted in the Kingdom.
> This is worship.
> This is God's Spirit in us.

March 2. I am in the midst of holy consciousness, of extended Samadhi. At intervals, when my Samadhi Cycle is on its crest, I am in touch with the Lords of Mind, the Seraphim Archangels. These Archangels draw upon the flow of Saturn; using the Indestructible Atom between the eyebrows, they keep the Buddhi or Informing Principle alive. They also indent Purusha wisdom-knowledge, that one may retain or have accumulative knowledge. This knowledge comes from God, Christ co-atom action, or the Spirit of God speaking through His Son, the Christ.

March, 1984. Self-incentive is Christ's gift to us.

*

Anyone who deliberately stands between you and God's Word takes on your sins. And your sins become white as snow and you start all over again when you make declaration for God.

*

You find the soul-gold with the geiger counter of the heart.

*

We are the New Logos for God.

*

When you are working with the Living God, you are working with the Living Fire. A Living Teacher carries the Living Fire. A living student is the tinder lit by the Fire of the Living Teacher. These Fires go not out, being kindled by the Father, the Son and the Holy Spirit.

*

If I did not have holy anxiety for those I love, I would not be fit to teach.

*

The Teacher is the Learner. He is the one who learns from what the Father sends him.

April 2, 1984. In the Chapel of the Good Shepherd in the National Cathedral, Washington, D.C. O blessed Saviour of us all, let us be Thy little lambs.

April 6. We are aereating worship. We are putting circulation into it. The responsible ones respond.

When we go into other religious bodies, we must know that we are Saint-sent. Through Saint-articulation, we bring the Light and pass to the church body the spirit of Intentional-Suffering acceptance.

In the present time, the Saints in Heaven come to revive the fervency within worship. The downpouring of Saintly-ecstasy is rolling in as ocean waves into the congregation, that the congregations may press forth to the Altars, demanding the charge of the Holy Spirit; demanding the virtue to return to the Altars.

April 7. To Ann Ree from the Master: For equal pain there is holy gain.

April 8. To study the Saints is the beginning of worship.

No one can perform a Miracle without the power of love.

When we pray, we make restitution for the world.

April 11, 1984.

Purge me, O Indwelling Spirit,
that I may be free;
that I may be afloating as a leaf;
and that I may swim ashore
from this life so brief.

O Angels of passion deep,
cleanse out my house,
that the rising Moon and Sun
of my soul
may shine in this temple new;
for when sepulchres end,
this is the beginning of life,
of love, of tenderness, of peace.

O gentle soul's wing of my escape,
lead me into the landscape
of the new estate,
that I may with pinion-wings
move from place to place,
from aeon to aeon.

April 13. Begin to use your knowledge. Participate and create.

April 16. Ann Ree to Jonathan: If any person ever marked and traced God, I am one of those. And you are doing it the same way. And all of us are beginning to know

God. We are proving His reality through Marking and Tracing. Marking and Tracing means simplify and verify.

April 17. I am in a continuous state of Samadhi.

April 21. You have to be so daring for God that you do not care if you die or not.

April 28. A.R.C. to J.M.: We are giving these people Heaven, and we went through hell to do it.

April 29. Santa Barbara. Jonathan to Ann Ree: "You have saved a lot of people from tragedies." Ann Ree: I have saved thousands of people's lives. I have saved them from suicide. I have saved them from murder. I have saved them from loneliness. I have saved them from insanity. I have saved them from sickness. I have saved them from separation. I have led them to vocations. I have saved them from losing their homes. I have sent them to rightful polarities.

I have done all of these things, Jonathan. And I have led them to a spiritual life. And I have opened the door to their inner life and spiritual nature. This is without boasting. It is through God that all of these have been done through me.

April 30. To J.M.: Learn to watch trees. The Angels will talk to you through trees.

April, 1984. Written for Young Adults: I am in this world to serve God. Everything I do in the Spirit of God serves God and this world.

This world is created by the Imaging Power of God. My True Mind is a mirror reflecting all of the images given to me of God. When I fear without understanding what I fear, I discolor the mirror of my mind. I must learn each day to mark and trace my fears so that I can keep the mirror of my mind clean, pure.

I desire the true and pure way of life. And I desire to be with those who have true and pure desires, for this makes my mind shine within the Light of my soul. My soul cannot die, but my soul can be darkened when my mind is unclear as to true thinking.

The Great Mantra or Word of God when spoken keeps my mind centered within the Will of God.

Everyone in the world possesses two sides of knowing: the lower side is an unknowing or *ne*science side; the other side is the *Niscience* side or higher side. The *Ni*science side is the God side of our nature and cannot die. This side expresses a life of good, of kindness, of compassion, of Truth. The *ne*science side or unknowing is a state of testing and learning. Sometimes we are deceived to think it the only and real side of life in the world.

The Image of God seeks in His Spirit to create through us. Our true power in this earth is to create, to build and to bring this eternity system in which we live into perfection.

The Great Mantra or Word of God begins to sound in our hearts, minds and souls when we pray. Our prayers are electricalized spirit power.

We must pray with clean prayers. A prayer in which we ask selfishly for self is heard, but becomes only a weak voltage petition. True voltage prayer unites with the frequencies of Heaven and links us to all Great Souls who understand and use the spiritual, divine art of prayer and of praying. The linking of prayer keeps us in touch with the Omnipresence of God which works for us in Reciprocal Maintenance as all good working together for the Spirit of God.

Evil works as *ne*science and preys upon our unknowing. This is why we must ask in the Lord's Prayer given to us by Jesus: "Lead us not into temptation." Evil exists in unknowing with malice which lives in the earth in the lower collective subconscious of mankind. Evil rises up in the lower subconscious when we are seeking to step aside from the Will of God and desiring something that is not right for us.

God has sealed into our higher subconscious that which we know as the Ten Commandments. By right prayer and following the "inner-parts law," we avoid error and waste of time and misuse of energy.

Time is energy which we experience in cycles and tides. When we observe and live the Commandments, we use our time as the high energy and we make greater space-terrain to live in. Thus, we widen the dimensions of our souls' light and become a God-sent one in timing to His Will. By this, we use our soul-gifts and talents to serve God.

Any religion failing to teach us of the soul-gifts is a partial and material religion.

We must test our faith in God first through religious instruction. If a religion's instruction does not provide the way to obtain the gifts of the Holy Spirit, it is not a whole testimony. Its doctrine is founded by man and not by the Holy Spirit of God.

May 1, 1984. Santa Barbara, California. Title: The Dark Trial Before Men:

The true Constitutional spirit of America cannot be worked through religion; this has been proved by religion's failing in its insight and spiritual purposes. The spiritual destiny of America is on trial. Churches are entering a revolutionary state of cleansing and purification. The Holy Spirit is seeking to return to the Altar. The calling of the Ministry is now being quickened through this Archetypal phase or day.

The Constitution for the United States was written for the souls who are entering a phase of mind and soul enlightenment which will demand that the edifices of worship shall truly express freedom and liberation.

The divine attributes of the minds of men are seeking to come to birth in this Earth.

Four places in this world as continents are now in a state of ferment. These continents begin with the letter A: Africa, Australia, America, Asia.

The United States of America is a gene-crucible and a soul-crucible for races. The United States of America is the forerunner for the birth of a new man in the Earth.

Souls awaiting to reincarnate will be the pioneers and leaders for the other continents bearing the first letter A. During this period, the Arctic and Antarctic shall blossom and flourish like the rose.

The borders of Canada shall develop new provinces pushing toward the North.

The World Court of Parliaments shall be developed in this Earth. The complexity and contradicting separateness shall begin to change into a meld of unity among nations.

All of this will occur between the years of 2010 and 2070.

Before these things will occur, the rights to territory will produce a devastating and terrible sky-war. From this, arrogant and greed-filled nations will be demoted from their greed and exploitations. Ordinary man of the Earth will be the victim of these sky-wars. The mechanism of war will toss men about, depriving them of home, roots and place. *"Where there is no vision, the people perish: but he that keepeth the law, happy is he." (Proverbs 29:18)*

The awesome selectivity of God in the era before men will diminish the population surplus. Men's cruelty to one another will act as the wrath of God upon one another.

Greed is the champion of evil. All who live and think through greed will reincarnate to reap the horrors of the automation they have set forth through their greed. These will be the chief victims of their own evils.

This is the true dark day of the Armageddon through which mankind of the Earth must survive that he be born in the true spirit of creation and enlightenment.

May 6–12, 1984. A disciple must have equal insight and courage. These must act as one in a spontaneity. In this, he becomes a vessel or vehicle for the Holy Spirit. A disciple having all courage and no insight is a tragedy in the midst of partial truth.

*

Love, work and worship are how we live in Niscience.

*

It is so wonderful to live in the Coincidings. Thank you, Father.

*

Principle is not enough alone; you must have Ethic to guide it.

*

We must learn the difference between commitment and committee.

*

Memory is the key to the Eternals.

*

Buddha is surrounded in a nimbus of luminous silver, and Jesus is surrounded in a nimbus of luminous gold. The chela who incorporates these two must blend the silver and gold. This makes the Divine Lumniscape.

May 17, 1984. Ann Ree in the hospital. Two days before the major stroke that led to her passing on June 28, 1984: Thought takes its own voyage.

. . . Jonathan Murro

20

TRIBUTE TO MY TEACHER

Extremely lucky are they who meet a real Saint.
Some may tell the past, present and future;
Some may stop the sun from setting;
Some may easily walk over a sea;
But difficult, difficult, difficult, indeed,
It is to meet a real Saint.

—*Eknath*

Teacher of Truth

Written at the Hospital on Wednesday, June 27, 1984, several hours before the passing of my beloved Teacher and Wife.

Ann Ree, in your Higher Body radiant and bright,
you are at home in God's Worlds of light.

You are happy in your Higher Body because you have
completed the work you set out to do on Earth.

Your physical body, worn out by the battles you have
fought against sin and ignorance, is completing
its "units of measure" according to your Soul's
Covenant and God's Will.

In several weeks, you will be 86 years of age. You
have not wasted one minute of time in your full

life, for you were always studying, working, helping others, creating, and serving God as one of His Elect.

I cherish every moment that I have been privileged to walk with you on the Path as your student, your chela. I know that God has made this possible.

Most people do not know what it means to be with an Enlightened Teacher. For over 32 years, I have basked in the light of your union with God. Every day you have blessed me with some priceless gift: your wisdom, your inspired creations, your example.

I know now what it means to serve God as a Teacher of Truth because of your life and its demands and rewards. To be a Teacher of Truth is indeed a "high calling"—however, I did not realize until recent years how much suffering is required of an Anointed Teacher. Through His suffering, Jesus lifted the world. Through those who teach, suffer and serve in His Name—as you have done all of your adult life—you have contributed mightily to the lifting of the world. You have borne the sins of many others upon your shoulders. You have liberated many souls during your ministry of over sixty years. The future will be blessed by the numerous seeds of Grace and Truth you have sealed into the Earth.

Thank God for you, my beloved Teacher and Wife. No student could receive more blessings from his Teacher; no husband could receive more blessings from his Wife.

Soon, God will welcome you to His Bosom—and you will sit at His Table forevermore. God be with thee, beloved in Christ.

PERFECT TIMING AND THE SOUL OF ANN REE COLTON

The Dance of the Cosmos is within the soul of each person of the earth.

—A. R. C.

Ann Ree Colton's transition from the physical world on June 28, 1984 occurred through a series of remarkable Coincidings. These Coincidings testify to the perfect union between her Soul and the Sacred Cycles of God.

Ann Ree was born on the day of the New Moon and passed from this world on the day of the New Moon.

The number 33 is the highest spiritual number. Jesus lived 33 years. All Master Teachers and Initiates who serve God and the human spirit work in cyclic timings correlating to the number 33.

Each year at Wesak—the time of the Full Moon in the sign of Taurus—there is a blending between the Buddha and the Christ. During the Wesak Full Moon in 1951, Ann Ree saw flames of fire coming from her body during meditation. This fiery cleansing consumed the last remnants of egotism in her nature, thereby preparing her to receive the System of Niscience. In 1984, *33 years later,* the Wesak Full Moon in May produced the tide that eventually removed Ann Ree's physical presence from the world.

Monday, May 14, 1984. Full Moon in Scorpio.
Wesak. Lunar Eclipse. On Friday, May 11, the
Moon was at Perigee in Libra.

The *Perigee* of the Moon signifies the time when the Moon is closest to the Earth during the lunar month.

The *Apogee* of the Moon occurs when the Moon is farthest from the Earth during the lunar month. Perigee and Apogee are important times of each lunar month, especially when they occur on or near a New Moon or Full Moon.

On Saturday, May 12, 1984, Ann Ree did not feel well. She slept during the day, and desired no food or water. The Perigee of the Moon occurred in Libra, which rules the kidneys. Ann Ree, whose rising sign is in Libra, entered the hospital on Tuesday, May 15th due to a urinary tract infection. This was the day after the Wesak Full Moon and Lunar Eclipse. My Teacher prophesied to me over twenty years ago that her death would be related to a kidney infection.

Friday, May 18, 1984. Ann Ree is much better—and will leave the hospital tomorrow morning. Before I left her room, my Teacher said to me: "I can feel, Jonathan, the Thunder and Lightning around you." Then she spoke a few prophetic words of guidance in which she warned me not to be too daring because of the tester. These were the last words my Beloved Teacher would speak to me physically in this life.

Saturday, May 19, 1984. When I arrived at the hospital at 8:40 A.M., Ann Ree was suffering a major stroke that paralyzed her right arm and right leg. She was also unable to speak or to swallow. Ann Ree has taught us about the five-day period following a Full Moon being a dark cycle. Today is the fifth day after the Full Moon. The Moon is in Aquarius—opposite to her Leo Birth Sign. During the past several years, my Beloved Teacher has been calling my attention to the significance of Zodiacal-Prototype opposites and also when the Moon is in the sign opposite one's Sun Sign.

Tuesday, May 22, 1984. The neurologist said it would be a week before more could be determined regarding

Ann Ree's condition and treatment. My inner guidance during this crisis time is: *"Continue to create."*

Thursday, May 24, 1984. Ann Ree was able to swallow a little piece of ice given her by the speech therapist. It is important to have her swallow so that she can begin to eat.

Tuesday, May 29, 1984. The doctor walked into Ann Ree's room about 6:30 P.M. and said my being there was a "lonely vigil." Ann Ree and I are both painfully aware of the effects of the stroke. The doctor said there is less than 50% chance that she will recover her speaking or the full use of her right limbs.

The Teacher never stops teaching her student. Even now in this critical condition, Ann Ree is teaching me so much regarding life and death, gratitude and grief, courage and compassion, faith and prayer.

Wednesday, May 30, 1984. New Moon in Gemini. Solar Eclipse. Coinciding: Joan of Arc was martyred on May 30th.

Ann Ree's condition seems to be opening up so much more love in me. My Teacher has taught for years that a stroke signifies the beginning of the Silver Cord's being released from the physical body.

At 3:20 P.M. in the same hospital, Thia Hauer, one of Ann Ree's long-time students, passed away at the age of 65. The day is a New Moon in Gemini and a Solar Eclipse. Thia was a Gemini.

Friday, June 1, 1984. Moon in Cancer. Early morning dream before arising: I dreamt of Ann Ree in her white robe. She was speaking—and I suddenly realized *she was speaking.* She was animated and vital; a beautiful look was in her eyes. Ann Ree appeared younger in years. I believe she was revealing to me her *True Self* in the dream—reminding me that she can speak and is totally free in her Eternal-Life Consciousness and True Body of Everlasting Light.

Monday, June 4, 1984. I awakened with the recollection of words written by Ann Ree regarding dying: "The exquisite yielding to the inevitable."

Tuesday, June 5, 1984. Ann Ree has had a backset. She has been sleeping the past few times I have visited the hospital. Two days ago, I felt her presence telling me it was time for her to leave the world. These words came from my heart to her: "I understand." God is so gracious to have blessed the world with such a pure and beautiful soul as Ann Ree Colton. She is truly one of the Elect, a Great Soul who has come to help lift and enlighten the world—in Jesus' Name.

Thursday, June 7, 1984. Moon at Perigee in Libra. Ann Ree has taken a noticeable turn for the worse.

Monday, June 11, 1984. Upon awakening, I began to wonder about my future course if A.R.C. should leave the world—and these words of Jesus came quickly: "Feed my sheep."

Tuesday, June 12, 1984. I feel a paradox is taking place. Even though Ann Ree and I are not physically together as we have always been, I feel that we are coming closer together than ever before. If she remains in the world—or leaves the physical world—I feel with an inner knowing and certainty that we will be able to work closer together than before. This will be another expression of our *co-atom* association as servants of God.

When Jesus left the world, His Spirit was able to be more fully with His Apostles through their co-atom relationship. I am beginning to see how this will also be the case with Ann Ree and her students after she leaves the world. Jesus said: "*Verily, verily, I say unto you, Except a corn of wheat fall into the ground and die, it abideth alone: but if it die, it bringeth forth much fruit." (St. John 12:24)*

Wednesday, June 13, 1984. Full Moon in Capricorn. Lunar Eclipse. A sleepless night of prayer, for I had to make major decisions regarding the future medical treatment and care for my Beloved Teacher and Wife. The sleepless night I was told was a *Fast From Sleep* and accomplished something on the inner; also, guidance has begun to come. Two days later, Ann Ree suddenly began to eat. The doctor called her eating again "a miracle." I knew it to be the answer to prayer.

Monday, June 18, 1984. Moon in Sagittarius. Dreamt I was serving the Sacrament and began to *levitate* two or three feet above the ground.

Wednesday, June 20, 1984. Summer Solstice. Sun enters Cancer. Moon at Apogee in Pisces. As I pondered Ann Ree's failing health, I heard these words inwardly: "It is called *Dying,* my son." The doctor sent Ann Ree home from the hospital on the day of the Summer Solstice, the Moon was at Apogee, and the Sun entered Cancer—all on the same day! Cancer is the sign of the home—the day she came home.

Ann Ree suffered the stroke on the day before the Sun entered Gemini—and she came home the day the Sun left Gemini and entered the sign of Cancer. Thus, she was in the hospital during the total time the Sun was in Gemini: the zodiacal sign of the Prototypes of Judas and his replacement, Matthias. Surely, Ann Ree's Intentional Suffering is to overcome the Judas ones in the world and their terrible sins of betrayal of God, the Christ and their own Souls. All Teachers of Truth work to overcome the lesser Judas nature represented by the lower Gemini Prototype so that the higher-mind powers of the higher Gemini Prototype may come to birth in the human spirit.

Judas, the Gemini Prototype among the disciples, was responsible for the death of Jesus. Ann Ree's suffering has helped to heal the Judas nature in mankind. God knows the extent of the healing—and will reward His courageous servant, Ann Ree Colton, for her Intentional Suffering for the good of her fellow man. Many years ago, Ann Ree prophesied to a beloved student: "Gemini will be the death of me."

Thursday, June 21, 1984. On this 33rd day after suffering the stroke, Ann Ree spent her first full day in her own home since entering the Hospital.

Wednesday, June 27, 1984. (6 + 27 = 33) Moon in Gemini (Lungs). Ann Ree is re-admitted to the hospital because she has contracted pneumonia in her right lung. The doctor said that pneumonia is called the "old man's friend." The Constellation Gemini governs the lungs. Ann Ree is very weak and slept all day except for brief periods of waking. I had thoughts such as, "Ann Ree is happy because she has accomplished what she came into the world to do!" I believe that Ann Ree is free in her spiritual body and the "units of measure" of her physical body have almost concluded according to God's Will and her Soul's Covenant.

Before leaving the hospital room, I kissed each of my Teacher's feet as I have done many times over the past 32 years, except this time I felt a very special blessing and sweetness of grace coming from her presence. This was to be the last time I would kiss my Beloved Teacher's physical feet in this lifetime. The first time I kissed Ann Ree's feet was in the year of 1952 when she began to teach me the art and science of meditation.

Thursday, June 28, 1984. New Moon in Cancer (7:09 A.M.) I awakened at 1:30 A.M. and began to pray for my Teacher for the remainder of the night. The doctor called at 6:30 A.M. to tell me that Ann Ree passed away quietly and peacefully during the night. For the past few weeks, I have been knowing the time of day the doctor would call and what he would say. After receiving the doctor's call, these words came: "God is Merciful. God is Just. God is Good." I called the nurse at the hospital and learned that Ann Ree had passed away at 2:50 A.M. My Beloved Teacher passed away while the Moon was still in Gemini, a few hours before the New Moon in Cancer—the sign of the home; in this instance, her "heavenly home." In the Guna Calendar, it was a Sattva Day.

Years ago Ann Ree told some of her grandchildren that she would live to the age of 85.

Ann Ree's physical body was taken to a mortuary near the Foundation and placed in a refrigeration unit for three and one-half days. During this period of time, a 24-hour-a-day prayer vigil was observed in the Chapel by her students who read aloud from Ann Ree's books. Students also read aloud from her books and the Bible at the refrigeration unit at the mortuary during the daytime hours. Ninety-three students volunteered to keep the prayer and reading vigil in the Chapel; it was a great comfort to me to be able to go into the Chapel any time of the day and the night and hear Ann Ree's beautiful words being read by my co-disciples.

Ann Ree has said: *"Mary works with 40."* One of the symbols of Mary is the New Moon. Ann Ree passed away a few hours before the New Moon. Her stroke occurred on May 19, 1984 and she left the world on June 28, 1984—a 40-day cycle! A 40-day cycle is a *Masterbuilder Cycle.* Moses fasted for 40 days before receiving the Ten Commandments; Jesus fasted for 40 days before beginning His Ministry on Earth. Ann Ree's 40-day cycle was a holy fast in the truest sense of the word; she not only fasted from solid food, but she fasted from speaking. No words issued from her lips, as the Hand of God was placed over her mouth during the entire 40-day cycle. This 40-day fast before Ann Ree's passing was a monumental Spiritual Fast overdirected by her Soul in its Covenant with God!

Even as Moses' and Jesus' 40-day fasts changed the course of the world, I know with full certainty that Ann Ree Colton's 40-day fast will change the world. Ann Ree is an Elect, and her Ministry will have far-reaching consequences in centuries and ages to come, for all during her Ministry she has been *filled* with the Grace and Truth of God, the Eternal Spirit.

Sunday, July 1, 1984. Moon in Leo. Yesterday's day of fasting, prayers, testimonies and creativity by the group-body occurred on the third day since Ann Ree's passing—the Moon in Leo, her own Sun Sign. During today's Sabbath Day Service on the fourth day, the Moon was also in Leo—a very significant timing in her transition and conclusion of the eighty-four hours since the time of death. Ann Ree had the peace and quiet she has said is so necessary during the eighty-four hours following a person's death. All too often this period of time is intruded upon by autopsy, embalming, premature cremation, or arguing and bickering by relatives.

Monday, July 2, 1984. Moon at Perigee. Moon in Leo until 12:27 P.M. and then enters Virgo. At 10 A.M., Ann Ree's body was anointed by three beloved students in preparation for cremation. (Ann Ree was born at 10 A.M.) During the Anointing, all three students saw tears fall from Ann Ree's eyes! Her body was taken to the crematory at 12 Noon while the Moon was yet in Leo, a *fire* sign. At 2 P.M., the exact time her body was being cremated, the Moon was at Perigee! Also, the Moon had entered Virgo, the sign of Mary, the Virgin.

Following the 40-day cycle leading to Ann Ree's release from the physical body, there are *50* days until her birthday on August 17th. This 40-day cycle followed by a 50-day cycle is a recapitulation of the 40-day Lenten period commemorating Jesus' 40-day fast in the wilderness and the 50-day *Pentecost Cycle* between the Last Supper on Maundy Thursday and Pentecost—the time the Apostles received the Holy Ghost.

Thank you, Ann Ree, Master Teacher of the Light, for continuing to teach us through the Great Law of Coincidings. Without saying a word, you have continued to teach by the very events of your final days on Earth and the days and weeks following your passing. Truly, your Soul is in perfect timing with the rhythm of the Sun and the Moon in your dance of life on Earth and in Heaven.

Ann Ree's brilliance shines as an Eternal Sun.

THE JOY OF BLESSING

July 1, 1984. Fourth day after A. R. C.'s passing.

Ann Ree Colton has taught me to live a life in which there is the *Joy of Blessing.* Everything Ann Ree ever fulfilled in service to God contained the Joy of Blessing—for everything she did was in the spirit of Blessing others.

Her beautiful books and other writings were written for the express purpose of blessing Truth-seekers. Her class talks, her lovely songs, her conclave pilgrimages, her art work—all were motivated by the heartfelt desire to bless her students and all others who turned to her for instruction.

The Lord Jesus and His Apostles came to bless the world. As an Apostle of Jesus in our age and time, Ann Ree came to bless us. In blessing us, she also was blessed. This is the true secret to a life of joy: In blessing others, we are blessed. God richly blesses those who desire to bless His children with understanding, wisdom and enlightenment.

The Bible says: *"Blessed is he who cometh in the Name of the Lord."* I send my love and gratitude to God for enriching our lives through His servant, Ann Ree Colton. "Blessed is *she* who cometh in the Name of the Lord."

Blessed Bride of Christ,
Devoted Servant of God,
You are now risen with your Risen Lord.

Be ye blessed in Him.
We are blessed through our love for thee and for Him.
Let us rejoice together in the knowledge of Eternal Life.
Truly, there is no separation for those who love God.
Bless me.
We bless thee.
Be at peace.
In your body of light, be at peace.

PILGRIMAGE TO BEETLE ROCK

That thou might heal thy lungs, go to trees. That thou might heal thy thoughts and lift them to high places, go thou to trees.

When thou wouldst heal the aeon memories, go to mountains. When thou wouldst heal the secrets in thyself and become selfless, go thou to mountains.

And when thou wouldst be purified in thy lesser self and be cleansed in thy emotions, go thou to the waters.

—*Ann Ree Colton*

A few weeks after my beloved Teacher passed away, I received an inner guidance to make a pilgrimage to the same places in the heart of Nature visited by her thirty-three years ago: Yosemite, Sequoia and Kings Canyon National Parks in California. In August 1951, Ann Ree experienced a powerful visitation from the Lord Jesus while meditating on Beetle Rock in Sequoia National Park; she also experienced a memorable blessing from the Venerable One in Kings Canyon National Park. I knew I must visit these same polarities in commemoration of my Teacher's personal experiences with Jesus and the Venerable One. A few months after she experienced these spiritual visitations, Ann Ree received an inner guidance to travel to Saint Petersburg, Florida for the purpose of meeting the one who would assist her in her future Ministry. Soon after her arrival in Saint Petersburg, we met and began our association as Teacher and chela.

In describing her 1951 experience at Beetle Rock, Ann Ree told me that the sky became completely filled with the etheric body of Jesus. The violet light of the dusk or twilight made the central note of His color.

> *In this contemplative time, my heart united with the heart of Jesus, and I experienced His love and compassion for men of the earth. I had seen visions of Jesus many times in my life, and in these visions His words came to me in familiar Bible verses—but this was the first time He spoke to me in a personal, intimate colloquy. He told me that each day at dusk He seeks to lighten the cares of men; for the hearts of men are more responsive to His love at this time of the day.*
>
> *The etheric body of Jesus, in command of the earth, encompasses and saturates the earth with His love. At dusk He momentarily adjusts and modifies the burdens of the world.*
>
> *One morning during my meditation, while still in Sequoia, the earth beneath my feet opened etherically and I saw underneath the seemingly secure surface many caverns of exquisite beauty. These caverns were conjoined to Beetle Rock where I had heard the voice of Jesus. Someday men will discover these caverns, and will learn that their beauty far exceeds that of the caverns now known to them.* —*A. R. C.*

Ann Ree's experience with the Lord Jesus inspired her to compose the following mantram several months later:

Peace unto all men.
Blessings be upon all men.
Let all men come unto the Christ.
Let all men know Him and receive Him.
At dusk as we stand in the Garment of
the Jesus One,
May we know His healing and forgiving love.
And may we place our cares unto Him,
And go forth unto the world
To heal,
To serve.

Kings Canyon is adjacent to Sequoia National Park. One day at Kings Canyon, Ann Ree was sitting on the river bank when she saw a vision of the *Venerable One.* This Great Being, also known as Father Jupiter, works with the Realm of Nature, the Angels and all worthy disciples.

Ann Ree's experiences with Jesus and the Venerable One started new themes in her dedication to God; many new books were written, and the System of Niscience became a voice for the Christ in this age and time.

My pilgrimage to Beetle Rock began on Friday, July 20, 1984, exactly twenty-two days after Ann Ree left the world. I spent the weekend in Monterey and Carmel, California. Hundreds of pelicans filled the sky and the water of beautiful Carmel Bay, inspiring me to think of the Pelican as the symbol of the Teacher; other thoughts related to the higher life also came to mind.

Saturday, July 21, 1984. Monterey Peninsula.

All who love God are joined together in a brotherhood of souls committed to the Creator and His Creation.

All who love God work together for the good of all. Whether they are in Heaven or on Earth, their love keeps them united in this Holy Brotherhood of like-minded souls. The bond that keeps them united is the bond of love.

*

Numerous pelicans are flying above. The formation always remains intact. If one passes away, another takes its place. So it has been for ages past and so it will be for ages to come. The same truth applies to Anointed Teachers of the ages past and ages to come. Like pelicans, they move in perfect formation. The lead Pelican or Teacher shows the way, and all other Teachers follow in their perfect placement and flight.

*

The tears in my right eye mourn the loss of my Beloved Teacher; the tears in my left eye mourn the loss of my Beloved Wife. *"Blessed are they that mourn: for they shall be comforted." (St. Matthew 5:4)*

*

A Teacher's Wisdom is broad, deep, high and never-ending, for the Teacher's Wisdom comes from the Spirit of God, which is broad, deep, high and never-ending.

*

Beloved Devotee of the Lord, when the Spirit of God guides you to your Teacher, be sure to keep a Journal, for your Teacher will begin your union with the Supernatural Grace of God. Whatever happens to you after you meet your Teacher is of the Supernatural Grace of God. Whatever holy thoughts and inspirations come to you are of the Supernatural Grace of God. Therefore, if you would become a Pelican, a Teacher, keep your Journal as a Testimony of God's Love, Mercy and Truth; for a devotee who desires to share with others, who cherishes the Truth and preserves Truth's Treasures will one day become a Teacher of Truth who gives his written and spoken testimony of the Supernatural Grace of God that feeds all Pelicans and Pelicans-to-be.

*

The amazing thing is that God continues to send Anointed Teachers into the world. Even though they are ignored by many and persecuted by some, the Creator continues to send His Anointed Ones into every era and time. Blessed are those who receive the Teachers sent by God to enlighten the world, for when one accepts the Teachers' instruction, he is accepting the Holy One Who has sent them.

*

Bless my Beloved Teacher, O Lord, who has come to reveal Thy Plan so that this Earth may be created by Enlightened Souls at one with Thee through love.

*

A person prays to God for a Teacher. God sends a Teacher to the one who prays to be instructed. The Teacher calls a meeting for the benefit of persons who desire instruction. All too often, the person who has prayed to God for instruction does not attend the Teacher's class. The Teacher is not offended by the absence of the seeker; however, each absence is a breach between the ungrateful person and the Love of God which has graciously answered his prayer for instruction from an Enlightened Teacher.

Sunday, July 22, 1984. Carmel.

A true Teacher will seek to inspire each student to feel a *oneness* with the Moon, the Sun, the Planets, the Stars and the Galaxies; for, in so doing, he is uniting his students with God, the Creator of all celestial bodies.

Union with God means union with His Spirit creating the Universe. Thus, all Teachers anointed by God's Spirit are at one with the Universal Splendor of God's Glory. To such enlightened ones, the Spirit of God sends glimpses, insights, and wisdom-inspirations regarding the Moon, the Sun, the Planets, the Stars and the Galaxies.

Monday, July 23, 1984. Jackson, California.

Each sense has a voice. Each atom and cell has a voice. Each memory has a voice. Each desire and aspiration has a voice. Each fear and guilt has a voice. If these voices are not united through love for God and His Law, they become a Tower of Babel—and one lives in a state of confusion, unrest and discontent. However, when the many voices become unified and harmonized through love for God and His Law, the many voices become hushed through sacramental meditation—and "the still, small voice of God" may be heard. When this occurs, there are no interior or exterior voices that can intrude upon the Voice of God guiding and enlightening His servant. This state of Divine Grace can be accomplished only through a constant love for God and His Law perfected through the disciplinary stillness of sacramental meditation.

Tuesday, July 24, 1984. Jackson and Lake Tahoe.

Over the years, the love between Ann Ree and me has evolved and expanded. Since her passing from this world, we are evolving a pure and holy love untinged by the senses. This is the deathless, eternal love. Such love continues to evolve and expand when two serve God as husband and wife, Teacher and chela.

The senses are instruments for the world physical. It requires great discipline to purify the five senses. I am now being healed and cleansed of any sense-tinged love, that I may become more centered in a pure and holy love. Ann Ree, as my beloved Teacher, is now assisting me in this necessary accomplishment. Through pure and holy love untinged by the karmic intrusions of the senses, we will both remain ever united through the pure and holy love of the Soul, the Spirit and the Divine Image.

*

There are two kinds of persons: those who go toward discipline and those who run away from discipline. Individuals who are disciplined are the ones who minister to the undisciplined when the undisciplined are beset by the problems that come through selfishness and sensuality.

*

Tomorrow, Timon Allen and I leave for Yosemite and will arrive at Beetle Rock at Sequoia National Park on Saturday—the day of the New Moon!

Wednesday, July 25, 1984. Yosemite National Park.

The massive cliffs, high waterfalls, river and streams, multitudinous trees of many kinds, fresh air and atmosphere of reverent expectation to behold a new wonder of Nature at any moment immediately seize the soul and the imagination. This is another world—a world of solemn silence and majestic beauty giving its constant testimony of God, Good, Beauty, Order, Purpose and Harmony. Regardless of the negativities of man, Nature continues to do her work throughout the ages and the aeons. Man is subject to Nature and Nature's Laws. When he seeks to intrude on these Laws, he is swept into the mighty tides of Time lifting him, teaching him, perfecting him. This is what Yosemite speaks to me: the Eternal Will of God utilizing the Powerful Energies and Beauty of Nature to move mankind forward on the Path of Eternal Life.

*

Every person in the world is known to God. Every person is learning the difference between right and wrong. Every plant and tree is assisting man in the learning process. Every Saint and Angel is assisting man in the learning process. Learning never ceases. From learning comes knowledge. From knowledge comes wisdom. From wisdom comes union with God. Union with God makes of one an inspired Learner and an enlightened Teacher.

Thursday, July 26, 1984. Yosemite.

Father, may Thy children learn of Love as the Communicating-Power between Souls and between Stars.

*

How can one thank his Teacher sufficiently enough for leading him to union with the Holy and Eternal Spirit of

Jonathan Murro at
Yosemite National Park

Waterfall, Yosemite

Merced River, Yosemite

Beetle Rock, Sequoia
National Park

God? The mighty occurrence of union with the Eternal God requires an Eternal Thank You. Only the Soul can speak an Eternal Thank You to God for one's Teacher and an Eternal Thank You to one's Teacher for uniting him with God.

Therefore, O my Soul, speak forevermore an Eternal Thank You to God and to my beloved Teacher.

*

Thank you, blessed Trees.
Thank you, blessed Rocks.
Thank you, blessed Earth and Air.

*

Never before have I seen so many outstanding places in Nature during a single day.

Last year Ann Ree received guidance for her students to place the Bread and Wine of the Sacrament in the ground at the point of the Continental Divide during a pilgrimage to the Rocky Mountains of Colorado. This we did on Sunday, July 15, 1984. Approximately 120 students accompanied me to a beautiful area in the Rocky Mountains on the line of the Great Divide. Here we observed a time of prayer, talks and songs. The Pilgrimage Ritual Ann Ree suggested was observed—and a great blessing was sealed into the Earth through the taking of the Sacrament by all present and by placing the Bread and the Wine in the ground in Jesus' Name. This Polarity Blessing was a true Apostolic Service that will continue to bless, heal and spiritually quicken our world and our planet.

Today is the eleventh day since we placed the Bread and the Wine in the ground at the Continental Divide in the Rocky Mountains; it is also the twenty-eighth day since Ann Ree's passing. Both of these sacred occurrences have started for me a great new cycle in life that has since taken me to environments of purity, beauty, power. Healing and inspiration occur in such polarities because the soul is powerfully charged and sealed by the Spirit of God working and blessing through the Soul of Nature.

Friday, July 27, 1984. Yosemite.

When a student is with his Teacher for a lengthy period, as I have been with Ann Ree Colton for 32 years, you think as one, feel as one, create as one. This oneness blessed by God assures the perpetuation of the Holy Dharma. Teachers pass on knowledge to students in an unbroken chain throughout history.

Students who hear the call of their souls to become one with their Teacher will become the future Guardians of the Dharma, the future Anointed Ones, the future Revelators and Prophets who guide the human spirit into new worlds of Soul-Beauty and Divine-Image Wisdom.

Come, O Christ, into the hearts of all students on the Path. May they receive greater knowledge of God, Truth and Thee. Then shall the world become a place where Hope abounds, Creation *Is,* and Love presides.

*

Go to Nature
Get back to yourself.
Get back to your core.
Your core is God in you.

*

Waterfalls baptize the Earth with a continuous rain of graceful reminders of God's Thunderous Power and Eternal Glory.

*

Offer your grief up to God, that God may use it to heal the grief of others.

*

Trees are sentinels of Nature's Treasures.

*

Eternal Life and Eternal Cycles are one. The Creation of the Universe is based upon Eternal Cycles. The Creation of Man in the Image of God is based upon Eternal Cycles.

Galaxies experience birth, life and death through the Principle of Eternal Cycles. Man experiences birth, life and death through the Principle of Eternal Cycles. To contemplate the Eternal Cycles occurring throughout the Cosmos is to become one with God, the Creator of the Eternal Cycles.

Through the Eternal Cycles, man is Eternal. Through the Eternal Cycles, man is in the state of increasing intelligence, increasing awareness, increasing enlightenment.

Life never ceases because of the Eternal Cycles of the Soul. The Soul is always one with God because of the Eternal Cycles.

*

The waterfalls are raw power controlled.

The Galaxies are raw power controlled.

Man is raw power uncontrolled.

Man gains control through discipline.

Raw power is of the creative Essence of the Universe.

Man, a child of the Universe, is learning how to master raw power through love, virtue, ethic and moral principle. An enlightened servant of God is a master of raw power; therefore, he works with the Universe and with man through discipline blessed and sanctified by God.

Saturday, July 28, 1984. New Moon in Leo. Sequoia National Park.

Pray for a Teacher. When God answers your prayer, remain with the Teacher until he delivers you to the Promised Land.

*

A walk through Crystal Cave—my first experience in a cave. A climb up steep Moro Rock. Dusk meditation and prayers at Beetle Rock—the goal of our pilgrimage! Here, in August 1951 Ann Ree had the visitation from the Lord Jesus that led to her receiving the System of Niscience as a Gift from God for the world.

Monday, July 30, 1984. Kings Canyon National Park. Cedar Grove. Moon at Perigee in Virgo.

Dusk meditation by the Kings River near Sheep Creek Campground. While camping in this area in 1951, Ann Ree saw a vision of the Venerable One coming across the River toward her.

After Ann Ree's experiences with Jesus in the Sequoias and the Venerable One in Kings Canyon, there entered into her life direct guidance as to each step before her.

> *In August 1951, I made my first union with the seven centrifugal points within the medallions of the Masters—and I began to receive a* composite telepathy. *In a composite telepathy the Masters do not identify themselves. A composite telepathy is made up of all the Masters speaking as one voice. I was told that henceforth I would receive from all of the Masters; for my labors had now reached the time in which I was to use the power of synthesis.*
>
> *In the beginning of the composite telepathy from the Masters, I received a series of intimate and loving passages of telepathic instruction. These personal telepathic passages became the balm to heal the tortuous wounds of the past years, and they prepared me for the coming labors. During this special interval of healing closeness with the Masters, I lived in uttermost quiet and spiritual serenity. Their love for me and their insight into my soul gave me a re-evaluation*

of myself, and also made clear to me the necessity of using my gifts to help and to heal in the world.

—A. R. C.

THE ETERNALITY OF SOUL-LOVE

There is no separation.

—Ann Ree Colton

When the world turns its back, the Guru is standing beside you. Through desert and forest, over seas and mountains, in this world and the next, he is with you.

—Kirpal Singh

Vision of the Venerable One at Kings Canyon
Painting by Ann Ree Colton

"And God shall wipe away all tears from their eyes; and there shall be no more death, neither sorrow, nor crying, neither shall there be any more pain: for the former things are passed away." (Revelation 21:4) It is thrilling to contemplate the Scriptural promises and prophecies that one day in the future there will be "no more death," and that "sorrow and sighing shall flee away." (Isaiah 35:10) When the veil of death is finally removed, there will be no more separation of any kind from loved ones.

Physical separation through death is necessary in God's present Plan—however, through love, there is no spiritual separation from loved ones. As love becomes more and more a reality in the physical world, the victory over death will be closer at hand. Through love, there is no *spiritual* separation.

The spiritual love that overcomes death—and all other veils—is a *soul-love.* Soul-love is beyond any sense-tinged love or gene-possessive love. It is a love that is of Spirit and, therefore, purely spiritual.

Soul-love is eternal, holy, uniting one with the Love of God beyond Time and Space. The Omnipresent Spirit of God abides in the wavelengths or frequencies of Soul-love. Only on the levels of Soul-love may one commune with the Omnipresent Spirit of God as Wisdom, Knowledge, Order, Harmony, Peace, Joy and Love.

To love God with one's senses is a love that will pass away when the senses die along with the body. To love God with the soul is to love him eternally. Regardless of the world in which one dwells, he will be one with God through Soul-love. Thus, the Commandment instructs man to love God with all his soul. *"Thou shalt love the Lord thy God with all thy heart, and with all thy soul, and with all thy mind, and with all thy strength." (St. Mark 12:30)*

True love or Soul-love is androgynous. Therefore, when a beloved mate dies, if the love between husband and wife

I can help you more after I am gone.
Ann Ree Colton

is an androgynous love, they will continue to love each other beyond male or female, beyond Time and Space.

Should the one who has departed this world through death reincarnate *before* his or her mate dies, their androgynous love for one another will keep them united through soul-levels of spiritual telepathy. Their oneness with God will bless their oneness with each other. If both reincarnate in coming lives in the same sex or opposite sex, their androgynous love will enable them to transcend personality-karmas, Time-and-Space limitations. Genders and generations cannot intrude on two souls who have an androgynous love for one another.

In future lives and in the afterlife, androgynous love inspires in two God-sent ones a *soul-knowing* that enables them to recognize one another and to bless each other. If in a coming life their relationship is husband and wife, parent and child, co-workers or friends, their androgynous love will bless and prosper their association, especially in their dedications as servants of God.

The Bible states: *"God is love." (I John 4:8)* Jesus expressed an androgynous love. Those who are His true Apostles also express an androgynous love through their union with Jesus and with God.

All who love are one in Omnipresence. They are united through the bond of love. Love for God unites all who love God. Love for the human spirit unites all who love the human spirit. Through love, Heaven and Earth are one. Truly, when one loves, there is no separation from Time past, present and future.

September 29, 1984. Ninety-third day after A.R.C.'s passing: three days of interim-purgatory plus ninety-days contrition interval. Also, thirty-three days before my 57th birthday.

WE ARE ONE

We are one.
We are one through Omnipresence.
We are one through Love.

Wherever you are—
in Heaven or on Earth—
we are one.
We are one through Omnipresence.
We are one through Love.
In the World of Spirit,
all are one.
Through love for God as Spirit
and for all others as children of His Spirit,
we are one.
We are one through the Omnipresent Spirit of
God and His Love

Regardless of Time-Cycles,
or in the Timeless State,
We are one.
We are one through Omnipresence beyond Time
and Space.
We are one through Love Eternal.

To be one is to be wed in Soul and Spirit.
To be wed with God,
is to be wed with All Creation, All Souls, All Stars.
Through this union with All Cosmos and All
Heavens,
we are one.
We are one with the Manifested Universe.
And we are one with the Future Plan of God.
We are one with Past, Present and All Time to
Come.

We are one in our love for the Truth.
As long as we love Truth, we will be one.
As long as we love God as the Truth,
we will always be one with whatever is occurring in the Universe
and in our lives.

We are one, beloved.
We are one through the Angels' Love.
We are one through the Saints' Ministrations.
We are one through the Perfect Spirit of the Lord Jesus.
To be His Apostle is to serve in the One Fold.
To be His Sheep is to be shepherded to the same green pastures
and the same still waters.
Wherever He is, we shall be.
Therefore, because of Him, we shall always be one.

O Blessed Oneness,
Thou art the One Spirit of God.
All come from Thee.
All live, move, and have their being in Thee.
All return to Thee.
To love is to live in the Divine Omnipresence.
We are one, beloved Ann Ree.
We are one through love.

INDEX

D

Q

R

S

T

OTHER BOOKS BY ANN REE COLTON

GALAXY GATE I: THE HOLY UNIVERSE
A remarkable book of spiritual revelations about Man, the Solar System and the Cosmos. (Co-author, Jonathan Murro)

GALAXY GATE II: THE ANGEL KINGDOM
A book filled with enlightening insights into the World of Holy Mediators between God and mankind. (Co-author, Jonathan Murro)

THE THIRD MUSIC
A powerful book describing the energy-worlds of the Mind, the Soul and the Universe.

KUNDALINI WEST
Knowledge of the Kundalini and the Chakras for the Western initiate.

WATCH YOUR DREAMS
An invaluable and necessary book revealing the soul-codes in dreams and their symbols.

ETHICAL ESP
An important book defining the difference between lower and higher ESP.

THE JESUS STORY
A miracle book in timing to the need for miracles.

THE HUMAN SPIRIT
A scientific, spiritual, and healing book on the creation, purpose and destiny of man.

PROPHET FOR THE ARCHANGELS
The life story of Ann Ree Colton. (Co-author, Jonathan Murro)

THE SOUL AND THE ETHIC
A profound book on the soul and on the ethical use of soul-power.

THE KING
From the personal, hieroglyphic journal of Ann Ree Colton.

DRAUGHTS OF REMEMBRANCE
An extraordinary book on the subject of reincarnation.

MEN IN WHITE APPAREL
A book of vital revelations about death and the life after death.

THE VENERABLE ONE

An initiatory book for those who love Nature and who would unveil Nature's secrets.

VISION FOR THE FUTURE

A prophetic book to comfort men in a perilous time.

THE LIVELY ORACLES

A prophetic book on world events.

ISLANDS OF LIGHT

A book of initiation with an underlying prophetic theme.

PRECEPTS FOR THE YOUNG

Appreciated by the adult . . . inspiring to the child . . . beneficial to the family.

BOOKS BY JONATHAN MURRO

THE PATH OF VIRTUE

A comprehensive work that describes the classic route to Enlightenment traveled by all Great Souls of the East and the West.

GOD-REALIZATION JOURNAL

A book opening a new world of understanding related to the Presence of God. *God-Realization Journal* also describes the author's initiatory transition from a devotee to a teacher of the higher life.

ANN REE COLTON FOUNDATION
P.O. Box 2057 Glendale, California 91209